The Ultimate Book of
Notes & Queries

D1422227

The Ultimate Book of
Notes & Queries

Edited by Joseph Harker

ATLANTIC BOOKS • LONDON

First published in 2002 by Atlantic Books, on behalf of Guardian Newspapers Ltd.
Atlantic Books is an imprint of Grove Atlantic Ltd.

10 8 6 4 2 1 3 5 7 9

A CIP catalogue record for this book is available from the British Library

ISBN 1 84354 008 8

Printed in Great Britain by Mackays of Chatham Ltd
Design by Katrina ffiske

Grove Atlantic Ltd
Ormond House
26–27 Boswell Street
London WC1N 3JZ

Contents

Foreword   vii

In the Beginning   1

Weird and Wonderful   50

Time and Place   94

Lifestyle and Society   149

Life, the Universe and Everything   218

Odds and Ends   277

Index   317

Foreword

In your deeper moments, have you ever wondered what the essence of life is? Or spent hours meditating on the concept of one hand clapping? Or deliberated on whether it is wrong to be wealthy?

Well, if not, don't worry, because the answers are right here in this book. Some of the best brains and most inquisitive minds in the world have come together to solve the biggest puzzles of our time. Things like: why don't Kansas and Arkansas rhyme? Can you use the word 'figment' without 'imagination'. Why do wine bottles have an indent in the bottom?

Readers of the *Guardian*, the *Guardian Weekly* and the *Guardian* website (guardian.co.uk/notesandqueries) have been sending in questions and answers since the Notes & Queries column began in the paper in November 1989. This volume brings together the very best of the contributions from these years. As you will see, there are no restrictions on the kind of queries that can be sent in: readers tackle issues of political philosophy, scientific theory, major historical events... and even the everyday trivia, such as does anyone ever buy a car in response to those 'for sale' notices in the windscreen?

Though not all earth-shatteringly significant, the answers often offer invaluable advice, such as why you should beware if you come across Inspector Sands at the train station. In some cases, readers simply cannot stop arguing. Just when you think you have a definitive answer on the benefits and virtues of homeopathic medicine, another response comes along to confuse things all over again. A few heated exchanges later, and the final answer is . . . well, decide for yourself.

But we don't want to make everyone hot under the collar – life's stressful enough, isn't it? Our hope is that here you will find all the answers you seek and, if not, you can always turn to page 168 where, we promise, you will at least find 'peace of mind'.

Joseph Harker, September 2002

1

In the Beginning

Who invented the T-shirt and why? And who first stuck a logo on?

According to *The T-Shirt Book* by John Gordon and Alice Hiller (Ebury Press, 1988), the first T-shirt dates from the 1899 US Navy uniform regulation. 'This specified a revolutionary "lightweight shortsleeve white cotton undervest" at a time when most men still wore shirts and drawers. These subsequently gave way to the one piece Union Suit, but it took another twenty years before athletic dress styles and the spread of central heating in the 1920s began to establish the T-shirt in America . . .

'T-shirts began to be used as sportswear, principally by the athletic departments of universities which started producing flocked shirts for their teams. Michigan date theirs from the 1920s and UCLA followed suit in 1931. The 1930s also saw the first promotional and souvenir shirts. The 1939 *Wizard of Oz* film T is now highly prized by collectors, but back then the public were not so keen.

'America's entry into World War II produced 11,000,000 new recruits all requiring regulation underwear and in 1942 the US Navy issued their suppliers with the first official specification for what they called the "T-Type". They had been designed as vests, but the troops also wore their T-shirts outdoors as protection against sunburn and when off duty in the evenings. Although most were still plain, Ts printed with the names of army camps and individual divisions became very popular.

'T-shirts acquired a certain combat glamour during the war and a generation of American males went home sold on what the army termed their "better appearance – and greater sweat absorption under the arms". The post-war period saw T-shirts becoming America's No.1 vest. While the conservative fashions of the day limited their potential as adult outerwear, kids were soon wearing printed Ts featuring contemporary heroes like Joe DiMaggio, Davy Crockett and Roy Rogers.'
George McCall, London W3

George McCall didn't mention that they weren't called T-shirts when they first arrived in the UK. I can remember my mother getting a 'Sloppy Joe' for me to wear. I assume the name came from the standard nickname for an American GI ('Joe'), and the fact that Englishmen in the 1940s and 1950s generally wore a shirt and tie, even for leisure activities. Wearing a vest in public was not the done thing.
Geoff Freeman, Bracknell, Berks

Geoff Freeman is off beam, I'm afraid. 'Sloppy Joes' were never T-shirts, but shapeless sweaters. Indeed, the OED refers to the Sloppy Joe, quite specifically, as 'a woman's baggy sweater'– although, as I recall, it was adopted by both sexes, quite possibly making it one of the first unisex garments.
Ron Graves, Prenton, Merseyside

Sorry, Ron Graves, but I have a photo of myself aged eleven at Easter 1949 wearing what I distinctly remember was the first Sloppy Joe I had ever seen or heard of. It was pale yellow and was what we would nowadays call a T-shirt. I thought I was incredibly trendy (though that word hadn't been invented), having been brought up to wear Aertex shirts. It wasn't until around the mid-1950s that they became fashionable, by which time they were called T-shirts. In the USA I'm sure the word was in common usage long before that date.

There were no such things as jeans in 1949 so I wore grey flannel girls' shorts. Jeans (known as denims) came in a few years later, but for women and girls they had side fastenings. I remember, around 1960,

the first time I saw a woman wearing jeans with a zip at the front – it was considered very daring.
Penny Aldred, London SE13

When and why did 'classical' musicians first start dressing for their performances as if they had been invited to a posh dinner?

The practice began when most musicians were employed by aristocratic patrons. Many court orchestras in Europe were also opera orchestras; the dress code was dictated by what the nobles and gentry wore. At the time, the music played was often contemporary. Today, most classical music dates from a previous century, and dress has retained this historical flavour.

Although readers might think that classical musicians are longing to dress otherwise, there is strong resistance to change, from both players and audiences around the world. I can't say why audiences wish to see musicians formally dressed, but as a player myself I can report that my colleagues somehow feel that the thought, care and preparation that go into a high-quality classical performance are best reflected in formal clothes. We have tried dressing down, but are disappointed by the result. Formal modern dress would do just as well, but there seems to be no agreement about what this would be. Clothes designers, please help!
Susan Tomes, London SW19

In Schubert's time he held 'Schubertiads' – evenings of his own music for close friends – which were indeed dinners and all-round social events. Schumann and Chopin adopted similar practices. It was probably Liszt who started dressing for his solo recitals, for which he was world famous.
Douglas Cole, Tunbridge Wells, Kent

If the natives of Afghanistan are Afghans, those of Uzbekistan are Uzbeks and those of Tajikistan are Tajiks, why are those of Pakistan not Paks?

The name of Pakistan, the Muslim-majority state created out of the partition of India that followed the end of the British Raj, consists of two elements, both derived from Persian: *Pak* and *stan*. The Persian language has exerted a powerful influence on all the languages of central and south Asia, and it was the administrative language of India before the British Raj. *Pak* means 'pure' and *stan* is a suffix meaning 'land' or 'place of'. Thus, Pakistan can be translated as 'Land of the Pure' or 'Place of Purity', the purity in question being religious (Pakistan was the first state to describe itself as an 'Islamic Republic'). To call someone 'Pak' (or 'Paki') is to call them 'pure'.

The Tajiks speak a dialect of Persian, whereas the Uzbeks (Turkish *uz*, meaning 'great' and *beg*, meaning 'prince') are a Turkic people. Accordingly, Tajikistan is 'Land of the Tajiks' and Uzbekistan is 'Land of the Uzbegs' (or 'Land of the Great Prince').

Other 'stans' include Almanistan (Germany), Bulgharistan (Bulgaria) and Inglestan (England). Apartheid South Africa had 'Bantustans' – nominal 'homelands' for the country's various 'Bantu' peoples – and the term has passed into English to refer to an unviable or inequitably divided state. The 'stan' suffix can also be applied to places other than countries; hence *mimaristan* (hospital) and *bustan* (garden, or 'place of nice smells').
Mike Diboll, Rotherhithe, London SE16

Mike Diboll is right to say that *Pak* means 'pure' and *stan* is a suffix meaning 'land' or 'place of'. However, this is a coincidence. The official Pakistani government website says that, in 1933, 'a group of Muslim students at Cambridge, headed by Chaudhry Rehmat Ali, issued a pamphlet, "Now or Never", in which, drawing letters from the names of the Muslim majority regions, they gave the nomenclature of "Pakistan" to the proposed State ... Many people believe that Pakistan only derives its meaning from the words that translate into Land of the Pure. However this is not the primary derivation but a secondary one.

'C. R. Ali first wanted freedom for the five Muslim "Indian" homelands in North West British India ... namely Punjab, Afghania, Kashmir, Sindh and Balochistan from British colonial rule, followed by their re-integration with the three Muslim "Asian" homelands of Afghanistan, Iran and Tukharistan (P.A.K.I.S.T.A.N.).'
John Dean, Headington, Oxford

My mother had a saying about the weather, which included the phrase 'enough blue in the sky to make a sailor a pair of trousers'. Does anyone know the full saying and anything about its origin?

I remember well a fairy story from my 1937 Christmas annual, *The Cat's Trousers* by Rose Fyleman. The disconsolate cat had no smart trousers for the Fairy Queen's party. The weather clerk pushed the clouds apart and the cat was able to cut out enough sky for his new trousers.
E. M. Selvey, Sheffield

My mother always used to say the sky had 'enough blue in it to make a Dutchman a pair of trousers'. The implication was always that there was blue sky between the clouds – or maybe Dutchmen always wore trousers made of small pieces of material. The blue refers to the *bleus de travail* that continental workers always wore before the advent of denim jeans.
Maggie Woolley, Hitchin, Herts

In south-west France, a small patch of blue in an overcast sky is often referred to as *une culotte des gendarmes*.
Julie and Peter Barnett, Tintwistle, Derby.

This expression was certainly proverbial by the mid-nineteenth century. In her 1860 novel *The Trail of the Serpent*, novelist Mary Elizabeth Braddon describes a cloudy day as having 'not enough blue in the gloomy sky to make the smallest article of wearing apparel – no, not so much as a pair of wristbands for an unhappy seaman'. Braddon evidently expected her readers to recognize the phrase.
Chris Willis, London E1

When I used to dither over things as a child, my father would hurry me up by saying: 'Come on Fred Frenacapan, get a move on.' I've since learned that other families used the term Fanny Frenacapan. Who, or what, were Fred and Fanny and how did their names come to be used in this way?

I was called Fanny Finickerpants for the same reason.
Alix Smith, London N11

Fred Frenacapan was the hero of a comic song by Gracie Fields, sung in the 1930s and 1940s. The theme was the formal first visit of a girl's 'young man'. It started: 'Pa was there, Ma was there and sister Mary Ann,/All of them waiting for Fred Frenacapan.'

The second verse described all the fine things to eat at the high tea. The last verse tells us that Fred has just come from the dentist, with the final line: 'And the only one who couldn't eat was Fred Frenacapan.'
Jean Bould, Hartshill, Stoke-on-Trent

Spike Milligan once recited me a poem he'd written, which went:

My name is Fred Frenacapan,

I walk about the town

Sometimes with my trousers up,

And sometimes with them down.

And when they were up they were up,

And when they were down they were down.

And when they were only halfway up,

I was arrested.

Perhaps the questioner's father was trying to save his dithering son from a similar fate?
Garry Jenkins, London SE12

What are the respective origins of the words, Kansas and Arkansas? And why don't they rhyme?

Both Kansas and Arkansas are named after native American Indian tribes. Kansas is named after the Kansa tribe, who called themselves Ni-U-Ko'n-Ska, which means 'children of the middle waters'. Arkansas is named after the Quapaw tribe. The Quapaw were called Arkansa (meaning 'south wind') by the Algonquian-speaking Indians.

The spelling and pronunciation of Arkansas are the result of a resolution passed by the state's General Assembly in 1881. Its two

senators at the time were divided on the issue. One senator was always introduced as the senator from 'Ar-kan-saw' and the other as the senator from 'Ar-Kansas'. The resolution declared that the state's name should be pronounced 'Arkansaw' in memory of the original native American inhabitants, but spelled Arkansas, in the French manner, as the French were the first Europeans to explore the area. (Sources: Kansas State Historical Society, Arkansas Secretary of State.)
Philip Sills, Plainsboro, New Jersey, USA

For some years after the war, popular ski-bindings bore the name 'Kandahar'. As that Afghan city may get a lot of snow but seems far removed from the world of skiing, how did the name arise?

The name is derived from Lord Roberts of Kandahar, who was in command of the British army that concluded the second Afghan war with a victory at the city. He was persuaded by Henry Lunn to donate a trophy to a skiing race that took place in the Swiss resort of Crans-Montanaz in 1911. Lunn's son, Arnold, was later to establish a skiing club in Murren, also in Switzerland, to which he gave the name 'Kandahar'.

Arnold Lunn's pioneering of downhill and slalom racing led to the organization in 1931 of the first world skiing championships, also at Murren, and to a close association with Hannes Schneider of the St Anton-based Arlberg Ski Club. From the late 1920s, the Arlberg–Kandahar ski races became an annual event and were later to be incorporated into the Alpine skiing World Cup circuit.
Glyn Evans, Ellesmere Port, Cheshire

Which is the oldest Act of Parliament still to have modern-day powers?

Two statutes date from the reign of Henry III. The first is the Statute of Marlborough (1267). This deals with the seizure by lords of their tenants' goods for default in payments. Among other provisos, the statute prohibits causing such distress upon the king's highway. This provision has been applied in a county court case within the last two years.

The second statute is the contemporary, but undated, Statute of the Exchequer. This also deals with distress for debts, and forbids the seizure of plough beasts and sheep by bailiffs.

John Kruse, Walthamstow, London

Who invented the drum kit?

In nineteenth-century New Orleans, percussion for popular entertainment was provided by two musicians. Traps, the diminutive of 'trappings', was the original term for what we now call a drum kit, and refers to a set of drums operated by a single person. This contrasted with the bass drum fitted with a cymbal hit by a wire beater, played by one man, and the snare drum played by another, as in the parading brass bands. The Alliance Brass Band was reported in 1889 as playing at dances at the Globe Hall in New Orleans.

What is now known as a drum kit, with everything played by a single musician and the bass drum operated by a pedal, is said to have been first assembled by Edward Dede Chandler, born around 1866. He is also credited with being the first to play jazz-style drums in a 'sit-down' dance band, that of John Robichaux, sometime around 1894–5.

Brian Wood, Walmer, Kent

Black is not found on the New Zealand flag, so why was it chosen for the country's official colours in rugby and most other sports?

The all-black outfit first appeared in 1901, when the players who played in New South Wales, Australia, were dressed in black jerseys with a silver fern leaf on the left breast, black shorts and black stockings. When the 1905 tour of Britain, now known as the 'Original All Black' tour began, the players were referred to as New Zealanders and occasionally as Maorilanders.

The first reference to All Blacks was in the London *Daily Mail*'s report of the Hartlepool match that New Zealand won 63–0. The reporter referred to the 'All Black camaraderie'. From then on the new name was gradually accepted.

An alternative version of the origin of the name was given by one of the surviving players of the 1905 tour, who claimed that it was due to a printer's error. The *Daily Mail* reporter at the Hartlepool game wrote that the whole NZ team played with speed and precision, as if they were 'all backs'. Several games later, when the team arrived in Taunton to play Somerset, they were met with placards saying: 'Welcome to the All Blacks.'
Bob Allen, Chevington, Suffolk

The name 'All Blacks' for the New Zealand rugby team certainly originated during the 1905 tour of Britain but the theory that it is based on a misprint for 'all backs' has long been rejected. The name was simply based on the colour of the uniforms and newspapers of the time found 'All Blacks' to be convenient journalistic shorthand for what had formerly been described as 'the New Zealand representative rugby team'.

Incidentally, that 1905 tour was not the first. In 1888–9 a 'New Zealand Native' team (almost all its members were Maori) toured the British Isles, playing an astonishing total of seventy-four matches with forty-nine wins, including a victory over Ireland and reasonably narrow losses to Wales and England. It was a member of that team, Tom Ellison of Otago, who suggested in 1893 that the black jersey with a silver fern be adopted as the national colours.
Jim Sullivan, Dunedin, New Zealand

Why are the occupations of fishmonger and ironmonger the only ones with this particular suffix? And what is their connection with warmongers, rumourmongers and panic-mongers?

The questioner is presumably too young to remember costermongers – fruit and veg barrow-boys, whose wares included 'costards', a kind of apple. However, he's probably seen the word 'whoremonger' at some time; it was certainly in use in Liverpool when I lived there – apart from its being in the Bible. 'Monger' was the Old English word for a seller (its use was first recorded in 975), and of the many combinations of words that have existed for different trades, possibly fishmongers and ironmongers are the only ones to have survived using this suffix, and the latter seems to be on its way out.

One reason for this is that in the Indo-European language system, the origins of the word 'monger' (like the homely 'mangle', a word derived from the name of a stone-throwing weapon, the mangonel) can be found in the idea of 'deceit' (*mangevo* is modern Greek for 'bewitch'). The word 'monger' gradually came to denote disreputable forms of trade, so the supposedly modern belief of anti-capitalists – that selling is a fundamentally deceitful occupation – seems to have a very long history.

'Panic-monger' goes back to at least the first half of the nineteenth century, and 'war-monger' to 1590.

Michael Martin, Chatham, Medway

What was the first book to be protected by a dust jacket?

Probably the instruction manual for the first vacuum cleaner.
Geoffrey Rider, London SW20

Dust jackets as an advertising medium were the most striking innovation in the presentation of books in the first half of the twentieth century. Printed dust jackets began to appear sporadically during the nineteenth century. The earliest example was probably English (the printed paper jacket that protected Heath's *Keepsake* for 1833) but they were also used occasionally in Germany from the 1860s onwards. Printed dust jackets became common in the 1880s. (Source: Philip Gaskell, *A New Introduction to Bibliography*, OUP, 1972.)
Joanna Moody, Pateley Bridge, North Yorks

It is possible that medieval chemise bindings, made of leather or textiles such as velvet, could be considered the precursors of the modern dust jacket. Many manuscripts from the fifteenth century onwards have survived, protected by limp paper bindings. The earliest known limp paper covers and other paper wrappers are documented in Michele Cloonan's book *Early Bindings in Paper*. The British Library houses one of the finest collections of paper and decorative wrapped covers.

In the nineteenth century, book jackets were used as a protective covering for cloth-bound books. These cloth bindings were prone to damage from abrasion and general handling in shops. Early nineteenth-century covers used plain or decorated papers and eventually had labels affixed to the paper in order to identify the book in question. The earliest known printed book jacket still in existence was a jacket for *The Keepsake* of 1833, as mentioned by Joanna Moody. The earliest example of the use of advertising 'blurb' on a dust jacket is attributed to Admiral Dewey by Hon. John Barrett. During the Second World War, jacket covers were used by various ministries to spread information about programmes such as *London Calling Overseas* or to inform the public of safety measures.

Tragically, many libraries removed and discarded the jacket covers of their books, so much bibliographical information has been lost. The National Art Library of the V&A Museum houses numerous boxes of dust jackets, accidentally found by staff at the British Library while packing items during the move to new premises.

Maureen Barcham, Staplehurst, Kent

What is the significance of the Russian craft names Sputnik, Vostok, Soyuz, etc.?

Russian names for their spacecraft are meaningful: Sputnik means 'companion' or 'fellow traveller'; that is, a satellite of earth. Vostok (the single-seat type that Yuri Gagarin travelled in for the first manned space flight) is usually simply translated as 'East', but I have also seen it referred to as something more like 'rising in the east'. Voshkod (Vostok's short-lived twin- and triple-seat successor) means 'ascent' or 'rising' (as of the sun or moon).

Soyuz means 'union'. The USSR was the Union, or *soyuz*, of Soviet Socialist Republics. The name was picked not in homage but because the Soyuz flights' first task was to pioneer docking (or union) of two manned spacecraft. Due to a fatal accident on the first attempt in 1967, the first docking of this sort did not take place until January 1969. Soyuz spacecraft are currently used as International Space Station rescue vehicles; at least one is always docked to the ISS, with a fresh replacement sent up every six months.

Salyut, the series of space stations started in 1971, means 'salute'. Almaz, the military space station built in the 1970s, means 'diamond'. Mir, the long-lasting successor to Salyut, means something like 'peace' or 'world' or 'community'. Zarya, a module of the ISS, means 'sunrise' or 'daybreak'.

Nick Waller, Villetoureix, France

Why is Mothering Sunday on a Sunday, thereby making it impossible for my card to be delivered on the right day? Why not Mothering Saturday? Or Monday?

I don't know and it doesn't matter. My younger son sent his card first class to his mother on the preceding Thursday from Leeds and it arrived in Leicester on Monday.

Robert Bracegirdle, Stoneygate, Leicester

It is on a Sunday so that you actually have to go and see your mother, instead of just sending a card!

Flora Howard, Tunbridge Wells, Kent

The Mothering Sunday 'tradition' as we presently experience it dates from the beginning of the 1950s, according to folklorists Peter and Iona Opie (*The Lore and Language of Schoolchildren*, OUP, 1959). Its origins lie in the seventeenth-century practice, in rural areas, of recognizing the fourth Sunday in Lent as a day when apprentices and daughters in service were free to return home for the day, and they would typically take a small gift for their mother. The custom appears to have all but died out by the nineteenth century.

In the early twentieth century Anna Jarvis of Philadelphia successfully lobbied to establish a day in the American calendar to honour motherhood. In 1913 the Senate and the House of Representatives identified the second Sunday in May as a national holiday – 'Mother's Day'. American servicemen in Britain during the Second World War who celebrated this day revived interest in the idea, and the significance of the earlier date was re-established. This was then seized upon by commercial interests. The Opies note that 'in 1956 the majority of High Street shops were displaying Mother's Day gifts in their windows: confectioners had special purple-printed bands around their everyday tins of toffee, florists were accused of increasing their prices, and stationers who as little as three years before had ignored the occasion now offered for sale a glory of tinselled sentiments.'

At the church near Portsmouth that I attended in the 1950s, the service on Mothering Sunday included a time when we children went to the chancel steps to be presented with a small bunch of violets to give to our mother. There was a rhyme that went with this little ceremony along the lines of: 'We who go a' mothering find violets in the lane.'

Peter Barnes, Milton Keynes, Bucks

Our postmen also object to working on Christmas Day, Easter Sunday and New Year's Day, as well as an awful lot of birthdays.

Robert Rushworth, London SE22

Why not post your card to arrive on Saturday and mark the back: 'To be opened on Mothering Sunday'. Increase the anticipation.

Jill Clarke, Rochester, Medway

There's more to its background than your correspondents revealed. It is part of Mothering Sunday observance, yes; but this mid-Lent Sunday (the fourth in Lent) is named thus not only for the custom of visiting one's mother. *The Concise Oxford Dictionary of the Christian Church* cites also the 'practice of visiting the cathedral or mother church on this day', and 'the words in the traditional Epistle for the Day' as read at Holy Communion are: 'Jerusalem which is above is free, which is the mother of us all' (Galatians 4: 26). Why this somewhat obscure reading was used is another question.

Frank McManus, Todmorden, Lancs

Who first described aristocratic blood as 'blue', and why?

The Arab Moors subjugated Spain in the early part of the eighth century. The indigenous Spaniards possessed relatively pale complexions, and intermarriages between the Moors and Spaniards resulted in a gradual darkening of the 'typical' Iberian skin. The Spanish aristocracy, doing their best to avoid the Moors, removed themselves to northern enclaves such as Aragon and Castile. It is thought that they went as far as shunning the sun in order to heighten their chromodermal uniqueness. So the aristocrats developed very white skin, through which their veins were clearly visible. Dark red venous blood appears blue through skin, therefore these well-bred Spaniards were handed the moniker of blue bloods (*de sangre azul*).

Mike Fisher, Tadworth, Surrey

Why were so many English music halls and theatres called 'Hippodrome', a word that means horse race in the original Greek and is the French word for a racecourse?

The first structure in modern times to be called a Hippodrome resembled the original Roman chariot-racing circuit. It was an arena built in 1846 in Paris by Victor Franconi (of the French circus family), seating 10,000 spectators, and it was used for historic spectacles, mostly involving horses.

The name was briefly used in England for Batty's Hippodrome (also the Royal Hippodrome). It was built in 1851–3 in Kensington to house a circus with the aim of cashing in on the Great Exhibition. In 1900 H. E. Moss chose the name for his new theatre in Cranbourne Street, Westminster. (It was later called the London Hippodrome and most recently the Talk of the Town.) Designed by Frank Matcham, it contained a circus-ring backed by a stage, after the style of Astley's (which had been demolished in 1893), allowing a performance to include music hall, circus acts and melodramas with horses.

The circus ring was covered by stall seats in 1909, losing its equine association but keeping the name. The building was an early move in the transition from music halls, which were associated with public houses and predominantly male audiences, to family-oriented and luxurious theatres of variety. Public companies were set up to finance circuits of suitable theatres throughout the country, accounting for the provincial Hippodromes. It is likely that all theatres called Hippodrome (or Empire or Palace) acquired their name as variety theatres.

Philip Astley, who virtually invented the circus and defined the standard size of ring, in 1779 called his building Astley's Amphitheatre (though it had several other names later). He also built many more such circuses on the continent; the one in Paris was taken over by Antoine Franconi. Astley's ex-employee and rival, Charles Hughes, opened the Royal Circus in 1782, the first use of this word for a building. It was later converted into the Surrey Theatre.

I. N. Anderson, Bournemouth, Dorset

Why is the green room, that haven of pre- and post-show drinks, so called? I was in one the other day and the only green things were the wine bottles.

In Shadwell's play *The True Widow* (Drury Lane, 1679) a character says: 'I have enjoyed the prettiest creature just now in a room behind the scenes.' Later it is described as 'a green room behind the scenes'.

The mundane explanation is that it was a waiting room adjacent to the stage and was decorated in green — as, perhaps, were most theatres. From Britain's première theatre the name may have caught on across the country by touring actors. It may also, however, be connected to the theory that the stage was covered in green baize; green was considered an 'unlucky' costume colour well into the twentieth century, perhaps because it would have been lost against such a background.

I have also heard that it's connected to rhyming slang (greengage = stage), and I have known older actors leaving the dressing room to say: 'See you on the green.'

Antony Tuckey, Ipswich, Suffolk

Further to Antony Tucker's reply, the origin of the green room perhaps lies in a warrant of 1662 'to deliver 110 yards of green baize for the upper tyring rooms of the Cockpit, which in their present state are unfit for rich clothes', noted in Nicoll, *A History of English Drama*. Tiring rooms were dressing rooms, and the Cockpit Theatre, at Whitehall, was used occasionally for plays performed for the court. Baize, a coarse woollen cloth, was usually dyed red or green (its natural colour is beige, which may account for its name). It is one of the cheapest materials with good opacity and weight, ideal for covering rough plaster or planked walls. It was also used in many provincial theatres to cover the walls of the more expensive parts of the public areas.

Whether the court use of this material was copied by the public theatres or merely reflected current practice remains to be discovered, but for over two centuries green baize was universally used for the stage curtain; the Olympic Theatre in Wych Street, which closed in 1904, was the last London theatre to have one. 'Greeny', or 'the green rag', was theatrical slang for a stage curtain and 'behind the green' meant going backstage.

In the late eighteenth century at least, the stage was also carpeted in green for tragedies, reputedly to protect the costumes of the 'victims' from the normally bare boards. Covent Garden used a black curtain for tragedy in the 1820s, perhaps to contrast with this.

The rhyming slang 'greengage' for 'stage' originates from the 1880s, a happy allusion to a colour once almost endemic to the British theatre, in front, on stage and behind.

Noel Anderson, Bournemouth, Dorset

What is the oldest, still-functioning, commercial organization in the world?

I have a bottle of wine purchased in France last year. The label says: 'Alphonse Mellot Père et Fils CHK depuis 1513, Sancerre.' This must be a contender.

Jim Watson, Woodley, Reading

The Shore Porters' Society of Aberdeen, which was founded as a haulage contractor in 1498, is still in business.

David Harvie, Dumbarton

When economic historians look for the predecessors of modern multinationals, the closest parallels they can find are the great cathedrals whose fund-raising and construction were enterprises

dwarfing anything else at the time.
Richard Hilken, Exeter

The wine bottles of Ernst Minges bear the legend: 'Weinbau in der Familie seit 1285.'
Brooke Harvey, Dunmow, Essex

Stora Kopparberg is the oldest share company in the world and can be accurately dated as having started up in 1280 in Falun to exploit the copper deposits there. It is still one of the mainsprings of the Swedish economy.
John Cummins, Bridgend, Callander

The Weihenstephan Brewery at Freising, near Munich, began life as the monastery of St Stephen and has been brewing beer since 1040. It appeared in the 1997 *Guinness Book of Records* as 'the oldest brewery in the world'. Nearer home, the Royal Mint has been making coins since the reign of Alfred the Great. In 1986 it published *The Royal Mint: An Illustrated History* to mark its 1,100th anniversary.
Henry Button, Cambridge

What is the origin of the expression 'to paint the town red'?

The four dictionaries I have looked at agree that this originates from US slang. The earliest recorded use is 1884, and the OED quotes the *Chicago Advance* (1897): 'The boys painted the town [New York City] red with firecrackers [on Independence Day].'
B. C. Rowe, London NW1

The expression is American slang, meaning to go on a reckless debauch, to be wildly extravagant. Originally the metaphor applied to bonfires painting the sky or scenery red. An old Irish ballad contains the lines:

'The beacon hills were painted red/With many a fire that night.'

The immediate source of the phrase may be traced to the times when a Mississippi steamboat captain would strain every nerve to make his boat defeat his rival. 'Paint her, boys,' would be his command to his men as they heaped fuel upon the roaring fires at night, casting a red glare upon the surrounding scenery. Undoubtedly the phrase was helped into popularity by the fact that 'to paint' (that is, to paint the nose red) was an old slang term for drinking. (Source: William S. Walsh, *Handybook of Literary Curiosities*, Lippincott, 1892.)

Peter Whitehead, Shaw Heath, Stockport

This phrase actually originated from Melton Mowbray in Leicestershire. In 1837, after a day of sporting activities, the Marquis of Waterford and friends had a little too much to drink and decided to paint several buildings in the town, as well as the toll gate and the toll-keeper, bright red! There are many paintings by local artists depicting the events of that evening, and also a locally brewed bottled beer, named Melton Red.

Joanne Pagett, Tourism Officer, Melton Borough Council, Leics

Why 'a load of cobblers'? Were cobblers once regarded as deceitful people, much like estate agents are today?

'Cobblers' is rhyming slang for balls, the full and unexpurgated version being 'cobblers' awls' (balls). The dictionary defines an awl as an iron instrument used for piercing leather but the word itself has been in punning use since time immemorial. One of the rude mechanicals at the opening scene of Shakespeare's *Julius Caesar* utters the immortal line, 'All that I live by is with the awl,' which would no doubt have had Elizabethan audiences in stitches.

The Cockney pun becomes obvious in the expression 'kick him in the cobblers'; although this has fallen out of common parlance, I recall it being used by Harold Steptoe's father in the eponymous 1960s TV sitcom.

Stephen Hoare, Farnham, Surrey

> A young man who lived near St Paul's
> Kept referring to Cobblers' bodkins.
> When they said: 'Come along!
> You know that's not right!'

He replied: 'You're all talking rubbish.'
Andrew Nelson, Bishop's Stortford, Herts

There appear to be few instances where a job lends itself to a home-made Cockneyism. 'Merchants' (as in 'merchant bankers') is the most obvious. Estate agents, sadly, do not appear to rhyme with very much. But would the image of schools be improved if they employed good (or bad) 'lays' (preacher = teacher)?
A. Barnes, Chester

The shoe-repairing department at Harrods used to have a sign that said: 'Shoemakers to HRH the Duke of Edinburgh.' I understand that this has now been replaced by: 'Cobblers to Prince Philip.'
John Oakes, Barnet

Why 'hot dog'?

In his book *Made in America*, Bill Bryson says that the hot dog, 'memorably referred to by H. L. Mencken as a cartridge filled with the sweepings of abattoirs', was an established food item in the USA in the early 1800s. But it was not until the early part of this century, when the popular cartoonist T. A. ('Tad') Dorgan drew a picture of a dachshund in an elongated bun, that the term 'hot dog' caught on. It was helped by the fact that the catchphrase 'hot dog' as a cry of delight or approbation was also sweeping the USA.
Douglas McNicol, Bridge of Weir, Renf.

Further to Douglas McNicol's reply, according to *The Encyclopedia of Word and Phrase Origins* by Robert Hendrickson, the cartoonist Tad Dorgan had in mind the fact that many people believed frankfurters were made from dog meat, and no doubt heard the vendors crying out: 'Get your red hots!' on cold days. When Dorgan drew the hot dog as a dachshund on a roll, the indignant Coney Island Chamber of Commerce banned the local use of the term 'hot dog' by concessionaires (they could be called only 'Coney Islands', 'red hots' or 'frankfurters').
David Havenhand, Rawdon, Leeds

The published replies (28 October and 11 November) used outdated information. I spotted the first 'hot dog' citation at Yale University, dated 1895. In 1894, the Yale Kennel Club opened for business. In the 1890s, the 'lunch wagons' were called 'dog wagons' by college students, first at Yale and then at Harvard, Cornell and elsewhere. 'Frankfurters' were called 'hot dogs' by college students before that name caught on at Coney Island.

Leonard Zwilling of *The Dictionary of American Regional English* did an exhaustive study of the language used by the cartoonist 'Tad' Dorgan, and found that Dorgan first used 'hot dog' in 1906.

Barry Popik, New York, USA

The name of the eponymous hero of Nigel Kneale's classic *Quatermass* TV serials of the 1950s was said to have originated in the London phone book. In the introduction to the 1970s reprints of the scripts, Mr Kneale comments that there are none left now. Are there any Quatermasses around and what is the origin of this curious name?

I understand that the name has a very long history. It is first found in France in 1011 when it was Quitrimala, becoming Quatormaus in 1180 and finally Quatremares in 1207.

My grandfather was Richard Paul Quatermass who moved to Walthamstow when it was mainly green fields and ran a newsagent's there for many years. His side of the family came from Ireland.

I have been in contact with John Quatermass of Kingaroy, Australia, who is collecting the history of the Quatermass family, in fifteen volumes with a proven pedigree chart.

Corinne Venner, Ferndown, Dorset

When and where was the first museum? What did it contain? Who thought of such an idea and why?

The first ever known museum may well have been in China, but the first one I know of is that of Princess Bel-Shalti-Nannar, sister of the Biblical Belshazzar, who saw the Writing on the Wall (Daniel 5).

In his book, *Ur of the Chaldees*, Leonard Woolley described how the archaeologists in the 1920s at Ur found in a room dated around 500 BC a group of objects that were all much older. Some were from about 2000 BC, two inscribed stones were from 1400 BC and 2280 BC, and another could have been 2500 BC. A clay object dated about 600 BC recorded inscriptions copied, so its writer claimed, 'from bricks found in the ruins of Ur ... which the Governor of Ur found and I saw and wrote out for the marvel of beholders'. Woolley interpreted this miscellaneous collection as the Princess's personal museum. The room was in her official house close to the temple of which she was priestess.

Incidentally, the Romans are usually credited with inventing the arch and the dome; but Woolley recorded finding domed chambers and arched doorways among the royal tombs at Ur, dated between 3500 and 3200 BC.

J. A. P. Dutton, Ellesmere Port, South Wirral

How did 'canard' come to mean a false report? Was shooting a duck in France somehow unsatisfactory?

The idea comes from the Middle French expression, *vendre un canard à moitié* (half-sell a duck). The falsehood lies in the fact that you cannot half-sell something; the duck is purely coincidental. In German, the expression could equally come from mythology, which speaks of 'marvellous beasts from distant lands'. Numbered in these mythical beasts are *blauen Enten* (blue ducks).

Terence Hollingworth, Blagnac, France

Who first coined the euphemism 'ethnic cleansing' for racial murder and persecution? Surely it must have been a dictator?

The Nazis, as Fritz Spiegl has pointed out, used the term *Rassenreinigung* – the immediate predecessor of the expression 'ethnic cleansing'; this looks less like a euphemism if it is properly translated (from its Serbo-Croat or German form) as 'ethnic purging'.

Robin Milner-Gulland, Professor of Russian and
East European Studies, University of Sussex, Brighton

'Ethnic cleansing' is a literal translation of the Serbo-Croatian phrase *etnicko ciscenje*. Drazen Petrovic of Sarajevo University Law School says in a 1994 article (*European Journal of International Law*) that the preponderant role of military officers in the process suggests that the term originated in military vocabulary.

The English phrase 'ethnic cleansing' does not appear to have been used by any of the major Western media earlier than 31 July 1991, a few days after Croatia declared its independence from Yugoslavia. In a despatch regarding a decision of the Croatian Supreme Council to mobilize extra police reservists in the conflict with Serbian guerrillas in Croatia, Reuters reported that the Supreme Council had accused Serbian guerrillas of wanting to drive Croats out of towns that were mainly populated by Serbs. Reuters quoted the Council as saying: 'The aim of this expulsion is obviously the ethnic cleansing of the critical areas ... to be annexed to Serbia.'

The obviously related expression 'ethnically clean' (as in 'ethnically clean territory') appears in the Western media nearly a decade earlier. At the time, and for at least five years thereafter, it was used exclusively to describe the efforts of Albanian nationalists to drive Serbs from the autonomous Yugoslavian province of Kosovo with the goal of merging Kosovo into Albania.

William Dunlap, Quinnipiac College School of Law, Hamden, Connecticut, USA

During the Arab–Israeli war of 1948, a number of Zionist military operations were given 'cleansing' and related names: Operation Cleansing (Mivtza Nikayon), Operation Broom (Mivtza Matate), Operation Passover Cleaning (Mivtza Bi'ur Hametz). The net result of such operations was the expulsion of 700,000 Palestinians from their towns and villages, rendering large portions of what became Israel empty of Arabs (see Benny Morris, *The Birth of the Palestinian Refugee Problem, 1947–1949*, CUP).

Muhammad Ali Khalidi, American University of Beirut, Lebanon

What is the origin of the word honeymoon?

The word first appeared in print when Richard Huloet in his *Abecedarium*

Anglico Latinum (1552) defined it as 'a term proverbially applied to such as be new married, which will not fall out at the first, the one loveth the other at the beginning exceedingly, the likelihood of their exceeding love appearing to assuage, the which time the vulgar people call the honeymoon'. His description suggests not only that the term had already been around for some time, but also that it was probably inspired by the notion that, although married love was at first as sweet as honey, it soon waned like the moon. (Source: *Bloomsbury Dictionary of Word Origins*.)
Elizabeth Bagheri, Bradford, West Yorks

It was common practice in Babylonia 4,000 years ago that for a month after the wedding, the bride's father would supply his son-in-law with all the mead he could drink. Mead is a honey beer, and because the Babylonian calendar is lunar-based, this period was called the 'honey month' or what we know today as the 'honeymoon'.
Peter Ferrie, Reykjavik, Iceland

Although the words 'honey' and 'moon' are Germanic in origin, the expression is Latin. The equivalent in German (also first appearing in the sixteenth century) is *die Flitterwochen*. The idea is the same – weeks of kissing and canoodling – but the root is different. The French, however, do have the same expression (*la lune de miel*), as do the Spanish (*luna de miel*) and the Italians (*luna di miele*).
Terence Hollingworth, Blagnac, France

I have heard that British volunteers fought for Germany during the Second World War. Does anyone have details?

The only bona fide British combatant on the German side was Thomas Mellor Cooper whose sympathies were due to his mother being German. He fought as part of the SS Wiking Division and was awarded a medal after being wounded on the Eastern Front.

Around fifty other Britons (and some Canadians and Australians) either volunteered or were press-ganged into joining the British Free Corps, often erroneously referred to as the Legion of St George. They were supposed to form the basis of Britain's contribution to Germany's

'Crusade against Bolshevism' alongside other foreign contingents. Apparently several hundred British POWs expressed an interest in fighting the Russians, but were deterred by the notorious reputations of the Free Corps and the Waffen SS.

Although the Germans went as far as issuing the fascists, drunks, cowboys and anti-Nazi infiltrators with their own insignia (including an armband, a Union Jack badge and a collar patch with the heraldic lions of England), the unit was never officially issued with live ammunition. However, several more active members apparently fought to the bitter end in the Berlin bloodbath of May 1945. Their leader, John Amery, was captured and hanged for treason after the war; his trial is covered in Rebecca West's book *The Meaning of Treason*. Rumours persist of an even tinier SS unit, the Stars and Stripes Legion – six pro-Nazi Americans.

David Barnett, London NW5

Did they ever 'shoot the messenger'? If so, how bad was the news?

The trouble is that the messenger is often implicated in the message. In the Bible (2 Samuel 1) an unnamed messenger brings to David news of the death in battle of his arch-rival King Saul, even handing David the crown, so clearly convinced was he that his news was good. On being interrogated, however, he admits that he killed Saul himself, albeit at the mortally wounded monarch's request. Horrified that the man had 'lifted his hand to destroy the Lord's anointed', David had the hapless messenger killed on the spot. Even messengers have to learn discretion.

Michael J. Smith, Swaffham, Norfolk

Bahá'u'lláh, the founder of the Baha'i faith, was exiled from Persia for upsetting the Muslim clergy. He was eventually imprisoned in Akka, in Palestine, by the Sultan of Turkey. From there he wrote to the Shah of Persia: 'We hope, however, that His Majesty the Shah will himself examine these matters.' The messenger, a seventeen-year-old youth, was brutally tortured to death at the instigation of the same Muslim cleric in July 1869.

Mrs A. Bainbridge, Flinders Island, Tasmania

Well, they crucified Christ and they shot Gandhi and Martin Luther King. How bad was the message? 'Love, equality and justice'... How bad can it get?

John Young, Al Ain, Abu Dhabi, UAE

When and why did popcorn become an essential part of the cinema-going experience?

In the Americas, there is a long and glorious history of consuming popcorn at entertainment spectacles, such as baseball games, which long pre-dates the advent of cinema. In fact, it is not inconceivable that the Aztecs happily munched popcorn and sipped chocolate drinks while watching a particularly gruesome immolation. The reason is simple: there are no other foods, save perhaps prawn crackers, that can stick to the end of your tongue like Velcro.

Glen Hearns, Vancouver, Canada

I don't know why, but I do know when. My father has given me a family heirloom of one can of Yarling's Popcorn. It contains unpopped kernels of popcorn that he and his father grew, harvested, dried and canned, then sold to the cinemas in their area. My father said that his father invented the system of canning and promoting it at cinemas. This was in Indiana, USA, and my father said he was about ten to twelve years old, which would have been 1932–4.

Pamela Yarling Dodd, California, USA

In *Shared Pleasures*, his history of movie-going in America, Douglas Gomery explains that popcorn was introduced in the Depression as a way of augmenting the declining revenues of movie theatres. Popcorn was also cheaper than confectionery and so in part replaced it as the preferred movie snack. Gomery records that the popcorn harvest grew from 5 million pounds in 1934 to more than 100 million pounds in 1940.

Ed Buscombe, London NW6

When was the first passport issued, and by whom?

Passeporte is the French for a gate- or door-pass. The first systematic and generalized use of permanent passports in Europe goes back to the time of Louis XIV, when his Foreign Office issued them to foreign diplomats accredited to France. As standing letters of introduction in French, they were eagerly sought after by foreign diplomats for making it easier to secure introductions and facilitate business.

At the same time there was a built-in code, depending on the tint and shape of the paper (square, rectangular, lozenge-shaped, etc.), that immediately indicated to any French official the country of origin of the bearer. His variety of Protestantism could be detected in the punctuation following the addressee's name in the greeting; and his noble rank was revealed in the decorative border pattern. The system enabled the French government to watch where the diplomats went and whom they saw.

F. Adam, Prestwich, Lancs

According to *The Shell Book of Firsts*, the first recorded passports were issued in Britain in 1414, their issue being regulated by Act of Parliament, although there is no record of this in the index of statutes for that year. The more up-to-date format, requiring photographs, was also first issued by Britain, in February 1915.

Arthur Clifford, Southall, Middx

Today's passport is derived from its medieval counterpart, the *guidaticum* (from the Arabic term *widaad*, meaning love, affection, or friendship). The *guidaticum* was a protective passport or safe-conduct that was proclaimed or issued by authorities, especially the king, to Muslims, Christians and Jews, either individually or collectively. In Spain this mini-institution can be traced from the eleventh century into Early Modern times. Several different forms developed in response to commercial and military needs.

The *guidaticum* facilitated surrender agreements between Muslims and Christians, as well as diplomatic embassies, foreign travel, settlement projects, debt and bankruptcy resolution, asylum for felons, licensing, and the conferral of privileged status on students or soldiers.

The etymology of *guidaticum* suggests that our modern passport is linked to the cosmopolitan world of medieval Islam. (See Robert Burns, *The Guidaticum or Safe-Conduct in Medieval Arago-Catalonia*, 1995.)
Paul Chevedden, Los Angeles, USA

The document referred to by Mr Chevedden is indeed a travel piece but is by no means a passport. Its status is that of the laissez-passer used throughout the Renaissance (in Germany and Italy as well as Spain). The passport is a modern identity document, involving information about nationality, personal appearance and (crucially) the existence of a centralized bureaucratic issuing agency, such as the Foreign Office.

The first extant British passport was issued during the reign of Charles I and was personally signed by him. The earliest known French passport dates from the middle 1500s; the first passport issued by the US Department of State bore the year 1796.
Stephen Werner, Professor of French, University College, Los Angeles, USA

What's so terrible about snake-oil salesmen? Why have they become a byword for untrustworthy conmen?

Snake meat contains almost no fat, so snake oil does not exist. A snake-oil salesman is therefore a synonym for a con artist.
David Gibson, Leeds

One would think that snake meat contains little fat, snakes being cold-blooded, but in *The Long Walk* Slavomir Rawicz describes crossing the Gobi Desert and surviving on snakes: 'The clear fat which oozed out over the heat of the fire we used as a balm for our lips, our sore eyes and our feet, and the soothing effect lasted for hours.'
Jeremy Light, Mens, France

David Gibson is logical – but wrong. The oil in question is oil in which a snake has been marinating. It is (alleged to be) efficacious for almost all ills, whether taken internally or applied externally.

Such salesmen are to be seen in Japan, at the monthly flea markets in the Toji temple, Kyoto, for example. The snake concerned is a *mamushi* – a kind of viper, which is poisonous – and it is also to be seen, dried, in the windows of old-fashioned shops selling traditional medicine. I have often seen these salesmen surrounded by eager crowds, with handfuls of cash, ready to buy. There's one born every minute!

Richard Lock, Westmount, Quebec, Canada

The jelly baby is a rather macabre kind of sweet. Who invented it?

Jelly babies were first introduced to this country in 1864 by an itinerant Austrian confectioner who took a job at the Lancashire firm of Fryer's, most famous for their Victory V lozenges. Unclaimed Babies, the original name, carried unfortunate connotations for Victorian moralists and the name was changed to Bright Babies.

Originally a northern taste, they became increasingly popular when one of the characters in radio's *ITMA* kept up a running joke about them. The idea was never trademarked and many firms subsequently cashed in. Over the years we've seen jelly Daleks, jelly cowboys and indians and jelly guardsmen. Bassett's version, complete with authentic belly button, also had a name – Reg. Not in honour of Reg Varney, but because it was Registered Design 885406.

Nicholas Whittaker (author of Sweet Talk:
The Secret History of Confectionery), Burton, Staffs

When and how did bulls and bears become associated with financial matters?

In the phraseology of the Stock Exchange, a 'bear' is a person who sells shares for future delivery, hoping that prices will fall and that s/he will be able to buy them at a lower price before having to deliver them. A 'bull' is a person who buys shares in the hope that prices will rise and that s/he will be able to sell them at a higher price before being required to pay for them.

The term 'bear' was current at least as early as the South Sea Bubble – which burst in 1720 – when the term was the longer 'bearskin jobber', its origin being in the sixteenth-century proverb, 'Do not sell the skin before you have caught the bear/beast/lion'. In *Henry V* (1599) Shakespeare wrote: 'The man that once did sell the lion's skin/While the beast liv'd, was kill'd with hunting him.'

The associated term 'bull' appeared a few years later when the eighteenth-century English comedic dramatist, Charles Johnson, wrote in *Country Lasses* (1724): 'You deal in bears and bulls.'

The continuing animal allusion is probably analogous to the aggression attributed to both animals. Both 'Take the bear by the tooth' and 'Take the bull by the horns' were in common usage in the seventeenth century, with the same meaning of 'to meet a difficulty rather than to evade it'.
Arthur Clifford, Southall, Middx

When was the word 'quack' first used to describe a bogus doctor, and what is the association with ducks?

As the *Oxford English Dictionary* acknowledges, the word is of Dutch origin and was originally 'quacksalver', from the Dutch *kwakzalver*. The OED suggests this as meaning 'someone who boasts about the virtues of his salves' – salve (Dutch *zalf*) being an ointment. The *Woordenboek der Nederlandsche Taal* (the Dutch equivalent of the OED) gives *kwakken*, which, unlike the English 'to quack', does not mean 'to sound like a duck', but 'to move like a duck', to move around unsteadily, to reel, lurch, stagger. So the meaning 'to bungle', also suggested by the OED, seems more appropriate.
Redgy van Hove, Merelbeke, Belgium

Bailey's *Interpreter of Hard Words* (1721) confirms the derivation from 'quacksalver', but gives a Teutonic root. However, it is more likely that 'salve' originated in the word quicksilver (*quecksilber*); toxic mercury was initially lauded as a panacea before eventually being denounced as a symbol of medical malpractice.

Bailey also offers this definition: 'Quacking of Titles (amongst Booksellers): the putting of new and different Titles to Books that

have not had a good Sale, and publishing them for new.'
David Stephens, Brussels, Belgium

I'd always understood that it derived from 'aquatic', as in the aquatic doctors who tended to the wealthy, often with more money than sense, who flocked to spa towns like Bath in the eighteenth and nineteenth centuries.
Judi Hodgkin, Montpelier, Bristol

What is the origin of the song 'The Twelve Days of Christmas'?

Catholics in England during the period 1558 to 1829 were prohibited from any practice of their faith by law – whether private or public. So 'The Twelve Days of Christmas' was written as one of the 'catechism songs' to help young Catholics memorize the tenets of their faith and to avoid being caught with anything in writing.

The 'true love' refers to God Himself. The 'me' refers to every baptized person. The 'partridge in a pear tree' is Jesus Christ, the Son of God. In the song, Christ is symbolically presented as a mother partridge, which feigns injury to decoy predators from her helpless nestlings, much in memory of the expression of Christ's sadness over the fate of Jerusalem.

The 'two turtle doves' are the Old and New Testaments; the 'three French hens' – faith, hope and charity, the theological virtues; the 'four calling birds' – the four Gospels and/or the Four Evangelists; the 'five golden rings' – the first five books of the Old Testament, which give the history of man's fall from grace. The 'six geese a-laying' are the six days of creation; 'seven swans a-swimming' – the seven gifts of the Holy Spirit, the seven sacraments; eight maids a-milking – the eight beatitudes; 'nine ladies dancing' – the nine fruits of the Holy Spirit; 'ten lords a-leaping' – the ten commandments; 'eleven pipers piping' – the eleven faithful apostles; 'twelve drummers drumming' – the twelve points of doctrine in the Apostles' creed.
Mykal Shaw, London E1

My godfather, the late Revd Peter Wyld, told me that 'a partridge in a pear tree' was a corruption of the Latin *Et parturit in aperto*, which translates as: 'And he was born in the open air'.

A similar corruption is the name 'Elephant and Castle' for the place where the 'Infanta of Castile' lodged on a visit to London.

Sebastian Graham-Jones, London SW1

Who sent the first email? When? What did it say?

Ray Tomlinson, an engineer at Bolt Beranek & Newman Inc. (BBN, Cambridge, Mass.), sent the first email message between two computers in 1972. (Tomlinson is also credited for creating the @ sign in email addresses.) I have no idea what the contents were, but if the first email was anything like the billions that followed, it was probably (a) some unrequested information about a BBN product; (b) an unsolicited invitation to visit an X-rated web site; or (c) a message asking whether the recipient got Ray's earlier email.

Stephen Saunders, New York, USA

Who was the first authenticated named individual in history?

Aside from early Biblical figures, who are historically unverifiable, the first named individual was Mes-anni-pad-da, King of Ur in southern Iraq. This name was found on a clay tablet dating to around 3100 BC, and his existence is historically corroborated by later 'king-lists' of the third millennium BC.

Tom Cosson, Norwich

History is the written story of mankind, as opposed to prehistory, which relies on archaeological evidence. According to J. M. Roberts in his *History of the World*, the *Epic of Gilgamesh* is the oldest story, dating from about 2000 BC. Gilgamesh ruled in Guruk in Lower Mesopotamia, part of the Sumerian Empire, and was a real person. At one point he builds an ark to save himself and his family from a great flood that obliterates the rest of mankind.

Neil Martin, History Today Magazine, London W1

Contrary to Neil Martin, Gilgamesh was the legendary king not of 'Guruk' but of Uruk (modern Warka); his reign is placed some time between 2800 and 2500 BCE; and his existence as 'a real person' is not authenticated outside king-lists and poetic fragments dating from several centuries later. There are several earlier named rulers in Mesopotamia whose existence is better corroborated. Also it was not Gilgamesh who was said to have built an ark to survive a flood, but another legendary individual (variously called Ziusudra, Atrahasis and Utnapishtim), one version of whose story was incorporated into the Gilgamesh epic.

Nicolas Walter, London N1

Our £2 coins have 'standing on the shoulders of giants' stamped on to the milled edge. Why?

This is a quotation from a letter by Isaac Newton, a top scientist who later became Master of the Royal Mint. It appears on £2 coins (and on the cover of a book by Melvyn Bragg) because of a misconception about what it means. According to a press release about the coin issued by the Mint, the words refer to Newton's work on gravity and indicate the modest way in which he described his success as being based on the work of his predecessors. None of this is true.

The words come from a letter written to Robert Hooke many years before Newton's work on gravity was published. They are part of a bitter correspondence between the two. Hooke claimed that Newton had stolen his own colour theory of light. It happens that Hooke was a very short man, with a twisted back. Newton's reply was to the effect that 'if I have seen further' it is by standing on the shoulders of giants – meaning 'I have no need to pinch ideas from a little runt like you' and implying that Hooke was an intellectual pygmy.

John Gribbin (author of Newton in Ninety Minutes*), Brighton, East Sussex*

John Gribbin ascribes the phrase to Isaac Newton in a letter to Robert Hooke. But Newton certainly did not coin the phrase (so to speak). He was, knowingly or unknowingly, quoting the saying of a twelfth-century scholar, Bernard of Chartres, which has come down to us via John of Salisbury:

'We are as dwarfs mounted on the shoulders of giants, so that we can see more and further than they: yet not by virtue of the keenness of our eyesight, nor through the tallness of our stature, but because we are raised and borne aloft upon that giant mass.'

As to why the words of a Frenchman should appear on the new £2 coin, perhaps we are being subliminally prepared for the euro.

Heather Lloyd, French Department, Glasgow University

When was food first preserved in tin cans?

In 1795, the French Directory, faced on all sides by the threat of military and naval action, offered a prize of 12,000 francs for a method by which food could be preserved in easily transported containers. It took the chef, confectioner and distiller, Nicolas Apert, until 1809 to develop a method for preserving food, using bottles or jars sealed with wax and heated. His method was a success but neither he nor anyone else knew why, until Pasteur explained the science many years later.

The tin can itself was invented in England in 1810 by Peter Durand, who used sheet steel coated with tin and soldered by hand. Square, oblong and round containers were used. Since the English at this time thought that iron could solve most problems, it was natural that this refinement of Apert's process should develop in England. By 1813, Durand was under contract to the Royal Navy and the patented cans were widely in use in the navy by 1820. They were introduced into America about 1819 but did not really catch on until the Civil War made them essential.

D. N. Mackay, London N10

The first patented can-opener wasn't invented until 1858, when Ezra J. Warner of Connecticut, USA, developed his device, based on the combined principles of the bayonet and the sickle. Until that point, people had used household tools to open their cans. On an 1824 Arctic expedition the explorer Sir William Parry took a can of veal bearing the legend: 'Cut round on the top with a chisel and hammer.' British soldiers, first faced with the new cans in 1812, resorted to using their weapons to open them. If they failed with their bayonets or knives, they shot at the cans with their rifles.

Karen Smith, Burnage, Manchester

Who gave the world's first benefit concert and what was it in aid of?

Joshua and his trumpets at Jericho. The beneficiaries were Rahab the harlot and her family.

Ted Webber, Cairns, Queensland, Australia

An early example took place on 2 July 1944, at the Philharmonic Auditorium in Los Angeles. It was in aid of the legal defence costs of young Chicanos who had been arrested in what came to be known as the Zoot Suit Riots.

On the bill were saxophonists Jack McVea and Illinois Jacquet, trombonist J. J. Johnson, pianist Nat 'King' Cole (under the pseudonym of Slim Nadine), guitarist Paul Leslie (aka Les Paul), bassist Johnny Miller and drummer Lee Young.

Mitch Mitchell, London SE20

Who invented playing cards and what is the origin of hearts, diamonds, clubs and spades?

Playing cards were invented by the Chinese before AD 1000. They reached Europe around 1360, not directly from China but from the Mameluke Empire of Egypt.

The history of suit marks demonstrates a fascinating interplay between words, shapes and concepts. The Mameluke suits were goblets, gold coins, swords and polo-sticks. As polo was then unknown in Europe, these were transformed into batons or staves, which, together with swords, cups and coins, are still the traditional suit marks of Italian and Spanish cards.

Fifteenth-century German card-makers experimented with suits vaguely based on Italian ones, eventually settling for acorns, leaves, hearts and bells (hawk-bells), which still remain in use today. Around 1480 the French started producing playing cards by means of stencils, and they simplified the German shapes into *trèfle* (clover), *pique* (pike-head), *coeur* (heart), and *carreau* (paving tile). English card-makers used these shapes but varied the names.

The spade (*pique*) may reflect the earlier use of Spanish suit marks, from *espadas* meaning swords, and clubs are what the Spanish suit of staves actually look like. Diamond is not only the shape of the paving tile, but may also perpetuate connotations of wealth from the older suit of coins.

David Parlett, Streatham, London SW16

Where and what was the original ivory tower?

The ivory palace in Psalm 45 (and elsewhere in the Bible) is probably that of King Ahab (869–850 BC). Ivory – for decoration rather than as a building material – was used in the ancient Near East as far back as the fifteenth century BC. The reference to the 'ivory tower' in the Old Testament's Song of Songs is not helpful, since it refers to the neck of the woman whom the writer is trying to impress.

Kieran Conry, Catholic Media Office, London

Princeton University's Graduate College tower, completed in 1913, became known as the Ivory Tower because one of the benefactors was William Procter (of Procter & Gamble), the manufacturer of Ivory Soap.

Jo Wood, Leicester

What is the derivation of the expression 'nitty-gritty'?

A few years ago I used the expression in a talk to a group of students. Afterwards I was told that it was, apparently, used by crew members on slave ships in the eighteenth century to refer to the (especially female) slaves held prisoner in the hold, who were no doubt plagued by both nits and grit. The cry 'Let's get down to the nitty-gritty!' was nothing short of a call to gang-rape.

Barry Stierer, Brighton, East Sussex

Barry Stierer's explanation is an urban myth. American dictionaries of slang state that nitty-gritty is an expression that first occurred in American black popular music in the 1950s. Its first use in its current sense was in a speech by the then president of the National Association for the Advancement of Coloured People. The entirely erroneous idea that it was a phrase used by slave owners to describe raping their female slaves seems to have arisen a few years ago on a training course for social workers.

Owen Wells, Ilkley, West Yorks

When were firemen's poles first introduced into fire stations, and who invented them?

According to an exhibit in the Fire Museum of New York City, the first sliding poles, made of polished wood, were used in Chicago in 1858. The first brass poles were installed in fire houses in Boston c. 1880.

Wolfgang Floitgraf, Boston, USA

What does humble pie consist of, and who baked the first one?

When the posh folks of old Northumberland tucked into a tender haunch of roast venison, everyone else made do with the umbles, or offal of the deer. Umbles are at their best when baked in a pie with beef suet, apples, currants, sugar, salt, nutmeg and pepper. But even if you love the taste, eating this pie is an acceptance of second best. For the recipe, see Jill Harrison's *Tasty Trails of Northumbria*.

Kathryn Leigh, London SE15

A pie made from the offal was called 'a numble pie' (from the French *nombles* and Latin *lumbulus*, meaning 'a little loin'). By mistaken word division this became 'an umble pie'. (By a similar process 'a nadder' became an adder, and 'a norange' became an orange.)

The superfluous 'H' seems to have been added, perhaps through error, before the invention of the phrase meaning to be humiliated or made to be submissive, with the implication that umble pie was the food of the lowly. People were certainly eating it in the mid-seventeenth century. 'Humble pie' (with the 'H' but without the metaphor) occurs as early as 1648, whilst Peacock mentions 'numble pie ... and other dainties of the table' in *Maid Marian* as late as 1822.

Nobody is sure whether 'to eat humble pie' is the result of further error, or a deliberate pun, though the latter seems likely. The phrase was in use by 1830 when it first appears in print in Forby's *Vocabulary of East Anglia*. Thackeray uses it in *The Newcomes* in 1855.

Ramin Minovi, Moseley, Birmingham

What actually is the oldest trick in the book?

'And God said "Let there be light"; and there was light.'
W. Huntley, Barnet, Herts

Send me a stamped self-addressed envelope and a cheque for £19.99 and I will tell you.
Lee Wright, Winchester, Hants

Does the oldest trick in the book relate to the oldest profession?
David Stewart, Hitchin, Herts

According to a satirical ditty ascribed to Seneca (a Roman philosopher of the first century) on the death of Claudius:
    Mourn, mourn, pettifoggers, ye venal crew,
    And you, newer poets, woe, woe is to you!
    And you above all, who get rich quick
    By the rattle of dice and the three card trick.
Hugh Sinclair, New York, USA

The oldest trick in magical terms is the cup and ball trick, which is recorded in hieroglyphics in an Egyptian tomb.

Most countries have a version of the trick, in which a magician starts with three cups and three balls; finally three surprise objects are produced under each cup. In Egypt the Gulli Gulli men end up with three live chicks; in Europe three lemons appear.

Steve Kliskey, Chelmsford, Essex

This is found in Genesis 3. A serpent made Eve eat fruit from the tree of good and evil, pretending that the tree was to be desired to make one wise.

Osmund Jacobsen, Torshov, Norway

When were the first fountains made and how were they operated?

An early example of a fountain, found in Mesopotamia, dates from around 3000 BC. It consisted of a series of basins and made use of a natural spring. A similar system can be found in Greek and Roman remains. Mechanically operated fountains became familiar during the fifteenth century in Italy. (Source: Gordon Grimley, *The Origins of Everything*, 1973.)

Ivor Solomons, Norwich

Further to Ivor Solomons's reply: growing interest in the use of water in the new grand gardens of sixteenth- and seventeenth-century Italy is attributed by Simon Schama (*Landscape and Memory*, 1995) to the publication in Venice in 1499 of *The Dream of Poliphilus* by Francesco Colonna. He drew on classical and pagan tradition to develop a mythical world in which water in general, and fountains in particular, played an important role. This dream was made concrete by the architects of Roman and Tuscan villas in the mid- and late sixteenth century, where fountains were conceived as 'stations en route to illumination'.

The 'new' technology of hydro-mechanics, employed to produce the fountains and special effects, was developed by *fontanieri*, whose talents had to combine mastery of both physics and metaphysics. Schama says that this knowledge was drawn from the writings of two physicist–mathematicians, Ctesibius and Hero, working in Alexandria in the third century BC. They were aware of the expanding properties of water under heat, and had experimented with the effects of air pressure and controlled vacuums in order to produce decorative waterworks. This work was known in the Middle Ages through manuscripts in Latin and Arabic, and was published in Italian during the sixteenth century.

The Italian *fontanieri* were soon called on by royalty in France, England and Austria to apply their expertise to their own palaces and

to develop the technology for public works including the supply of clean water.
Peter Mackay, London SE10

Who was Gordon Bennett?

James Gordon Bennett (1841–1918) was an American journalist, the editor of the *New York Herald* (in succession to his less well-known father, also James Gordon Bennett) and a sports enthusiast. He is probably best known now for being the man who commissioned Henry Morton Stanley to search for Dr Livingstone (thus presumably occasioning a telegram that began: 'Gordon Bennett – I've found Livingstone!')

Bennett also introduced polo to the United States and was involved in horse racing (in James Joyce's *Ulysses*, Leopold Bloom spends some time contemplating a bet upon a horse in the Gordon Bennett Handicap, which actually ran that day in Dublin).
Nicholas Graham, Teddington, Middx

In January 1876 Stanley saw a great mountain 'afar off' and named it Mount Gordon Bennett. This was later changed to the Ruwenzori, better known, perhaps, as the Mountains of the Moon.
Rennie Bere, Bude, Cornwall

When Bennett opened his newspaper's Paris office in 1887, he was unable to dine at a busy restaurant, so he bought it and sat down to mutton chops.
Paul Crowther, Knutsford, Cheshire

In 1900 he donated the Gordon Bennett trophy for a race between national teams of drivers and cars. The complex qualifying process for entry led to the exclamation: Gordon Bennett!
George Hartshorn, Badby, Daventry

Once after a heavy drinking bout at a party arranged by his fiancée, he took advantage of the blazing fire to relieve himself in front of the assembled guests. For this he was thrown out and later horsewhipped by his fiancée's brother with whom he had once fought a duel. So as the latest escapade spread among the gossips, all shook their heads in disbelief and despair and said: 'Oh, Gordon Bennett!'

Revd W. Webb, Guildford, Surrey

My sister-in-law, a born and bred East Ender, insists that 'Gordon Bennett' is just a politely extended form of 'Gawd', to avoid accusations of blasphemy.

Si Cowe, Pickering, North Yorks

What was the origin of the old debate about how many angels can dance on the head of a pin?

This poetical and interesting question was raised by Thomas Aquinas (1225–74). He is known as the Father of Moral Philosophy and also as the Angelic Doctor because of his preoccupation with the qualities, nature and behaviour of these celestial beings. He was canonized in 1323.

Muriel Cottrell, Wirral, Merseyside

It is often used disparagingly about theological speculation. In a long-past BBC *Brains Trust* programme, the late Professor C. E. M. Joad used the expression in that way. The following week he was firmly denounced for loose thinking by a listener who claimed, with apparent authority, that there was no evidence that this subject was ever debated. On the other hand, he said, monks in medieval times would, purely as a recreation, hold rigidly structured debates on all kinds of unlikely subjects. So the 'angels' debate could have originated from such a source. Joad had, it seemed, no answer to that. Nor have I – it just stays in the memory from the old *Brains Trust* days.

Stephen Fearnley, Halifax, West Yorks

I was interested to read the comments on this dispute. However, I think that the idea behind it was whether angels had dimensions and occupied space. If they did not, then clearly an infinity of angels could dance on the sharpest, most needle-fine point. Milton gets round the difficulty most beautifully in Book I of *Paradise Lost* when he makes the Fallen Angels appear first 'In bigness to surpass Earth's Giant Sons' and then to 'throng numberless' in Pandemonium like tiny elves — 'incorporeal Spirits'.

Laura Garratt, Uxbridge, Middx

Who was Riley and why does living his life sound so desirable, in spite of dissolute overtones?

The saying comes from a comic song, 'Is That Mr Reilly?' (sic), which was popular in the USA in the 1880s. There was also a music-hall song in England at about the same time: 'Are You the O'Reilly?' One was probably a variant of the other. The latter includes the lines: 'Are you the O'Reilly they speak of so highly? Cor blimey, O'Reilly, you are looking well.'

Stephen Pratt, Twyford, Berks

Why is the sequence of scoring 15, 30, 40 (but not 45) in tennis?

Originally, a point-scoring system was introduced, based on the quarters of a clock and divided into minutes, probably to avoid confusing point scores with game scores. This provided a neat, cyclic '15–30–45 game' system. However, the three-syllable '45' proved too much of a mouthful, so it was soon abbreviated to '40' and has stayed as such ever since.

Ironically, the estranged 'five' has made a comeback at club level, as an abbreviation for '15' when the players themselves are keeping score.

Peter J. Phillips, London E6

Why is New York known as the Big Apple?

The Big Apple was a bar on 42nd Street in New York, which was much used by jazz musicians in the 1920s. When musicians bumped into each other while touring in the States, they would always arrange to meet up again in the Big Apple, and in time this became synonymous with New York City.

Sharon Simpson, London W14

The city of New York for many years has had a large Spanish-speaking population. It is said that one member of this population saw the city (Manhattan in particular) as one large city block – 'una manzana grande'. In Spanish *manzana* also means 'apple'.

Rick Holland, Cheadle Hulme, Cheshire

The explanation that I once heard is that in the 1920s and 1930s jazz musicians in America referred to engagements in large towns and cities as 'a bite of the apple'. The largest city and most prestigious venue was New York – hence the Big Apple.

Arthur Hasler, London N22

To the early Protestant settlers in rural America, urban New York, with its confidence men and painted ladies, was seen as a den of sin and temptation, which threatened their new Garden of Eden. Hence 'The Big Apple'.

Simon Bendle, Upminster, Essex

The Big Apple was one of the many dances that proliferated during the 1920s and 1930s. It first appeared in New York about 1935.

Munroe Hall, Bury, Lancs

As a New Yorker born and bred, I never heard New York City referred to as the Big Apple before the mid-1970s. At that time, New York City was bankrupt. Businesses were moving out and tourism was plummeting. It was in the course of an expensive publicity campaign designed to improve the city's image that the phrase first came into common use.

Why the 'Big Apple'? Well, New York (the state) was at the time the country's biggest producer of the fruit. Patrons of supermarkets all over America were familiar with 'New York apples'. Thus the slogan 'New York City – the Big Apple' was developed to sell the

city to middle America. New Yorkers, of course, never use the phrase.
Maureen Basedow, West Germany

Who tested the first parachute and did he live to tell the tale?

Disregarding Chinese acrobats who, in order to entertain the emperor in the sixteenth century, were supposed to have jumped from various heights with umbrellas attached to themselves, and Fausto Veranzio of Venice, who is supposed to have tested a crude form of parachute in 1616, it is generally accepted that Sebastian le Normand of Montpellier in France was the first person to test a parachute. This he did on Boxing Day in 1783, jumping from the tower of Montpellier Observatory, attached to a rigid parachute made of canvas and wickerwork. He landed safely.

Balloonists developed and refined this form of rigid parachute, and made numerous descents, with varying degrees of success, as part of the general entertainment associated with ballooning. The originator of the folded parachute, which was capable of being stored in a container and opening on descent, was Major Thomas Baldwin of the USA. In 1850, he began successful demonstrations of his equipment, again by dropping from a balloon. However, the parachutes suffered from the limitation that they were attached to the balloon and could only be opened by the effect of the parachutist dropping away, his weight pulling the parachute from its container and, when it was fully extended, breaking the cord attaching the parachute to the balloon.

The reputed inventor of the self-contained manually opened parachute, capable of being worn on the body, was Leo Stevens of the USA. He is said to have demonstrated such a parachute in 1908, although it was not until the First World War that such parachutes became generally available.
Steve Day, Salisbury, Wilts

Why is a pirate flag called the Jolly Roger?

The Pembrokeshire pirate Bartholomew Roberts, known as Barti Dhu or Black Barti, had as his personal flag a skeleton on a black background. Other pirates liked the design and copied it. Because Barti wore a red coat, the French nicknamed him 'Le Joli Rouge', which was corrupted into 'Jolly Roger' and came to mean the flag rather than the person. Barti was a rather strait-laced sort of pirate who banned drinking on board ship, insisted on early nights for the crew and never attacked on a Sunday. He was killed in an encounter with a Royal Navy ship in 1722, aged forty. Yours with a yo-ho-ho and a bottle of rum.

Diana Salmon, Llanfyrnach, Dyfed

Yo ho ... er, hang on a bit. May I contradict Ms Salmon? The Jolly Roger, or Skull-and-Crossbones, was first used by a French pirate, Emmanuel Wynne, about 1700.

J. Claydon, Newmarket, Suffolk

Another possibility is that English pirates in the Indian Ocean began to refer to the red flag of the Tamil pirate Ali Raja by his name. 'Ally Roger' or 'Olly Roger' was later corrupted to 'Jolly Roger'. The English word 'roger', meaning a vagabond rogue, may be another explanation. David Mitchell, in his book *Pirates*, discusses this question and seems to prefer a derivation from Old Roger – a synonym for the Devil.

Graham Hulme, Leicester

'And Bob's your uncle.' Who is Bob? Why is he my uncle and what is the origin?

Attempts have been made to suggest that this catchphrase derives from those blatant acts of nepotism so commonly practised by former British politicians or prime ministers. Thus, in *Eminent Edwardians* (P. Brendon, 1979), we find: 'When, in 1887, Balfour was unexpectedly promoted to the vital front-line post of chief secretary for Ireland by his Uncle Robert, Lord Salisbury (a stroke of nepotism that inspired the catch-phrase "Bob's your uncle"), Parnell's supporters derided him as "the scented popinjay" ...'

It is possible that the phrase contains a punning reference to the early eighteenth-century adjectival use of 'bob' to indicate that things were 'pleasant' or 'nice', and to the late seventeenth-century usage 'all is bob', meaning 'everything is safe'.

Keith Cook, London E12

Why, when a footballer scores three goals in a game, is it called a 'hat-trick'?

The term originated in cricket and refers to the bowler's taking of three wickets in successive balls. George MacDonald Fraser (*Flashman's Lady*, set in 1843) claims the first use for Flashman. When he takes his third wicket (by cheating), the victim, Alfred Mynn, presents Flashman with his straw boater as he leaves the field with the words: 'That trick's worth a new hat any day, youngster.'

More seriously, Eric Partridge (*Historical Slang*), giving 1882 as the probable date of origin, says that it entitled its professional performer to a collection, or to a new hat, from his club. Being gentlemen, amateur players could, presumably, afford their own hats.

Ramin Minova, Moseley, Birmingham

David Harris, the great Hambledon bowler of the 1780s, was presented with a gold-laced hat after a fine spell of bowling, although not actually taking three wickets with successive deliveries. Around 1800 the first top hat, a white beaver, came into vogue and was awarded by some clubs to bowlers who took three wickets with successive deliveries. This practice grew until the late 1800s when the tasselled cap, boater and pillbox cap made the top hat no longer de rigueur. The expression 'hat-trick' was then coined by other sports to indicate a threefold success.

Steve Pittard, Langport, Somerset

When football was in its infancy, and hence footballers were not professional, top scorers were not rewarded for their goals. If a player scored three goals in a match, a hat, or similar container, would be passed round for donations. I presume that only the home supporters would actually chip in.

Peter Orme, Winchester, Hants

Where do the terms left-wing and right-wing come from?

The political terms right and left date from the early days of the French Revolution, and derive from the seating arrangements in the National Assembly in 1789. In the Estates General in May, the nobility sat in the place of honour on the right-hand side of the Chair. In the Constituent Assembly in July, the supporters of the Old Regime also sat on the right-hand side of the Chair, and their opponents therefore sat on the left-hand side, with the moderates in between.

Thomas Carlyle described the result in *The French Revolution* (1837): 'Rudiments of Methods disclose themselves; rudiments of Parties. There is a Right Side (Côté Droit,) a Left Side (Côté Gauche); – sitting on M. le Président's right hand, or on his left: the Côté Droit conservative; the Côté Gauche destructive. Intermediate is Anglomaniac Constitutionalism, or Two-Chamber Royalism.'

This pattern has continued in French and other assemblies, especially those with a circular or semicircular hall. Left and right 'sides' later became left and right 'wings', as the image of seats in a hall was replaced by one of units in a battle, and conventional political terminology was fixed for ever.

In the English Parliament, the government sat on the right-hand side of the Chair but it continued to do so whether its politics were 'left' or 'right'. This pattern has continued in assemblies copied from the British model, especially those with two sides facing each other in a rectangular hall.

Nicolas Walter, London N1

The terms come from the physical make-up of the Parliament in post-revolutionary France. The revolutionaries sat on the left side of the house (denoted by the colour red), the bourgeoisie sat in the centre (denoted by white) and the royalists sat on the right (denoted by blue) – a make-up that can be recognized in the design of the French flag.

Ann Moody, London SW6

Use of the terms 'left' and 'right' in fact pre-dates the French Revolution by over a century. They were used in the 1680s by the Societies United in Correspondence ('Covenanters'). The Societies used them in the opposite sense to ours, right being extremists and left moderates.

In the late nineteenth century the American and French revolutions and the first English working-class political organizations were influenced by the tradition handed down from the Societies of the seventeenth century. It is probable that the French Assembly adopted the phrase from this tradition, and in it the extremists sat on the right and the moderates on the left. But when the chairman called on a speaker, he called him from his right or left hand, with the result that the meaning of the words reversed.

C. Wason, Bridgwater

There is no connection between the layout of the seats in the French Assembly and the development of the red, white and blue tricolour, as suggested by Ann Moody.

It's true that red was associated with the left (a red flag was hung outside the Jacobin Club), and that white was the colour of the monarchists (it was the livery colour of the Bourbons). There is also a case to be made for identifying the colour with the Three Estates. But the development of the Tricolore was completely coincidental, and was based on colours originating in the municipal arms of Paris, combined with the Bourbon white. In any case the Tricolore was established well before the 'post-revolutionary parliament'. The cockade was officially adopted on 31 July 1789, and the tricolour flag on 24 October 1790, but the first revolutionary assembly did not open until 1791.

William Crampton, Director of the Flag Institute

What does OK stand for? Why is it such an internationally understood phrase?

The origins of 'OK' are still hotly debated by American professors. Bill Bryson, in his book *Made in America*, lists nine possible derivations, ranging from 'Only Kissing' to 'Olla Kalla' – allegedly Greek for 'all good' – to *okeh*, the Choctaw Indian word for 'yes'.

Some claim that OK was what President Andrew Jackson, who started life in the backwoods of Tennessee, wrote in the margins of documents, signifying 'Orl Korect', when he was in the White House in the 1830s. The initials first appeared in print in the *Boston Morning Post* in 1839 as a whimsical shortening of 'Oll Korrect' and were taken up the following year by supporters of Jackson's protégé and successor as president, Martin Van Buren, who set up OK Clubs to help his election prospects. Van Buren was known as Old Kinderhook, after his home town in New York, but that may have been a piece of tidying-up to improve the nickname of a rather fastidious politician.

Steve Bates, London SW1

One theory is that it originated among African Americans. Apparently, in Mandingo *o ke* means 'all right' and in Wolof (Senegal) *wav kay* means 'yes indeed'. Use of the term in New England c. 1840 (the first known use was in a Boston newspaper) has been put down to the steady influx of refugees from the Southern slave states.

Other suggestions about origins include: the Latin *omnia correcta*; the southern French dialect word *oc* (*oui*); *aux quais* ('to the harbour') stencilled on casks of Puerto Rico rum specially selected for export; Aux Cayes (a place in Haiti noted for the excellence of its rum); the Scots 'och aye'; and the initials of Otto Kaiser (a German-born US industrialist).

Basil Morgan, Uppingham, Rutland

It goes back much further than either of your correspondents suggests. When the Black Prince married Eleanor of Aquitaine, he became Henri II of France (which was in fact four different countries in those days). The local dialect of Aquitaine (the south-west of France) was Occitaine, which is still spoken today in more rural parts.

'Oc' is obviously a shortened form of Occitaine and also means 'yes'. Henri brought this word back to England and the rest is history.

Dave Novell, Leeds

Dave Novell's letter contains historical inaccuracies.

First, the Black Prince may have been Duke of Aquitaine (or Guyenne as it was known to the English) but he did not marry Eleanor of Aquitaine – he was Eleanor's great-great-great-great-grandson. Eleanor's husband became Henry II of England, but Henri II of France was the husband of Catherine de Medici and he died in a tournament in 1559.

France was never four different countries, just one country whose king was so weak that he had magnates who were more powerful than he.

Occitaine was never a dialect but a full language, spoken widely across all of what is now southern France, north-east Spain, the Balearics and north-west Italy. From Occitaine are descended Provençal, Mallorquin and Catalan. The great linguistic divide of France was typified by the word used for 'yes'. In the north it was *oeuil*, which has now become *oui* but was then pronounced something like 'aye'. In the south 'yes' was *oc*, hence the alternative name of the heartland of Occitanie – Languedoc.

But, if we are genuinely to believe that *oc* was the origin of the term 'OK', it has even older roots than Mr Novell suggests. *Oc* itself was derived from the Latin affirmative *hoc*.

Colin Pilkington, Ormskirk, Lancs

2

Weird and Wonderful

A refuse tip for Tendring council in Essex is directly opposite a holiday caravan camp called 'Shangri-La'. Do readers have other examples of inappropriate place or business names?

The funeral directors, F. A. Holland & Son, are based in Terminus Road, Littlehampton.
Bob Higham, Brighton

The Southern Water sewerage outfall to the east of Brighton leaves the shore at Portobello – the name was there before the sewers.
Bryan Moody, Hove, East Sussex

In Hemel Hempstead there is a small industrial estate called Paradise, and a business park called Dolittle Meadow.
Cecily Roberts, Hemel Hempstead, Herts

Some years ago I drove past a bed and breakfast establishment near Plockton called 'Nessun Dorma' (Let no one sleep).
Bernadette Newman, London SE13

York has a care home for the elderly in a road called Saint Peter's Close.
Steve Marshall, Usk, Monmouthshire

Mount Pleasant in central London derives its name from an ironic eighteenth-century reference to the rubbish dump on that site.
Will North, London E8

Bernadette Newman cites 'Nessun Dorma' in Plockton, in the Scottish Highlands, as an inappropriate place name. She does not mention that the B&B in question is adjacent to the Inverness–Kyle railway line and that the name is plainly ironic.

Might I suggest 'No Place' near Stanley in County Durham as a non-ironic inappropriate name.
John Price, Biddick Village, Tyne and Wear

One approaches our local crematorium via Charcoal Lane.
Kay Steward, Altrincham, Cheshire

At a coastal resort, where I happened to live some years ago, there was a boarding house called 'Park View', opposite a car park on a disused railway siding.
Janet Merrifield, Oswestry, Shropshire

Great Britain and United Kingdom.
Piers Beirne, Bowdoinham, Maine, USA

Bucks County Council operates a waste disposal and recycling facility at High Heavens between Marlow and High Wycombe. The name pre-dates the council activity, as evidenced by nineteenth-century maps.
Ian Bates, High Wycombe, Bucks

In Birkenhead the local family planning service runs their vasectomy clinic from a health centre in Balls Road.
David Coombs, Birkenhead

There's a bridge in Cornwall called Notter Bridge.
Bernadette Fallon, St Day, Cornwall

The Leeds Centre for the Blind is based in a building called 'Shire View'.
Nick Redfern, Leeds

A recent *Guardian* article mentioned the Theatrephone link, which relayed performances from the opera house direct to people's homes in Paris in the early 1900s. Does anyone have more information?

In 1881, Clement Ader staged a demonstration of the Theatrephone as part of the Paris Exhibition of Electricity. He installed a series of specially constructed microphones across the front of the stage of the Paris Opera. These microphones were connected to receivers in the exhibition hall of the Palais de l'Industrie by telephone lines laid through the Paris sewers. The design of the receivers was essentially similar to the hand-held units then used for telephones but each listener would hold two receivers, one to each ear – a clear precursor of stereo sound and the first ever 'broadcast'.

The system developed and remained in service until the 1920s, providing subscribers with 'broadcast' music via pay telephones. Other systems evolved, notably in Budapest where a Theatrephone service provided not only music but news bulletins and feature programmes.

Tony Gibbs, Lansdown Centre for Electronic Arts, Middlesex University, London

Is there a scientific explanation as to why fire-walkers don't seem to burn their feet, or is it simply a mind over matter thing?

Fire-walking is a circus stunt. The fire-walk always takes place outdoors, just after sunset. The fire-walkers stand around barefoot in damp, freshly watered grass for an hour or so, listening to a lecture about 'positive energy' and other nonsense. This ensures that their feet become cold and wet and that the dead skin on their soles absorbs a lot of water.

When the walk begins, the coals – which are just barbecue charcoal – are raked over a cold patch of ground, separate from where the fire was burning. The walkers then march smartly over the smouldering coals, completing the walk in around two seconds.

There is a distinction between the temperature of a body and the amount of heat energy it contains. Wood charcoal can be very hot but actually contains very little energy. Also, you have to get the energy out of the hot substance by conduction and wood is a poor heat conductor. However, a cold, soggy foot needs a lot of energy to heat it enough to damage the living tissue and this amount of energy simply cannot be transferred in the few seconds that the foot is in contact with the coal.

If fire-walkers were to try to walk over red-hot steel ball-bearings heated to the same temperature, they would experience a very different result.

Owen Boyle, Nyon, Switzerland

Professor Richard Wiseman conducted a notable experiment on fire-walking on a *Tomorrow's World Live* show some years back, where 'expert' fire-walkers were asked to walk over sixty feet of coal. The hypothesis was that if fire-walking truly was mind over matter, they should be able to handle any distance of coal – not just the usual fifteen feet. As it turned out, none of the fire-walkers could go the distance and they had to be treated for second-degree burns.

Adrian Hon, Cambridge

Some years ago I read about a nineteenth-century man who was a compulsive walker, daily covering great distances. As he aged he was able to walk less far, and ended up walking round and round his bedroom. Can anyone provide details?

The questioner is probably referring to an eighteenth- rather than a nineteenth-century walker. Foster Powell (1734–93), known as 'The Astonishing Pedestrian', was able to walk at amazing speeds and would terrify people by his sheer walking power as he zoomed past them. In 1787 he walked from Canterbury to London Bridge and back again in less than twenty-four hours. His favourite route was from London to York and it is recorded that at the age of fifty-eight he did this journey in five days, fifteen hours and fifteen minutes. Whether he took to walking around his room I don't know.

David Kidd-Hewitt, Great Missenden, Bucks

An article by Dr R. Conrad in the Long Distance Walkers' Association magazine, *Strider*, told the story of William Hutton, a Nottingham-based bookbinder who was born in the Midlands in 1723. In his early twenties, when he needed working materials from London he would walk there to buy them. In three successive days he walked fifty-one, forty and forty miles respectively, conducted his business in those three days and walked back home again.

At the age of seventy-eight he achieved his ambition to see Hadrian's Wall, walking all the way there from Birmingham. And at eighty-nine, though his sight was failing, he still managed to walk the three miles to the centre of Birmingham. Aged ninety-one, he complained: 'If I once give up walking I shall never recover it again.' Helped by servants, he continued to stumble around a quarter-mile course that he had measured out in his garden – although by then he was scarcely able to drag one foot after the other. Finally confined to his bedroom, he still made circuits of that, always needing support. He died in 1815.

John Jennison, Baildon, West Yorks

In 1805 a man named George Wilson set a new trend, that of 'pedestrianism' (sustained walking of a set number of miles in a certain time). Much of his walking took place on Blackheath, London. He was due to walk 1,000 miles in 1,000 hours (about twenty-four miles per day for over forty days). Unfortunately he was arrested before he completed his millennial mile, thanks to a rowdy and drunken crowd, a small herd of elephants and fear of a riot. More details can be found at Lewisham Reference Library.

Francesca Pont, London EC1

Years ago a man in his seventies told me that, at the beginning of the twentieth century, there was a land-based torpedo on the South Coast, controlled from the shore by trailing wires. He said that he had manned the weapon. Can anyone supply more information?

In 1885 the Irish-Australian marine engineer, Louis Brennan, introduced a coast-defence torpedo, which was not so much wire-guided as wire-driven. Hundreds of yards of eighteen-gauge piano-wire were wound around a drum in the body of the torpedo itself and led aft to a powerful steam-winch on the beach. The winch drew the wire rapidly ashore, which in turn spun a propeller that drove the projectile seawards. The torpedo, therefore, uncoiled along its own wire towards its target. Apparently, this bizarre contraption could achieve some thirty knots at a constant depth of ten feet.

The system was first deployed along the River Medway in order to protect the dockyards at Chatham, where some of the brick winch-houses may still be seen. This was obviously a very cumbersome operation and, in 1888, a simpler system was developed by Nordenfelt, in which the torpedo carried its own batteries and electric motor. It was still guided, however, by means of wires running ashore. I assume Mr Corbett's informant was referring to one or other of these systems.

By 1900, however, the compressed-air-driven 'free' torpedo became the norm, whether launched from shipping or from shore installations. Even today, however, some submarine-launched torpedoes are still wire-guided.

J. E. Muldowney, Haworth, Yorks

In Ballsbridge, Dublin, in the 1970s, I remember the Swastika Laundry. Down the sides of its tall red-brick chimney, clearly visible from the surrounding area, was painted the name in block capitals, with large swastikas at each end. Does anyone know the origins of this firm, and how such an infamous symbol could have survived for so long?

When the Swastika Laundry was founded in 1912, the symbol had none of the infamy that the Nazis were subsequently to dump on it. Another commercial use from the period was on the front covers of the Macmillan 'Pocket Editions' of the works of Rudyard Kipling, which continued to be reprinted until at least the late 1920s.

Growing up in post-war Dublin, I heard stories suggesting that the strong branding on the tall chimney had been designed to prevent German bombers targeting it. Given Ireland's neutrality, this could be seen as a bit excessive although it could also be argued that it worked, as the only wartime bombs to fall on Dublin (from a navigationally challenged Luftwaffe plane) landed several miles away on the other side of the Liffey.

Nick FitzGerald, Brighton

There's a comic scene in the *Irish Journal* of the Nobel prize-winning German writer Heinrich Böll, in which he describes his visit to Ireland shortly after the Second World War. For Böll, Ireland is a refuge from the horrors he has just lived through, so it comes as a shock when, walking the streets of Dublin, he is nearly knocked down by a laundry van and looks up to see a swastika emblazoned on its side.

Adam Dawtrey, London W14

In Copenhagen a few years ago I visited the Carlsberg brewery and saw its famous Elephant Gate. The elephants are all adorned with swastikas, which were at one time seen as a symbol of 'quality, cleanliness and purity' (perhaps something that the laundry was also proud to boast). The swastika was the symbol of the Carlsberg brewery – it can be clearly seen on old bottles – until the Second World War.

Darren Cawthorne, Scunthorpe, Lincs

Nick FitzGerald is wrong to claim that in 1912, when the Swastika Laundry was founded, the symbol did not have infamy attached to it. In 1910, Guido von List, poet and nationalist, suggested the swastika as a symbol for all anti-Semitic organizations, and the National Socialist Party duly adopted it in 1919/20. The fact that the laundry did not subsequently change its name, and carried this symbol high on its chimney for decades after 1945, is not insignificant.

Fred Lowe, Ballsbridge, Dublin

Further to Nick FitzGerald's letter, the Swastika Laundry was indeed founded in 1912, by my grandfather Jack Brittain. He had set up two laundries in Dublin before moving in 1910 to London, where he also ran one. Wanting to set up his own laundry back in Dublin he returned there in November 1911.

Many names for the new venture were discussed. One day he visited the White City Exhibition where my grandmother bought some highly ornamented hat pins, designed to hold the large picture hats then fashionable. My grandfather's attention was drawn to one in the shape of a swastika. A leaflet explained that it was one of the oldest good luck signs in the world ('swastika' is in fact a word of Sanskrit origin, meaning 'well-being') but it had to be depicted straight, not tilted, as this would bring bad luck. (The emblem used later by the National Socialist Party was tilted through forty-five degrees.) It is reported that my grandfather proclaimed: 'Mother, I've got the name of the new laundry.'

Regarding Fred Lowe's point, the significance behind the Swastika Laundry retaining its name after 1945 was purely commercial. The laundry had been a very successful and well-known business in Dublin for many years and it remained so until it was taken over in 1987; changing the name would not have been commercially sensible. Besides, the modern vogue for reinventing corporate identities had yet to be discovered.

Tim Graham, Bath

Further to previous replies: a slightly unsettling find in an antique shop a couple of years ago was an enamel lapel badge bearing a swastika and the words: 'National War Savings Committee: For Service.' Equanimity was restored when I realized that it must be from the First World War.

This particular use of the symbol was mentioned, in passing, during a 1996 Commons debate on granting a badge to the (disbanded) 273 Squadron. This fighter squadron operated in Ceylon and Burma in the Second World War, and the proposed badge design included a 'fylfot' as an Asian symbol of peace and goodwill. Chambers defines 'fylfot' as 'swastika'.

Ian Nolan, Eastleigh, Hants

I have heard of Jeffrey Hudson, an eighteenth-century 'dwarf', who ran with the pirates, constantly duelled with his detractors and was frequently presented to high society encased in a pie or a cake. Does anyone know more about him?

It is, perhaps, only right that Sir Jeffrey Hudson (1619–82), England's smallest man, should have been born in England's smallest county, Rutland (motto: *Multum in parvo* – much in little). The son of an Oakham butcher who was of normal proportions, Sir Jeffrey was only eighteen inches tall until well into middle age when he 'grew' to a height of three foot six.

He came to the attention of Henrietta Maria, the wife of Charles I, when he was hidden inside a venison pie at a banquet in her honour held at the Duke of Buckingham's home near Oakham, where he was a page. He remained a loyal servant to the Queen and saw service during the Civil War. However, a staunch Catholic, he was eventually caught up in the panic surrounding the Popish Plot, the invention of Oakham's other famous son, Titus Oates. After a spell in prison, he was released and lived off a pension supplied by the new Duke of Buckingham, the son of his first sponsor.

He was written into one of Sir Walter Scott's lesser-known Waverley novels, *Peveril of the Peak* (now out of print), where his appearance and eventful life are described in greater detail than is possible here.

The most famous painting of Sir Jeffrey is Van Dyck's *Queen Henrietta Maria with Sir Jeffrey Hudson and an Ape*, in the National Gallery, Washington DC. There are other portraits in a private collection near Oakham and also at Petworth House in Sussex, owned by the National Trust. His clothing can be seen at Sherborne Castle in Dorset; but the strangest artefact is a life-sized statue of the adult Sir Jeffrey on display in the public bar of the Boat Inn in Portumna, County Galway.

The house where Sir Jeffrey was born (The Dwarf's Cottage) has recently been given a blue plaque, although it is privately owned and not open to the public.

Michael Walton, Pordenone, Italy

In 'Some Famous Dwarfs', her contribution to *A Pageant of History* (Collins, 1958), Frances Collingwood gives the following information:

'When the Queen [Henrietta Maria] fled to Paris, [Hudson] went with her and there fought two famous duels. The first was against a turkey cock and the second against a Mr Crofts. The man did not take his little opponent seriously and turned up armed only with a squirt. Sir Jeffrey, mounted on horse-back to bring him up to Crofts' level, shot his opponent dead. Leaving Paris in a hurry, he tried to return to England, but pirates caught him in the Channel and he was sold into slavery.'

Mrs A. A. Hesson, Burnley, Lancs

What is the deepest that man has penetrated below the earth's surface, and what proportion does this constitute of the distance to the core?

The deepest that man has penetrated below the earth's surface is 3,777 metres at the Western Deep Levels gold mine in the Transvaal, South Africa. The earth is not spherical and the best approximation is an ellipse rotated about its minor axis, so the distance to the centre of the earth varies with latitude. The earth's equatorial radius is 6,378 kilometres; assuming that this is reasonably accurate for the Western Deep Levels, the depth mined represents little more than 0.05 per cent of the distance to the centre of the earth, although a latitude correction should be made. The depth to the core – as opposed to the centre – of the earth, is approximately 2,898 kilometres, so the mine depth is marginally over 0.1 per cent of this figure.

Dave Haynes, Lancaster

Further to Dave Haynes's reply, the deepest penetrations have been by boreholes, not mines. There is a 9.1 kilometre borehole in Germany, part of the Continental Deep Drilling Project (KTB), but deeper still is the 12.25-kilometre 'Superdeep' hole in the Kola Peninsula near the Arctic Circle in Russia, drilled between 1977 and 1989. The latter is roughly 0.4 per cent of the distance (2,900 kilometres) to the core of the earth.

Leib Wolofsky, Niagara-on-the-Lake, Ontario, Canada

The Mohole project in the early 1960s drilled to 124 miles (122 miles of ocean floor beneath two miles of ocean off the coast of California). The purpose of this project was to determine the nature of the Mohorovicic discontinuity, which is the boundary between the earth's crust (which makes up the continental land masses), and the earth's

mantle, on top of which it floats.
Philip Sills, Plainsboro, NJ, USA

Some of the earlier answers have been misleading. Project Mohole was funded by the US government in 1957, stoked by the belief that the USSR was planning deep drilling. The pilot project succeeded in drilling 197 metres – not 197 kilometres, as Philip Sills stated – into the bed of the Pacific Ocean from a drilling barge on the surface nearly three kilometres above. The project was abandoned in 1966 when unsavoury financial links came to light between the Texan oil-drilling company running the project and the Democratic Party.

The USSR had indeed planned since about 1960 to drill deep holes onshore. The Superdeep Number 3, in Kola, Russia, remains the world's deepest hole into the earth, at 12,261 metres. It took from 1970 to 1984 to get that far. One of the scientists in charge told me that they were keen to license their world-leading drilling technology to the West for hard currency. But the government decreed that since the West wanted the knowledge, it should be classified as a state secret – so no deal. The project was put on hold due to lack of funds, and the Russians' capability to drill to 15,000 metres will probably never be tested.

However, the results disproved outdated concepts held by influential conservative USSR geologists, and the plate tectonic paradigm came to be officially accepted.

The German deep-drill hole, the KTB in Bavaria, was planned to go down to 10,000 metres, but drilling was abandoned in 1994 at a depth of 9,100 metres, as the temperature of 280°C at the bottom turned out to be hotter than expected. Every time the drill-bit was withdrawn for replacement, the lower portion of the hole closed up due to the plastic flow of the rocks. Thus it will probably never be possible to drill much deeper unless you choose a region of cold crust, as the Russians did.

An ancient meteorite impact crater at Siljan, central Sweden, was drilled to test the hypothesis promoted by Thomas Gold that oil deposits can originate from abiogenic methane. Drilling stopped at a depth of 6,957 metres in 1988. Gold claimed that the minute amounts of methane recorded, together with an oily sludge, point to the origin of oil from a deep crustal source. Oil industry geologists dispute this.

They can account for the findings either by conventional theory for oil production from organic matter, or else by contamination from the drilling fluids. Gold's claims persuaded private investors to fund another deep hole nearby. He says that eighty barrels of oil were recovered, but his predicted 'giant oilfield' was never found.

(Professor) David Smythe, Glasgow

I have read of a nineteenth-century town clerk who inserted the words 'and the town clerk's marriage is hereby dissolved' in the technical clause of a municipal bill. No one noticed, the bill received the royal assent and he and his wife went their separate ways. Can anyone shed further light on this?

R. E. Megarry discusses this legal fable in his book *Miscellany-at-Law* (1955). After quoting true examples of errors in Acts of Parliament, he writes: 'Instances such as these give new hope to those who still have faith in the old story about a private or local bill into which an unauthorised and unnoticed insertion was made for personal reasons.' He quotes the town clerk story, from the days when divorce was only possible by Act of Parliament, adding the gloss that when the town clerk died the problem arose of whether the clause applied to his successors in that office.

Megarry then owns up to inventing the last bit himself on a previous occasion, concluding: 'It needs but a slight knowledge of human nature to suspect that the main corpus of the story was also knowingly evolved – by a man – to meet a long felt want.'

Philip Spruce, Hall Green, Birmingham

Whatever became of Joanna Southcott's Box? What were the contents? I recall seeing advertisements placed by the Panacea Society claiming that when the box was opened the problems of the world would be solved. Am I to assume that the box has remained closed?

The Panacea Society was created by the followers of Joanna Southcott, a nineteenth-century 'prophetess' who wrote more than sixty books of religious thoughts. She claimed to be pregnant with a messenger from God called Shiloh, and thousands of believers awaited news of the birth. Most of them melted away when it was announced that Shiloh had been taken up to Heaven immediately on being born. In fact it was a phantom pregnancy.

Before Southcott died, she said that the secrets of eternal peace and contentment had been left in a sealed coffer until twenty-one bishops of the Church of England should open it, at which point Christ would return to earth and bring with him perpetual peace.

After her death she still had some supporters, and after the First World War the Panacea Society enjoyed a resurgence. Believers moved to Bedford where they bought a number of Victorian houses in the town centre. In a room in one of them there is a table with twenty-one chairs waiting for the bishops to turn up. As Southcott demanded that they spent three days in prayer and debate before the opening of the box, there was an unsurprising reluctance to spend sixty-three bishop-days on this matter. However, at one point the box was opened by a smaller delegation and, according to report, all that was found was a primed pistol fixed to go off when the lid was raised. Fortunately for whichever bishop opened the lid, the pistol had rusted and did not fire. The Panaceans proclaimed that this was not the real box, which still awaited fulfilment of the condition of Southcott's will.

The Panacea Society still exists in Bedford, though its numbers are down to a few elderly people. They stopped advertising some thirty years ago (the *Daily Mail* would call them whenever it had some unsold space and offer them a cheap deal). Recently the society has started painting and renovating its houses in Bedford and a member confirmed to one of our reporters that this was being done in expectation that Christ would return for the millennium.

There is, apparently, another Joanna Southcott organization in Britain in addition to the Panacea Society.

Frank Branston, Bedfordshire on Sunday, Bedford

Frank Branston's explanation is not accurate. Joanna stipulated that the box could only be opened by twenty-four bishops, who had to study its contents for seven full days and nights. The box-opening to which Mr Branston referred was fake, part of an ingenious stunt set up by professional publicist Harry Price in 1927 to advertise his new National Laboratory for Psychical Research. Of the twenty-four bishops invited, only the Bishop of Grantham was present. There were fifty-six articles inside, one of which was a rusty horse pistol, but the story about it being primed to fire is not true.

The real box was held in the custody of a Yorkshire family called Jowett, from Leeds and Bradford, through five generations. Southcottians have campaigned vigorously since Joanna's death in 1814 for the box to be opened, maintaining that it is vital this is done before Judgement Day, in 2004. The box was eventually handed over to Annie Stitt, the head of the Southcottian Society in Blockley, Gloucestershire, who lived in Joanna's old home, Rock Cottage. In 1966 she put it for safe keeping in the British Museum. 'It is safe in their care and well guarded,' she wrote to a fellow Southcottian. 'The head man in London took me to see the big table with twenty-four seats round it, where the bishops will one day open the Box.'

But it was the Museum curators who opened the box, selecting any papers they felt were of interest. These were bound into two thick volumes and are now kept in the Museum library. The actual box and the rest of the contents were stored in the basements, after which Museum officials lost track of it.

The Panacea Society in Bedford, to which Mr Branston referred, is a schism group formed in 1920 and is regarded with suspicion by 'purist' Southcottians. Joanna died apparently in the throes of childbirth, but no child appeared and disciples claimed that she had in fact given birth to a spiritual child, named Shiloh; modern-day Southcottians believe Shiloh has already returned and is occupying the body of Prince William. My book, *Satan's Mistress*, tells the story of this extraordinary woman.

Val Lewis, Shepperton, Surrey

With regard to the explanations of Frank Branston and Val Lewis, there is in fact a third school of thought. Many Southcottians believe that the real box was not bequeathed to the British Museum but is still held by one of their very own members.

If it is, it would be in keeping with their original maxim as recorded by Mary Robertson in her 1929 book, *The Authentic History of the Great Box*. This decreed that each custodian since Joanna's death in 1814 would be chosen by special ballot, elected for their integrity, and placed under a solemn vow not to give up the box of sealed writings save to the proper authorities – that is, the twenty-four bishops. The handover to the British Museum would not meet this criterion.

Joanna was interred with great privacy on 1 January 1815 at St John's Wood. Her tombstone displayed an epitaph, ending with the line: 'Thou'lt appear in greater power.' Almost incredulously, it was her grave alone that was shattered by the Regent's Park explosion of 1874 – a circumstance that revived hopes of her return.

Richard Webber, Horfield, Bristol

In the 1960s I remember visiting a café called Gandalf's Garden in Chelsea where you could just pay what you felt your snack was worth (or could afford). Does anyone know who started the venture, how long it survived and why it closed? Do any cafés with a similar philosophy exist today?

At The Booth, one of Shetland's oldest pubs, the owner makes no charge for the excellent vegetarian meals that are served. Instead, she invites donations towards running a seal sanctuary in what used to be the beer garden. She cannot have misjudged too badly, for the sanctuary is well established and the restaurant is attracting increasing custom.

R. A. Hewitt, Fulford, Yorks

There is a restaurant on Finchley Road in London called Just Around the Corner, which has no prices on the menu but asks the diners to pay what they feel their meal was worth. In a discussion with the owner when I was last there, he commented that most people pay over the odds; and although very occasionally people will leave having only paid, say, a couple of pounds, they never come back.

Charles Levine, Hendon, London NW4

A factor in the demise of Gandalf's Garden may have been the frequent visits by fellow pupils at my school a few hundred yards away. Many of them were more familiar with the works of Desmond Dekker than those of J. R. R. Tolkien, and having eaten a plate of macrobiotic brown rice and yoghurt they would decide that it was worth nothing. Those customers who had genuinely embraced the hippie ethic will, of course, remember nothing at all.

Paul Dennehy (Sloane School 1966–70), Enfield, Middx

Gandalf's Garden Centre was not simply a café but a non-sectarian mystical community and a spiritually oriented magazine of the same name. I began it in 1968 as an antidote to the nihilistic 'underground' journals of the day and geared it towards a more positive world attitude. The magazine was created to give direction, especially to those among the 'flower-power children' who were lost in a limbo somewhere between society and spaced-out LSD trips.

At the Garden we offered food and drink at minimal prices, gave it free to those in need, tended to tramps and dossers on the streets, offered a safe haven for junkies on bad trips and helped to wean them away from drugs towards self-development. To this end – and perhaps for the first time in the UK – we created a forum for sages and spiritual teachers from every tradition and from all over the world, who freely offered us all new perspectives on life.

Our core of dedicated workers subsisted on 50p a week pocket-money each (from our third year only) after we had paid for our communal meals and clothing. We fondly remember the kindness of the up-and-coming Marc Bolan of T-Rex, and David Bowie, who gave a benefit concert to enable us to bring out the second issue of the magazine.

We eventually ran out of funds and steam in 1972, owing to too many stationers never paying us for the magazines they sold, street-sellers ripping us off and shoplifters purloining the handmade goods of those attempting to live outside the rat-race. Our overworked and exhausted community members dispersed to India and to other spiritual centres. Yet even today, all of them are still involved in similar work. For a while I stayed behind, to reorganize and train new members to take over. Then I too left for my own pilgrimage to India, where I journeyed and studied as a mendicant monk for the following three years.

In 1974, my hopes of returning were dashed when a gang of skinheads threw dustbins through the window and wrecked the shop. That was the final demise. However, Gandalf's Garden inspired a dozen Friends of the Garden seed-centres (spiritual discussion groups) across Britain, and mystic cafés of a similar nature such as Middle Earth, Merlin's Garden, etc., opened in Holland, Germany, Italy and Scandinavia.

Today our core offshoot, the Inner Garden, organizes a mantra and mysticism workshop tour across Europe and spiritual tours to India.

Muz Murray, Caveirac, France

I have read about Wojtek, a brown bear that 'fought' for the Polish army by carrying ammunition on his back. A hero among Poles, this bear lived and died in Edinburgh Zoo after the Second World War. Can anyone confirm this story and explain how this bear ended up in Scotland?

My father, Kazik Tkaczyk, served with the Polish Second Army in Persia (now Iran). The bear was found as an orphaned cub in the mountains by one of his comrades, who became its owner. Wojtek certainly did his bit around the army camp and did carry ammunition. Following his wartime adventures in Egypt and Italy, the bear was smuggled into Scotland disguised in a Polish army uniform.

For a time Wojtek lived with the same owner until he became too big and unmanageable, when he was transferred to Edinburgh Zoo. My father told my mother how, around 1946, he went to the zoo with a comrade. When they reached the cage, they started whistling the first bars of the Polish national anthem. The bear began shaking the bars of the cage and would not calm down until the bear's owner got into the cage with him and was hugged.

Today, there is a full-sized statue of Wojtek in the Polish Hearth Club in South Kensington.

Dominik Tkaczyk, Welwyn, Herts

After 1946 Wojtek spent some time with his human friends at Winfield Camp in Berwickshire near my childhood home, where I remember seeing him before he moved to Edinburgh Zoo in 1947. He spent the

rest of his life there and became the subject of a book, *Soldier Bear*, by
G. Morgan and W. A. Lasocki (Collins, 1970).
Sheila Cameron, Kelso, Rox.

Has anyone ever looked for a needle in a haystack?

I did find it, but I lost it in my flat.
Peter Stockill, Berwick Hills, Middlesbrough

I have taken part in a wild goose chase. About ten of us eventually
caught the bird, which was hampered by an injured wing.
Roger Moon, Princes Risborough, Bucks

I have looked for a signet ring in a sand dune! I was with a group of
friends in the Namib desert (in Namibia), which has the largest sand
dune in the world. We climbed it to see the sun rise one morning and
returned to camp for breakfast. One of the group noticed that his signet
ring was missing and managed to persuade us to go back to the dune to
look for it. Amazingly, after half an hour's hunting, I spotted it in the sand!
Edward Hillier, Fenham, Newcastle upon Tyne

Jim Moran, an American eccentric, put a lot of effort into disproving
popular fallacies. He unloaded fifty tons of hay in Washington and had
someone bury a needle in it; eighty-two hours and thirty-five minutes
later, he found it. He also sold fridges to the Inuit in 1938, and the
following year took a bull into a New York china shop. He ended the
experiment after an hour; two plates had been damaged.
Ivor Solomons, Norwich, Norfolk

For a physicist (funded by the military), the task is an easy one. Reduce
to two dimensions by burning the stack, and then use either a metal
detector or infra-red glasses. For some haystacks, it should be possible
to pinpoint the needle in 3D using short-wave radar. I asked an
economist friend in Singapore how she would do it and she said: 'I
would pay someone.' This profound problem goes to the very core of
who we are.
Joss Hawthorn, Mosman, NSW, Australia

My cousin lost one contact lens during a folk festival in a meadow. Even though it rained that night he went back to search for it the next day and found it hanging from a blade of grass much like a raindrop. He put it straight back into his eye and it was undamaged.

Saskia Wesnigk-Wood, Portslade, East Sussex

In 1955 as a ten-year-old, I went with my parents and brothers to an agricultural show in Levin, a farming town ninety-four kilometres north of Wellington. As part of the entertainment for the children, a needle in the haystack competition was held. A lorry dumped a load of hay in the arena and all the children were invited to find the needle. After a bit of wandering about my eye caught a red piece of wool with a needle at the end. My prize, which I still have today, was a clockwork Hornby train.

Warren Johns, Remuera, Auckland, New Zealand

Does anybody know who or what are the Shriners in the USA?

Shriners, or Shrine Masons, belong to the Ancient Arabic Order of the Nobles of the Mystic Shrine for North America (AAONMS). The Shrine is an international fraternity of approximately 610,000 members who belong to Shrine Temples throughout the United States, Canada, Mexico and Panama. Founded in New York City in 1872, the organization is composed solely of thirty-second-degree Scottish Rite Masons (which has nothing to do with Scottish Freemasonry) or Knights Templar York Rite Masons.

The Shrine is as North American as apple pie. It was tied to an Arabic theme by its founders – actor Billy Florence and physician Walter Flemming. They recognized that the fledgling fraternity needed a colourful, exciting backdrop and it is believed that Florence conceived the Shrine's Near East setting while on tour in Eastern Europe.

As the legend goes, Florence later attended a party in Marseilles, France, hosted by an Arabian diplomat. At the end of the party, the guests became members of a secret society. Florence realized that this might be the ideal vehicle for the new fraternity, and he made copious notes and drawings of the ceremony.

When Florence returned to the States, Flemming agreed to this idea, and together they created elaborate rituals, designed the emblem and costumes (the most notable of which is the red fez) and formulated the salutation.

Though the Shrine is not itself a secret society, it still retains much of the mysticism and secrecy of its origins.

Charles Levine, Hendon, London NW4

The Shriners are a charitable order who conduct much of their fund-raising on behalf of people with mobility problems. They are most commonly seen in parades driving miniature vehicles in formation, and the sight of fez-wearing middle-aged gents perched on motorized model boats, beeping horns and rushing about in complex manoeuvres down Main Street, presents a memorable scene of Americana.

Robert MacRae, Salford, Manchester

In his book *The Lost Continent*, Bill Bryson gives a rather different view of the Shriners from the previous replies:

'The Shriners, if you are not familiar with them, are a social organisation composed of middle-aged men of a certain disposition and mentality – the sort of men who like to engage in practical jokes and pinch the bottoms of passing waitresses. They get drunk a lot and drop water balloons out of hotel windows. Their idea of advanced wit is to stick a cupped hand under their armpit and make farting noises. You can always tell a Shriner because he's wearing a red fez and his socks don't match. Ostensibly, Shriners get together to raise money for charities. This is what they tell their wives. However, here's an interesting fact that may help you to put this claim into perspective. In 1984, according to *Harper's* magazine, the amount of money raised by the Shriners was $17.5 million; of this sum, the amount they donated to charities was $182,000. In short, what the Shriners do is get together and be assholes.'

Tim Brown, Kea, Cornwall

Every 31 December, families throughout Switzerland, Austria and Germany celebrate by watching Freddie Frinton and May Warden in a twenty-minute comedy sketch, 'Dinner for One'. It is broadcast –

in English – on up to six channels at different times throughout the evening. When and why did this become part of German-speaking Europeans' New Year celebrations?

In 1963 a German television presenter, Peter Frankenfeld, and his producer, Heinz Dunkhaser, were in Blackpool trawling the variety theatres for talent to present on Frankenfeld's show, which was broadcast by NDR in Hamburg. At an eleven o'clock performance on the morning before their departure they came across Freddy Frinton and asked him to do a sketch for their programme. Frinton, whose wartime experiences had left him decidedly hostile to all things German, agreed on the one condition that the sketch should be in English. He went to Hamburg only twice – to perform 'Dinner for One' live and for the filmed version, which has been shown on German television every New Year's Eve since then. (He died before the colour version could be made.)

Frinton plays a butler at a ninetieth-birthday dinner. The old lady sits alone and Frinton is required to assume the roles of her dead friends around the table while serving the meal, steadily becoming drunker and finding it ever harder to avoid tripping over the tiger-skin rug.

No one knows who wrote the piece, but Frinton gives a classic performance as the archetypal unflappable English butler perpetuating an eccentric tradition:

'The same procedure as last year, Miss Sophie?'

'The same procedure as every year, James.'

Germans quote these lines in the same way that British people quote Monty Python's 'Dead Parrot' sketch.

This sangfroid and fondness for ritual are alleged English characteristics, which are regarded by many Germans with great affection; and in broadcasting every New Year's Eve an alien television sketch that was rejected by the BBC, they have in some way created an eccentric tradition of their own.

John Davies, Redditch, Worcs

Has a fire station ever burned down?

In May 1941, the Central Fire Station in Bootle, Merseyside, was bombed and the upper floors burned out. At the last moment, water became available and the fire was kept away from the appliance room at street level, though the station was out of commission for months. In London, Wandsworth fire station was set alight in November 1940 and Redcross Street in December.

A. B. Sainsbury, London SE3

Our village station was badly damaged by fire a few years ago. I believe there were firemen there when it started and one of them asked a neighbour to use her phone to call the fire brigade.

David Holmes, Yatton, Bristol

In May 1973, at the Stevenston site of ICI, a fire started in a large open-air stock of nitrocellulose drums. The company's on-site fire station was next to the store and was put out of action within three minutes of the fire starting. Two firemen were burned leaving the station, as the roof was already alight and flames surrounded it; one died later in hospital. All the company's fire appliances except one were lost in the blaze; heat from the fire destroyed or damaged thirty other buildings, and there were forty further casualties. This incident led to much subsequent research into better packaging, and appropriate safety distances between a nitrocellulose store and other facilities.

Alan Tyldesley, Bootle, Merseyside

This query reminded me of a tape of ancient music played on the Aquincum organ that I purchased in the Museum of Budapest History. The accompanying notes state that this is 'the only organ from Antiquity in which so many of the individual parts have been preserved. The instrument was presented in 228 to the fire brigade by one of the foremost citizens of the city [Aquincum], Gaius Iulius Viatorinus. The inflagration [sic] which swept through the settlement in 294 did not spare the headquarters of the fire brigade either. Thus, the leather and wooden parts of the organ were consumed in the flames.'

Gwen Hersec, Bristol

I'm not sure about a fire station but the crematorium in which my father was to be cremated had a serious fire a couple of days before

the service that almost razed it to the ground. I know he would have seen the somewhat macabre humour in the situation!
Charles Stuart, Phoenix, Arizona, USA

When I was five the fire station in my home town, Venray (Netherlands), burned down. My father took us to watch the blaze. It has kept me confused for years about the actual meaning of 'fire station'.
Maarten Schim van der Loeff, Banjul, The Gambia

At Hornsby, about twenty-five kilometres north of Sydney, Australia, the Pacific Highway makes a ninety-degree right turn. At the apex of this turn there once stood the Hornsby and District Fire Brigade building, housing two fire engines, administrative offices and accommodation. Sometime in the late 1970s a petrol tanker, taking the turn at speed, rolled on to its side and slid into the invitingly open doors of the station, igniting an almighty conflagration, gutting the station and burning everything within. Miraculously no lives were lost. The fire station subsequently moved from that site.
Walter Slamer, Bali, Indonesia

Do or did zombies ever exist, or are they just a voodoo superstition?

A decade or so ago, Harvard University ethnobotanist Wade Davis claimed to have discovered the secret behind the legendary magic powers of voodoo sorcerers. In his best-selling book *The Serpent and the Rainbow* (1986), he presented evidence that sorcerers do indeed create zombies, allegedly by poisoning their intended victims with extract of puffer fish. These fish contain tetrodotoxin, a poison that is commonly fatal but which, administered in just the right dosage, induces a deep coma easily mistaken for death itself.

Davis's account envisions the grieving relatives being tricked into burying the comatose victim within a few hours of 'death' and, shortly afterwards, the sorcerer secretly breaking open the tomb. In a matter of hours, the poison wears off and the unfortunate victim awakes from the coma as the 'living dead', facing a lifetime of misery as the sorcerer's slave. Davis's extraordinary theory is today widely accepted – not least because it seems to explain why zombies behave in a zombie-like way, having become brain-damaged by a lack of oxygen while entombed and the long-term effects of poisoning.

But over the past few years I have spent many months travelling in Haiti, and my own investigations suggest that zombies are in fact mentally handicapped individuals caught up in a web of mistaken identity. My TV documentary, *Interview with a Zombie,* featured the case of two 'zombies' – one of whom had been officially classified a zombie by the Haitian High Court during a trial in which an alleged sorcerer was convicted of 'zombifying' him.

In both cases, the individuals, who had been homeless and wandering around in a zombie-like state, were recognized by their shocked 'families' as their long-mourned dead. Parents, siblings, children, entire villages, even the judiciary, were convinced of their identity. But when, with the permission of the individuals involved, blood samples were taken from the two 'zombies' and their 'families', and DNA tests were performed at a laboratory back in Britain, the results showed that the two zombies were totally unrelated to their so-called families. The zombie phenomenon seems to be Haiti's version of 'Care in the Community'.

Chris Ledger, London E9

Is it really possible to break a wineglass by singing at a particular pitch and volume?

Yes. The note sung has to be at or near the resonance frequency of the glass, and must be loud enough to cause vibrations large enough to shatter the glass.

The wineglass will generally have to be almost perfectly circular in cross-section so that its resonance frequency is in the correct vocal range. Occasionally you will see water in the bottom of the glass to modify its resonance frequency. In addition, such experiments will often use crystal, ostensibly because no prima donna could be expected to shatter an ordinary glass, but more correctly because crystal, being more brittle, is a good deal easier to shatter.

Andy Harbison, Dublin

I don't know about wineglasses and singing, but years ago our daughter, then an infant, was screaming on her mother's knee when an ordinary glass tumbler on the nearby table simply disintegrated.
Peter Parker, Ely, Cambs

A recent article in the German weekly *Die Zeit* stated that there is no documented instance of a person bursting a glass with the power of her or his voice. Caruso is rumoured to have done so, but his wife Dorothy always denied it. Wolfgang Eisenmenger, a Stuttgart physicist, breaks glasses in his lectures using a tone of 120 phons tuned to within one tenth of a hertz of the frequency of the glass. The human voice is only capable of at most 100 phons – this is acoustically 120 times less powerful than the tone Eisenmenger uses.
Bruce Collins, Kiel, Germany

Bruce Collins alleges that the human voice is insufficiently powerful to break a glass. If so, he might care to account for what happened when my wife and I had a row one evening. Our voices grew louder and louder and rose higher and higher. Suddenly a cut-glass goblet standing on the dining table shattered into many pieces.
Ron Isaacs, Barnet, Herts

I achieved this feat when, as a teenager, I was singing the title song from the film *Annie*. When I hit the top note, a large wineglass across the room shattered. I must point out that it happened spontaneously and was not thrown at me.
Claudia Freeman, Glasgow

Which playing card is known as the curse of Scotland and why?

The 'Curse of Scotland' was the name given to the nine of diamonds playing card but there is little agreement over how it earned this nickname. Innumerable references suggest that it seems to have been known in Scotland for 300 years and more.

The most frequently quoted story – which probably appeals most strongly to patriotic fervour – is that the Duke of Cumberland, the infamous victor of the Battle of Culloden, wrote an order in the field that no quarter was to be given to the Jacobite soldiers. He used the back of a playing card, which was the nine of diamonds. It helps the credibility of this attribution that Cumberland is said to have been an inveterate gambler who generally carried a pack of cards in his pocket.

Another (and earlier) story that finds favour in Scotland is that the nine lozenges in the heraldry of John Dalrymple, 1st Earl of Stair, bore a resemblance to the nine of diamonds. This recalled his part in manoeuvring the massacre of Glencoe in 1692, which earned him almost universal detestation. These and many other citations were gathered by the great lexicographer and editor of the *Oxford English Dictionary*, Sir James Murray (1837–1915).

Hugh Cheape, National Museums of Scotland, Edinburgh

The allusion to the Battle of Culloden is unsustainable, as the battle took place in 1746, and there is a reference as early as 1710 in *The British Apollo*, which simply stated: 'The Nine of Diamonds is called the Curse of Scotland.' The massacre at Glencoe is also an unlikely candidate, as the diamonds on the Dalrymple arms are of gold on a blue saltire and do not therefore significantly resemble the nine of diamonds.

The most likely, though somewhat dull, answer is that the nickname derives from the old card game of Pope Joan, where the nine of diamonds is designated the Pope (the Pope being held as the Antichrist in Scotland).

Roger Thomson, Brighton

Old maps reveal a railway station near Waterloo called Necropolis. Who did it serve and how did it acquire such a strange name?

Following the cholera epidemic of 1848, two industrialists developed a huge burial site for London's dead at Brookwood Cemetery, near Woking in Surrey – far away from city-dwellers anxious to avoid infection. Bodies and mourners were transported by train on the Necropolis ('City of the Dead') railway to the new burial site, consecrated in 1854.

It was a controversial project. The Bishop of London condemned the 'offensive' despatch of first-, second- and third-class corpses on the same train, while poorer relatives worried that they might not be able to visit their loved ones' graves very often because of the high fares.

Paul Vickers, Dorking, Surrey

The funeral trains comprised ordinary carriages for mourners and special hearse vans for coffins. The cost of a railway funeral varied: it could be several pounds. Yet the Necropolis Company gave paupers a decent interment in a separate grave for only fourteen shillings (70p), including the fare. Special tickets were issued: returns for mourners and singles for the dead.

John Clarke, Chairman, The Brookwood Cemetery Society, Surbiton, Surrey

From November 1896 to May 1897, mysterious large airships powered by propellers and decorated with electric lights were reported flying in California, Texas and the Great Lake states of the USA. Who built these craft and for what purpose?

In April 1897, Jon Halley and Adolf Wenke of Springfield, Illinois, reported a flying craft of a similar type, whose 'pilot' told them that it was a new invention that was flown at night to attract less attention. The pilot said he had left Quincy, one hundred miles to the west, only thirty minutes earlier – an impossibility for an aerial object of the time. Similar objects were reported in Indiana, where a crew were making on-the-spot repairs.

The pilot was tracked down by the press in Martinville, where he made the statement that he had an airship in Brown County undergoing repairs and that he also had three more machines flying in central states of the USA. Whilst many reports of the time are undoubtedly hoaxes dreamed up by local newspaper editors to increase circulation, there remain some tantalizing unexplained facts.

Also in April 1897, for a period of over thirty minutes, a huge airship was witnessed by jurors, judges and lawyers who had gathered outside the courthouse in Harrison, Nebraska. It had a bright white light, coloured lights around it, and was oval shaped with a box-like structure hanging from it, with a propeller at the stern.

To this day, though well documented, there has been no explanation for the sights observed.

Chris Picknell, Littlebourne, Kent

I'm sorry to say that these craft probably never existed. Considered to be the first widely reported UFO flap, this wave of sightings has been revealed, fairly conclusively, to be a string of hoax stories propagated by reporters and telegraph operators, and enthusiastically endorsed by a then less jaded public. It's possible that their stories may have been inspired by genuine reports of unusual lights (but not aircraft) seen flying in the sky, but it's probably too late now to uncover the necessary details of each individual case.

Like their disc- and triangle-shaped contemporary counterparts, the mystery dirigibles were then technologically a few years ahead of their time. Clumsy balloon flights had been made in Europe as far back as 1852, and by mid-1897 at least two airship patents had been awarded to American inventors, but it wasn't until 1900 that the first successful (and very short) Zeppelin dirigible flight took place in Germany. Again, like today's UFOs, balloons and dirigibles had long featured in popular contemporary fiction, such as Jules Verne's *Around the World in Eighty Days* (1873), and were also regularly depicted in drawings and cartoons of the time.

The mystery airships would return in 1909, visiting countries as far afield as the USA, Britain, New Zealand and Scandinavia, but their origins still remain a mystery.

Mark Pilkington, West Kensington, London W14

At what speed would Father Christmas have to travel to visit all the world's children (say, under eleven years old) in a twenty-four-hour period?

The following was first published in America's *Spy* magazine:

There are 2 billion children (persons under eighteen) in the world. But since Santa doesn't (appear) to handle the Muslim,

Hindu, Jewish and Buddhists, that reduces the workload to 15 per cent of the total – 378 million. At an average rate of 3.5 children per household, that's 91.8 million homes.

Santa has thirty-one hours of Christmas to work with, thanks to the different time zones and the rotation of the earth, assuming he travels east to west. This works out to 822.6 visits per second, so Santa has one one-thousandth of a second to park, hop out of the sleigh, jump down the chimney, fill the stockings, distribute the remaining presents under the tree, eat whatever snacks have been left, get back up the chimney, get back into the sleigh and move on to the next house. Assuming that each of these 91.8 million stops are evenly distributed around the earth, we are now talking about 0.78 miles per household, a total trip of 75.5 million miles.

This means that Santa's sleigh is moving at 650 miles per second, 3,000 times the speed of sound. By comparison, the fastest man-made vehicle on earth, the Ulysses space probe, moves at a pokey 27.4 miles per second – a conventional reindeer can run, tops, fifteen miles per hour.
Miss Blanaid McKinney, Macduff, Aber.

The question is completely hypothetical. Everyone knows that in reality Santa has many helpers who make it possible for him to visit all children.
Steve Dawson, Ipswich, Suffolk

Miss Blanaid McKinney and *Spy* magazine are wrong in assuming that Santa doesn't handle Muslims, Hindus, Jews and Buddhists. My six-year-old Hindu niece Parama – who lives in Calcutta and calls Jesus Christ Jishu Krishna – hangs out a pair of white socks every Christmas Eve and receives presents from Santa the next morning. Perhaps, given his busy schedule, Santa does not have the time to discriminate among children on the basis of religion.
Dipak Ghosh, Bridge of Allan, Stirling

In 1984 a High Court ruling meant that the last mortal remains of

Edward the Martyr, King of England, were deposited in a branch of the Midland Bank in Croydon. Are they still there and why?

The murdered king was first exhumed from Corfe Castle when healing miracles began to be reported at his grave. He was reburied in a shrine at Shaftesbury Abbey, to be venerated by medieval pilgrims until the Reformation, when he was again disinterred and reburied in a secret location within the Abbey grounds for safe keeping. The estate passed into the hands of the Claridge family, and in 1931 the bones supposed to be those of St Edward were again exhumed.

John Wilson Claridge wanted these bones, as the remains of a royal saint and martyr, to be appropriately laid to rest, and he invited a number of Anglican bishops to receive the bones for reinterment. His offer was declined. Subsequently, there was contact with English members of the Orthodox Church, who agreed not merely to receive the relics but proceeded to acquire a former chapel of rest at Brookwood, near Woking, for conversion into a basilica for the relics.

Claridge's younger brother Geoffrey disputed through the High Court the elder's ownership of the bones and his entitlement to surrender them to the religious order, hence their sojourn in the vaults of the Midland Bank. The Attorney-General's Office became involved in the affair because of the relics' supposed royal origin, but was satisfied with the security arrangements at Brookwood and allowed arrangements to proceed.

Bruce Purvis, Salisbury Library, Wilts

The spoof TV series *The Day Today* told of a secret tunnel between 10 Downing Street and Buckingham Palace. Are there really such tunnels in the vicinity of Parliament?

There have been several rumours over the years about escape tunnels leading from Buckingham Palace. These include: a tunnel running from the palace under Green Park where, rumours suggest, it intercepts the Piccadilly underground line, allowing the Windsors speedy access to Heathrow Airport; ditto to the Victoria Line, which conveniently runs directly under the palace; and a shorter foot-tunnel to Wellington barracks just across the road.

Most favoured, however, is the suggestion that a tunnel runs from Buckingham Palace under the Mall to a massive underground citadel, known as Q-Whitehall, which lies a hundred feet under Westminster and Whitehall, and extends as far north as Holborn. Evidence for this includes a huge extractor fan just outside the Gents loo at the Institute of Contemporary Arts – directly above the supposed site – which the ICA confirms is nothing to do with them.

The ICA building is immediately opposite a huge top-security fortress building, on the corner of the Mall and Horse Guards Road, which is generally accepted to be the service access to Q-Whitehall.

It is also known that a tunnel connects Downing Street to a massive atom-bomb-proof bunker constructed under the Ministry of Defence building in the early 1990s at a cost in excess of £100 million. It is also likely that this building connects directly with Q-Whitehall.

Therefore travel from Buckingham Palace to 10 Downing Street should be possible if the need arose.

David Northmore, London N6

Chapman Pincher, writing in the *Express* in 1959, refers to 'ten miles of reinforced tunnels built under London after the last war at enormous cost. These tunnels . . . are below Whitehall, Leicester Square, Holborn and Victoria.'

Beneath the City Streets, by Peter Laurie (Penguin, 1972), provides considerable evidence for the existence of secret tunnels under London, some of which were started as long ago as the First World War. The most famous is the one deep below Goodge Street underground station. On one of the platforms at one end is an obscure notice, which warns of a deep shaft. This complex of tunnels was used as a transit camp by soldiers on their way to Suez in 1956.

Ken R. Smith, Leeds

On a tour organized by Subterranea Britannica in 1995, we visited a former MoD bunker directly beneath Chancery Lane tube station in central London. We could hear the trains overhead, and there was a lift shaft along which the station could be seen. There was one inconspicuous entrance in High Holborn, and another in Furnival Street.

Hillary Shaw, London SW16

I think Ken Smith is wrong when he states that the Goodge Street underground tunnels were used as a transit camp during the Suez crisis in 1956. In November 1954 I stayed overnight at the Goodge Street camp, on my way to Egypt. But at the end of July 1956, on my return from Libya, I was billeted for a night in a school or church hall just off Tottenham Court Road. I was told that Goodge Street was no longer used and later found out it had been destroyed by fire in 1955. I doubt very much whether it was made habitable in time for the Suez crisis in October 1956.

Ken Light, Milton Keynes

The construction of the Jubilee Line was a highly visible and disruptive process, involving thousands of construction workers. If there really are ten miles of reinforced tunnels below central London, how could these be built and remain secret? Who built them, or is this a secret too?

David Powell, London NW1

David Powell, citing the Jubilee Line extension, implies that 'secret' tunnels cannot exist since we didn't notice them being constructed. But London Transport advertises what it is doing. Other utilities that build tunnels, while not necessarily being secretive, nevertheless create as little disruption as possible so as not to antagonize the public. London Electricity, for instance, has in the last few years built miles of three-metre-diameter tunnels under London. Did Mr Powell notice? How much more, then, could have been achieved by an organization that sought to hide what it was doing?

As it happens, we do know who built some of the 'secret' tunnels. The eight or so miles of tunnel, 5.5 metres in diameter, that link various places in central, east and south London, were built by William Halcrow. This system, which was later extended westwards to Shepherd's Bush, is also linked to the extensive system of tunnels in the Whitehall area (which may indeed have a connection to

Buckingham Palace) and to the massive telephone exchange deep beneath Chancery Lane.

All this information can be found in two books: *London Under London* by Richard Trench and Ellis Hillman; and *Secret London* by Andrew Duncan.

Geoffrey Taunton, Portsmouth

I can assure Ken Light that Goodge Street transit camp was open on 3 December 1956. I, and 200 other matelots, stayed overnight there on our way from Devonport to Mombasa to commission one of Her Majesty's frigates. It was a grim place and stank to high heaven.

James Stewart, Mannheim, Germany

History books often refer to 'fountains flowing with wine' during major celebrations. Is there any credible account of how these fountains were operated, or was the term merely an overblown way of saying that drinks were free?

One of the most famous of such fountains was at the court of the Great Khan of Mongolia in the city of Karakorum. William of Rubruck, who saw it when he visited the court in 1254, reported that it was in the shape of a tree and had been made in solid silver by William of Paris, a French silversmith captured by the Mongols in Hungary and then living in Karakorum.

At the base of the fountain were four lions, which gushed out mare's milk or *koumiss*, while at the top four branches, decorated with serpents, were ready to dispense wine, distilled mare's milk, mead or Chinese rice wine. When these drinks were needed, the chief steward signalled a man crouching inside the fountain, who then blew into a tube that sounded a note on a trumpet held by a silver angel atop the fountain. Servants would then pour the drinks into the appropriate channels and the liquid would ascend tubes inside the trunk of the tree to emerge from the mouths of the serpents and pour into silver basins.

William Ward, Muswell Hill, London N10

At the opening by the Marquis of Normanby of the Melbourne International Exhibition (1880–81) the fountains outside the purpose-built Royal Exhibition Building in the Carlton Gardens flowed with pink champagne. During the ceremonies, which included the performance of an interminable Exhibition cantata, everybody waiting outside got drunk and rioting ensued. Buckets of pink champagne were carried off to the suburbs. I do not think similar hospitalities have since been attempted in Melbourne.

Angus Trumble, Art Gallery of South Australia, Adelaide

For centuries Exeter's citizens were supplied with drinking water by a public conduit, an impressive edifice with taps, situated in the centre of the city at the Carfax. On special occasions, such as the visit by Henry VI in 1452 and the coronation of William and Mary in 1689, the conduit ran with wine. This was achieved by inserting a hogshead of claret behind the spout.

Hazel Harvey, Exeter

The town of Marino, near Rome, still has such a fountain. During the Sagra dell'Uva, at the grape harvest in August, the celebrated Fountain of the Moors in the main square is decorated with bunches of grapes, and it pumps out wine instead of water. We used to join in the scrum to fill glasses, carafes and jerrycans with the very drinkable local produce. Economic considerations mean that this free-for-all lasts only about an hour, but I am told that in the past it lasted several days.

Mark Langham, Bayswater, London W2

Henry Mayhew's book *London Labour and the London Poor* mentions a Professor Sands, who walked on ceilings using an 'air-exhausting boot', on the model of a fly's foot. Did such a person exist and, if so, how did the boot work?

The American Richard Sands introduced the ceiling act to his Sands' American Circus in 1852. He walked upside down on a nine-foot marble slab suspended about twenty feet above the ground. Later that year he is reported to have presented his ceiling-walking at the Surrey

Theatre, and again at Drury Lane in 1853, using rubber suction pads attached to his feet.

Henry Mayhew's informant suggested that the performer he saw was not the real Sands because he was killed on his benefit night in America. One version claims that this happened at Melrose, Massachusetts, in 1861. (When Sands was ceiling-walking in the town hall, a section of the plaster came away and he fell and broke his neck.) Another source says that Richard Sands died in Havana, Cuba.

There were a number of ceiling walkers in nineteenth-century Britain. A number used the suction pad method, which required a very smooth surface, but most used a system of hooks and rings, at such a height that the aids were invisible.

John Turner, Circus Friends Association, Formby, Merseyside

What is the minimum size for Noah's Ark on the basis of two of every known species and enough food for six weeks (assuming the animals wouldn't eat each other)?

The size of Noah's Ark is immutable, for God said (Genesis 6:15) that it had to be 300 cubits long, 50 cubits wide and 30 cubits high (450 feet × 75 feet × 45 feet).

If the questioner wants to know what size an Ark would have to be to fit the conditions laid down in the Bible, then this is completely different. Noah was told to take into the Ark seven of each clean beast, seven of each fowl of the air and two of each unclean beast. They were in the Ark for over twelve months, not six weeks. The animals would have to have eaten one another, for carnivores cannot live off hay. So for them to survive, space would not only be needed for the animals that were to be saved but also for the animals to be used as food.

There would also have to be space to store many, many tons of widely varying foodstuffs for them all. In addition, there would have to be space to store thousands of boxes in which to keep insects to feed to the insect-eaters that were being saved. Space would be needed too to grow plants for the pollen-, fruit- and nut-eaters, and space too for gallons upon gallons of fresh water. Also there would have to be tanks for freshwater fish and sea fish for feeding to the fish-eaters. And, of course, space would be needed for exercising. Room would have to be found for thousands of tons of fodder and animals to support them all when the deluge ended. Finally, there would have to be space in the Ark to store the millions of seeds, seedlings and cuttings necessary to replant the world, for 'every living substance was destroyed' (Genesis 7: 23).

How big was the Ark then? The size of the Isle of Wight?
R. Lord, Bolton, Lancs

I assume this correspondence is closed, now that we have had the definitive answer from R. Lord.
Steve Babbage, Newbury, Berks

I have heard that if you pass enough electricity through a pickled cucumber it will glow bright green. Is this true, and if so, how do I demonstrate it without endangering my life?

In south London pickled cucumbers used to be called 'wallys'. I would guess that the name refers to the last person to try this experiment.
Lorna Eller, Milton Keynes

A pickled cucumber will glow if you pass electricity through it – the Inspire Science Squad do it regularly in their science shows. We use a specially constructed 'Pickle Blaster', which puts 240 volts of mains electricity through the pickle. It consists of a wooden frame with two metal spikes – on which we mount the pickle – connected to a standard thirteen-amp plug. I have seen other people do it with just two wires connected directly to the mains, but I wouldn't recommend this. Incidentally, the pickles glow orange, not green, due to a sodium emission effect similar to that in street lamps filled with sodium vapour.

Various colleagues have tried other types of pickle, but not with such impressive effect, although someone claims to have achieved a magnificent yellow-green emission from the yolk of a pickled egg.
Ian Simmons, Director, Inspire Hands-on Science Centre, Norwich

Why is the augmented fourth the 'chord of evil' that was banned in Renaissance church music?

More accurately the *diabolus in musica*, the augmented fourth was the only augmented interval that appeared in the modes used before the emergence of the major and minor scales. Using only the white keys on a piano, the interval of F natural to B natural is the only augmented one (also known as the tri-tone) and it was considered so unnatural and discordant in pre-tonal times as to be known as 'the Devil in Music'. Oddly, the inverted chord of B to F (the only diminished interval in the modal system) was not stigmatized in quite the same way, although its use was avoided.

Jas Huggon, Knodishall, Suffolk

The augmented fourth (the interval between the two tones of a fire-engine klaxon) exerts its unsettling effect even when the notes are sounded in succession, in conventional harmony and in counterpoint. Its use is still subject to rules and regulations. While the interval, used judiciously, gives vigour and interest to what would otherwise be rather anodyne melody, the churchmen thought its disturbing effect 'apt to provoke lewd and libidinous thoughts'. Naturally the ban ensured that the augmented fourth became a favourite device of Church composers, and much later it was reinvented, labelled the 'flattened fifth' and somewhat overused by young jazz players anxious to dissociate themselves from traditional styles.

Robin Dow, Audlem, Cheshire

I remember children in 1930s Liverpool lighting bonfires in the streets early on Good Friday morning and 'burning Judas'. Did these activities take place anywhere else, and are they still going on?

In *The Lore and Language of Schoolchildren* (OUP, 1959) Iona and Peter Opie describe the custom of burning effigies of Judas as being centred in the largely Roman Catholic area around the docks in the south end of Liverpool. They cite a report from 1954 of attempts by the police to prevent fires being lit in the streets: 'It is comic to see a policeman with two or more "Judases" under his arm striding off to the Bridewell and thirty or forty children crowding after him shrieking "Judas".'

The origins of the custom are traced to Spain, Portugal and Latin America, and it would appear that aspects of it were transported to Liverpool and other ports by visiting ships. The Opies refer to a report in *The Times* of April 1884, describing crowds in London watching effigies of Judas being flogged on board Portuguese and South American vessels moored at the docks.

Peter Barnes, Milton Keynes, Bucks

In Lagos, Nigeria, in the late 1960s, I remember children on Good Friday morning parading an effigy of Judas to chants of 'Judasi ole o pa Jesu je' ('Judas thief had Jesus killed for money'). The effigy was flogged and later discarded or burned, depending on the exuberance of the group.

Adé Lawal, Hampton, Middx

In Northern Ireland in the 1950s, there was a tradition of 'burning Lundy' – represented in effigy – on the bonfires lit on the eve of the Twelfth (of July). This Lundy had been going to open the gates of Derry to the armies of King James and was therefore, like Judas, a traitor.

Hazel Martin, Edinburgh

In Brazil, Judas is usually made to resemble whichever public figure is particularly unpopular at the time.

T. J. L. Oxton, Colchester, Essex

On the south coast of Crete, an effigy of Judas Iscariot is burned on the night of Easter Saturday. He is given a black hat and an ugly face. Local children come to throw stones at the traitor during the afternoon, and he then goes up in flames to a fine display of exploding fireworks and out-of-date ships' maroons. After that, the otherwise very peaceable Cretans celebrate by firing shotguns, pistols and automatic rifles into the night sky. A church service follows towards midnight.

Bernard Stafford, York

Is it possible to have a dream which is sufficiently frightening to cause a heart attack, and for the dreamer to die without waking?

Yes, according to Drs Kartz and Melles of the San Diego School of Medicine, who conducted a study of physically healthy young Asian men who suffered from night terrors in the 1980s.

'What distinguishes night terrors from severe nightmares is that victims begin to shout in their sleep, toss and turn violently. Within less than a minute their heart rate shoots up uncontrollably, sometimes fatally, often in men with no previous sign of heart disease. If they survive the attack they remember having violent nightmares. This phenomenon seems to be associated with deep depression and usually affects refugees or immigrants, but as the young men become more established in their adopted countries the incidence of night terror decreases.'

Jacqueline Castles, London W2

Who were the Peculiar People? Have they ceased to exist, and what were their peculiarities?

According to Nelson's *Encyclopaedia* (1911) they were 'a sect of faith-healers founded in 1838 by John Banyard who reject medical advice except in surgical cases, relying on prayer and anointing with oils. Members have been frequently tried for manslaughter.' The title was also assumed by a London sect, the 'Plumstead Peculiars'.

Jim Miller, Redhill, Surrey

My wife and her mother were members in the late 1940s and 1950s. 'The Peculiars' had a great community spirit. My wife's parents had moved from Manchester to Grays, Essex, in the 1930s and many of the chapel members there became their closest friends. As a young girl, my wife enjoyed the Sunday services in our local chapel, despite their uncertain length – the Spirit might move anyone to give testimony. Often, the congregation would be chatting on the pavement outside the chapel after service, and the Spirit would move someone to sing – so they would all go back in and carry on, unaccompanied and with great gusto. As they were not supposed to do any work on a Sunday, many members would cook the Sunday meals on Saturday. The Sunday School was great fun, and often visited other Peculiar chapels by coach and train to share their Sunday worship and to go on picnics.

The Peculiar People took their name from Titus 2: 13 and 14: 'Looking for that blessed hope, and the glorious appearing of the great God and our Saviour Jesus Christ; who gave himself for us, that He might redeem us from all iniquity, and purify unto himself a peculiar people, zealous of good works.'

David Collins, Harpenden, Herts

The title also comes from 1 Peter 2: 9, which reads: 'But you are a chosen generation, a royal priesthood, a holy nation, a peculiar people, that ye should show forth the praises of Him who hath called you out of darkness into His marvellous light.' More modern translations have 'a purchased people', a 'special people', a 'people belonging to God'.

The Peculiar People still exist but are now known as the Union of Evangelical Churches. They are orthodox evangelical churches and in the mainstream of evangelical Christian beliefs.

L. B. Gunn, Claygate, Surrey

Would it be possible to construct an airship that was propelled and steered by sails?

A sailing boat works because it uses the opposing forces imposed on it by the air and the water. Because the hull (usually with a deep keel) is largely in the water, it resists the thrust of the sails. The rudder, too, is in the water. Thus, when a wind comes from the side, sideways movement is prevented by the water, and the boat goes forward like a dried bean squeezed from between the fingers.

An airship is not dipped in a more resistant medium: it is entirely immersed in air. Thus, there are no opposing forces involved. A sailing airship would simply be blown along, twisting and turning in an uncontrolled way – which is exactly what happens to an airship now if it loses its power.

Gerald Haigh, Project Editor, Association for Science Education, University of Warwick

It could be done. Gerald Haigh is right when he says that a sailing boat works because it uses the opposing forces imposed upon it by the wind and water. The problem is to generate these opposing forces in mid-air.

There are two intriguing possibilities. The first is to adapt the principle by which unpowered, sailless barges were once navigated on the River Hull in east Yorkshire. By dragging an anchor from the bow to reduce their speed to less than that of the tidal flow, such barges were able to steer effectively while travelling astern in the general direction of the current, the speed difference causing a steady flow of water over their rudders. An airship dragging an anchor over land, or a sea-anchor over water, could be steered in a similar fashion.

An even better possibility might be to exploit the fact that wind speeds and directions are far from constant at different altitudes above a given point on the earth's surface. Thus, an airship flying at, say, 10,000 feet might be driven by a fifteen-knot wind, while at 15,000 feet the wind might be thirty knots. Obviously a 'mast' long enough to exploit this difference would be impractical, but 'sails' resembling a large kite or a modern steerable parachute could be launched up into the zone of faster winds, and the tension between airship and kite used to navigate in the same manner as a sailing boat. There are obviously many technical difficulties with this approach, but theoretically 'tacking', that is, zigzagging into the wind, should be possible.

John Ramsey, London E3

When Shelley drowned in a boating accident, his wife Mary and Lord Byron burned his body on a funeral pyre. Mary rescued his heart from the flames and kept it in a casket for the rest of her life. What happened to the heart when Mary Shelley died and where is it now?

Shelley's cremation, stage-managed by his friend of only six months, Trelawny, was attended by Trelawny himself; Lord Byron; Leigh Hunt, who had travelled to Italy to join Shelley and Byron in a publishing venture; and various local officers. Mary did not attend and, according to Trelawny's account, the others could hardly face it – Byron swimming off to his boat and Hunt remaining in his carriage. Trelawny observed that Shelley's heart was not consumed in the fire and rescued it, burning his hand and risking quarantine in the process.

Hunt laid claim to it from Trelawny, justifying his action to Mary, who assumed a natural right to its possession in a letter: '... for [Hunt's love of Shelley] to make way for the claims of any other love, man's or woman's, I must have great reasons indeed brought to me ... In his case above all other human beings, no ordinary appearance of rights, not even yours, can affect me.'

Byron was asked to intervene but flippantly questioned Hunt's need for the heart ('He'll only ... write sonnets on it'). It was eventually through the efforts of Jane Williams, the Shelleys' friend, whose partner Edward had drowned with Shelley, that Hunt was eventually persuaded to part with the relic and Mary took charge of it.

At Mary Shelley's death in 1851, the heart was found in her desk wrapped in a copy of *Adonais*, Shelley's self-prophesying eulogy on the death of Keats. It was kept in a shrine with other relics at Boscombe Manor, the home of Shelley's son, and was finally buried in 1889 in the family vault in Bournemouth.

Abbie Mason, Cambridge

Amy Wallace, in the second *Book of Lists*, writes: 'There is a peculiar note of irony to the whole affair. The organ that longest survives a fire is not the heart but the liver — and no one present at Shelley's funeral knew enough about anatomy to tell the difference. This theory would explain the legend that the heart was unusually large.'

David Cottis, London SW15

A more precise location of Shelley's heart is the graveyard of St Peter's Church, Bournemouth, where it shares a resting place with the remains of other such worthies as Mary Wollstonecraft, eighteenth-century feminist, and Sir Dan Godfrey, founder in 1893 of the precursor of the Bournemouth Symphony Orchestra.

John Gritten, London

No one interested in Shelley's heart should omit to read Timothy Webb's 'Religion of the Heart' (*Keats–Shelley Review*, autumn 1992). The reader will learn that Shelley's heart was not unusually large, but unusually small – according to Trelawny, who snatched it from the fire. It was Leigh Hunt who changed Trelawny's account probably, as Webb plausibly argued, because he could not face the idea of a Shelley with a diminished organ of benevolence.

Hunt himself was well equipped to know the heart from the liver, having been much struck when young by some preserved hearts among the anatomical specimens of a Lincolnshire surgeon. So we must look for an explanation, other than anatomical confusion, for why Shelley's heart would not burn.

A condition leading to progressive calcification is one possibility that has been advanced. The irony of the whole affair might well be that Shelley's heart was becoming literally, though not metaphorically, a heart of stone.

Nora Crook, Cambridge

According to John Gritten, Mary Wollstonecraft is buried in Bournemouth. But whilst her body may be there, her memorial headstone is still in London's Old St Pancras churchyard, behind the station.

Paul S. Coates, University of East London

What was the last recorded instance of a duel being fought with seconds, at ten paces and using pistols?

My ancestor, Captain George Cadogan, avoided the police to fight a duel with pistols and seconds on Wimbledon Common on 30 May 1809. His opponent, Lord Paget, had seduced George's sister Charlotte, who was married to the Duke of Wellington's brother. The duel was fought at twelve paces, not ten, and they both missed (in Lord Paget's case this was deliberate).

David Colombi, Angmering, West Sussex

The Duke of Wellington fought a duel with pistols, and seconds, on 21 March 1829. His opponent was Lord Winchelsea, who had cast a public slur on Wellington's political honour. They met at Battersea Fields. The seconds were Sir Henry Hardinge and Lord Falmouth respectively. The duel was fought at twelve paces, and as the command 'Fire' was given, Wellington noticed that Winchelsea kept his arm close to his side. The Duke fired wide, accordingly, and Winchelsea fired in the air. A brief letter of apology was presented by Hardinge, and the matter was deemed concluded. (Source: Elizabeth Longford, *Wellington: Pillar of State*, 1972.)

Carol Ball, Aylesford, Kent

On 19 October 1852, in a duel with seconds, Emanuel Barthelemy shot and killed Frederic Cournet on Priests Hill, Egham, Surrey. The full ceremony was observed, with the combatants standing back to back and walking twenty paces before turning and firing.

Duncan Mirylees, Surrey Local Studies Library, Guildford

A confrontation involving Marcel Proust, the author of *A la Recherche du Temps Perdu*, and his literary contemporary, Jean Lorrian, took place in France at Bois de Meudon as recently as 6 February 1897.

The clash was occasioned by Lorrian accusing Proust of plagiarism and referring to him as 'one of those pretty little society boys who have succeeded in becoming pregnant with literature'. Two shots were fired, but – to quote *Le Figaro* – nobody was hurt and the seconds declared that the dispute was ended. (Source: Philip Kerr, *Fights, Feuds and Heartfelt Hatreds*, 1992.)

Bob Hays, Ripponden, Halifax

In December 1971 a duel was fought between a Uruguayan field marshal and a general, after the former had dubbed his colleague 'a socialist'. The protagonists met at dawn in a Montevideo public park and, from twenty-five paces, fired thirty-eight rounds at each other. Neither was hurt. According to the field marshal's second, the men did not put on their glasses before commencing the back-to-back walk. (Source: Stephen Pile, *The Book of Heroic Failures*, 1979.)

Dominic Gould, Hull

3

Time and Place

Most European countries converted to metric units in the early nineteenth century, often spurred on by Napoleon Bonaparte. What units of measurement had they previously used?

It is wrong to think that Napoleon was a great proponent of metrication in early nineteenth-century Europe. He is reported as saying to a lieutenant: 'What are metres? Speak to me in *toises*!'

The metric system did not become obligatory in France until 1840 and, despite many criminal proceedings, until the twentieth century the French continued to use the old units: the *toise*, the *pied* and the *ligne* (respectively equal to two metres, one-third of a metre or a foot, and one 432nd of a metre) as well as numerous other regional variations. It was only in 1870 that the French set up a commission to try to internationalize the metre, which had been dreamed up by a think-tank of eminent scientists during the Revolution.

But long after that date it was said that, though all the peoples of Europe admired and envied the French metric system, at least nine-tenths of the French people themselves ignored it. As late as 1895, a French priest is quoted as saying: 'Our villagers have passed their military service and our children have passed through school, but the metric system has not passed into custom yet.'

It is only after the First World War that there was a widely perceived need for standardization in Europe and even then it only triumphed in the non-Anglo-Saxon world. NASA, I believe, still use feet and inches in their space odysseys, and the revered Yankee cabinet-maker, Norm Abram, still abjures the inconvenient millimetre!

Ted Wilson, Department of History, Manchester Metropolitan University

In Germany people still occasionally refer to miles (*Meilen*), yards (*Ellen*), feet (*Füssen*) and ounces (*Unzen*), though they bear no relationship to modern measures. One still sometimes hears older people asking for a pound (*Pfund*) of fruit or vegetables when they mean half a kilogram.

Brian Smith, Darmstadt, Germany

In rural Brittany and a few Belgian bars in Paris, shellfish may still be bought in pints and I have been told that butter is sold in half-pound measures in isolated village markets in the Midi. The word *pouce* (inch) is also maintained in idioms to mean 'a very small amount' in the same way as it is in English (for example, 'I didn't give an inch').

Richard Stanton, Bromley, Kent

Not so many years ago, Swedes would always use the *mil* to describe distances. The Swedish mile was much longer than ours – something like the old English league. And they would still use the *tum*, the Swedish inch, to describe the thickness of a piece of wood.

Harold Lewis, Cobham, Surrey

Further to Brian Smith's and Richard Stanton's examples, I've often come across French market stalls where items are sold by the *livre* (pound), which equates to half a kilo. When I lived in Amsterdam there were cheese stalls on the Saturday market that priced items by the *ons* (ounce). It seems Britain is the only country that takes the metrication rules seriously.

Marc Wilson, Swindon, Wilts

Having just returned from St Helena, where Bonaparte died, I can report that metrification there has a long way to go. Potatoes were on sale near Napoleon Street at £1.60 per gallon.

Brian Robinson, Hutton, Essex

Ted Wilson believes that NASA still uses feet and inches in its space odysseys. Why?

Since November 2000 I have asked the NASA HQ – via an accepted web questionnaire, emails and half a dozen snail-mail letters – what units NASA used. I received some replies, but no one actually answered my question. I would guess that they use some sort of metric system, but why the secrecy? And what system of units do the UK and US armed forces use on joint exercises?

Norman Shepherd, Bristol

Like most people in my city I use *pinte*, *pouce* (inch) and *pied* (foot).

Louis Brazier, Paris

In the 1980s I owned an eighteenth-century house in Picardy that was built to imperial measurements. The French still refer to British Thermal Units (BTUs).

Bernard Batchelor, Liphook, Hants

I can ease Norman Shepherd's puzzlement; NASA, and, indeed, most of the West's aviation industry, uses feet and inches. However, this isn't a problem as an inch is defined as exactly 2.54 centimetres, and conversion to metric is thus easy and accurate in these days of electronic computation. On many machine tools the change between imperial and metric can be accommodated simply by pressing a button. No problems were encountered in the design of Concorde either, although the French used metric measures and the British imperial, and calculators then were the size of typewriters.

The standardization of the inch came about after the wartime discovery that the American inch and the British inch had become slightly different. The British standard yard bar was the culprit: it was made of an alloy of silver, copper and tin, which was not metallurgically stable; also it had partially recrystallized; and it had grown longer over a period of time. This discrepancy was discovered because Rolls-Royce parts had high failure rates when fitted to American Packard-built Merlin aero-engines.

Dick Bentley, Southampton

Harold Lewis wrote that 'the Swedish mile was much longer than the English mile – something like the old English league'. This is not entirely correct. First, the *mil* unit is very much a part of modern Swedish and is preferred over kilometres for longer distances. Second, it is a metric measurement of exactly ten kilometres.
Claes Harvenberg, Shamley Green, Surrey

Mark Wilson translates the Dutch *ons* as 'ounce'. The Dutch *ons* equals 100 grams, the ounce is 28.35 grams. The *ons* is part of the metric system and is the amount people have always used when buying small quantities. Holland has had a metric system for centuries. To fit in with the EU, the Dutch now have to ask for a kilo whereas before they might have asked for two *pond* (a *pond* being 500 grams).
A. Walsh, Bushey Heath, Herts

The growing interest in international exhibitions and commerce in the nineteenth century accelerated the use of the metric system, which was used by thirty-five countries by the beginning of the twentieth century. Britain signed the Treaty of the Metre in 1884, thereby recognizing the importance of a common international system, but has so far failed properly to implement it. Any similarity in attitude towards a common European currency is purely accidental!
Doris Mitchell, Tatsfield, Surrey

The station car park at Auffay, Normandy, is named Place Michel Hollard, with the explanation that Hollard was 'l'homme qui sauva Londres en 1943'. Who was he, and how did he save London?

Michel Hollard was a French engineer who, when the Germans occupied France in 1940, escaped to Switzerland. He made contact with the British Embassy there and began working for British intelligence, running a network of agents called AGIR who crossed the border to carry out espionage missions in occupied France.

In 1943, after hearing about a new factory in Normandy, Hollard and his team discovered dozens of sites across the North of France, all with concrete runways aligned towards London. Eventually, he uncovered the purpose of these sites: they would be used to launch the VI 'flying bomb'. Hollard and his agents infiltrated the plants and stole blueprints to send back to England. He is commemorated at Auffay, because it was there at the railway station that Hollard, disguised as a railway worker, examined one of the bombs and made detailed descriptions of it. He also found out where one of the VI designers was staying and had the RAF bomb the place, killing the scientist.

Using AGIR's vital information, the Allies were able to destroy many of the VI launch sites and factories. Although the 'Doodlebugs' caused much death and destruction in London in the later years of the war, the damage would have been far greater, had it not been for the heroic work of Hollard and his network.

Hollard continued his espionage work until he was betrayed and arrested by the Gestapo in 1944. He was tortured but refused to talk and eventually escaped when the ship he was being held in was bombed and sank. At the end of the war he was decorated by both France and Britain; he then quietly returned to his profession as an engineer. He died in 1993, aged ninety-five. His story is told in Georges Martelli's book, *The Man Who Saved London*. Perhaps Hollard would be the perfect candidate for that empty plinth in Trafalgar Square.

Duncan Harris, Chesterfield, Derby.

Why did Spanish dictator General Franco remain neutral during the Second World War and not support Hitler?

Spain's wartime neutrality is a myth concocted by Franco and his supporters after the event. Franco was an enthusiastic supporter of Hitler, without whose assistance in 1936 – in providing air transport for the Army of Africa from Spanish Morocco to the mainland – the nationalist *coup d'état* would have stalled and possibly failed. Germany (and Italy) went on to provide considerable amounts of manpower and material to assist Franco in defeating the Spanish Republicans.

In return, Spain provided assistance to Germany during the Second World War in the form of submarine refuelling facilities on the Spanish mainland and the Canary Islands, as well as selling wolfram to the

Germans, which was essential for the production of tungsten. Spain also sent thousands of troops, known as the Legion Azul, to fight for Germany against the Soviet Union.

Brian Ferris, Tunbridge Wells, Kent

Franco and Hitler met in October 1940 in Hendaye on the French-Spanish border for the first and only time. The exact details of the meeting are unclear and disputed; however, it would seem that although Franco was keen to join the Axis, he laid down certain conditions that seemed preposterous to Hitler. After the ravages of the Spanish Civil War, he insisted that Germany rebuild the Spanish army. Franco, whose military reputation had been created in Morocco, also demanded a North African empire, which would have been unacceptable to Hitler's existing allies, Italy and Vichy France.

Hitler left the meeting with his opinion of Franco greatly diminished, later saying to Mussolini: 'Rather than go through that again, I would prefer to have three or four teeth taken out.' When the tide of war changed, Franco's stance also changed; he would have liked to share in the Axis glory but he was never an ideologue in the Hitler/Mussolini mould.

Luke Baxter, Madrid, Spain

Why didn't the Canadians buy Alaska from the Russians 150 years ago?

The Russians did not offer to sell it to them, primarily because Britain was Russia's principal rival on the international scene, and also because the Russians wanted a buffer between Siberia and British North America in the event of war between the two powers.

By 1867, the Russians had virtually wiped out the Alaskan sea otter population, ending the lucrative trade in its valuable pelt, and the corporation that administered Russian America was facing bankruptcy. The Russian imperial government was in dire need of foreign currency to carry on its overseas adventures, and few officials in Moscow retained any interest in Russian America. The United States was the obvious choice for a buffer, as thousands of Americans were already there searching for gold. Also, talk of annexation was rampant: the Mexican War and the annexation of Texas were still recent history.

The Dominion of Canada, which achieved autonomy that year, was still a part of the British Empire and was therefore hardly a suitable buffer. Delivering Alaska to the Canadians would have extended the British Empire to within twenty-four nautical miles of Russia's eastern coast across the Bering Strait. Therefore Russia opened negotiations directly with the United States and sold what is now the State of Alaska for US$7,200,000, or about two cents an acre.

William Dunlap, Hamden, Connecticut, USA

In any purchase agreement there must be both a willing seller and a willing buyer. William Dunlap notes that the Russians, actively involved in the 'great game', were reluctant to sell Alaska to an element of the British Empire. The Americans were a useful foil for possible British expansion in the western Arctic. However, the Canadians were also less than enthusiastic about the idea of an Alaskan purchase. Canada, established as a self-governing Dominion in 1867 and eager to become a real country, had already made a far more attractive and profitable real estate deal in the same year.

While the Americans haggled with the Russians over the purchase of 'Seward's Folly', Canada purchased Rupert's Land, the Hudson Bay Company land grant, more than tripling the size of the country. The purchase included all the lands draining into Hudson Bay: that is, much of what is now northern Quebec and Ontario, the Canadian prairies, the North-West Territories and Nunavut. The purchase of Alaska was small potatoes in comparison.

David Neufeld, Whitehorse, Yukon, Canada

A recent *Guardian* obituary recorded the death of the Samaritan high priest in Palestine. Do the Samaritans have any extant scripture and, if so, how does it compare with the Christian Old Testament?

The Samaritans, whose religion is very close to that of the Old Testament Israelites, have as their scriptures the five books of Moses and the book of Joshua – the first six books of the Old Testament, which are probably the only part of the Bible to be written before the Jews' Babylonian exile.

The Samaritan version is written in the original, pre-exile Hebrew script (similar to ancient Phoenician), and differs only slightly from the Jewish–Christian version: notably in that it sites Abraham's attempted sacrifice of Isaac (Genesis 22) and Joshua's consecration of an altar (Joshua 8: 30) on their own sacred mountain of Gerizim at Nablus in the north of what is now the West Bank, rather than farther south in Jerusalem and near Jericho respectively. This difference probably reflects the tradition of the northern kingdom of Israel, created when Solomon's empire was split after his death and was destroyed by the Assyrians in 722 BC.

The Jewish – and hence the Christian – Bible, which follows the tradition of the rival southern kingdom of Judah, says (2 Kings 17: 24–41) that the Samaritans were not descended from the ('lost') ten tribes of ancient Israel, and that they mixed worship of the Israelite God with that of their own gods. This is unlikely to be true, however, given that the Samaritans of today follow only the God of the Old Testament, and follow the dictates of the five books of Moses much more exactly than modern Jews or Christians – they sacrifice animals as specified, for example.

They were almost certainly the descendants of the ordinary population of ancient Israel, who were left behind when the Assyrians carted off the aristocracy into slavery. Many were wiped out by the Byzantines following various rebellions, and most of the rest eventually converted to Islam, but there are two small communities of Samaritans today, totalling only a few hundred people, in Nablus and in the Tel Aviv suburb of Holon.

Daniel Jacobs, London SE15

Views as to the origins of the Samaritans have changed radically with the discovery of Bible texts with 'Samaritan' characteristics – old Hebrew script and expanded narratives – among the Dead Sea Scrolls. This proves that Jews and Samaritans shared common Biblical traditions until less than 300 years before Christ.

It is now thought most likely that the Samaritans were a conservative sect who rejected the worship of the Jerusalem priesthood at a time when this was tending to assimilate elements from pagan Greek culture. The Samaritans appear to have deliberately reverted to archaic Biblical forms, adopted a rigorously literal interpretation of the law; and taken themselves off to the most ancient of Israelite sanctuaries at Shechem (near modern Nablus), where they built a rival temple.

The Samaritans are absolutely rigorous both in refusing intermarriage outside the sect and in excluding all non-Biblical elements from their law and worship.

Tom Hennell, Withington, Manchester

In a book review in the *Guardian* a woman was said to have been prosecuted in 1944 under the Witchcraft Act of 1735. What did the Act say, and is it still on the books?

The 1735 Act repealed various earlier Acts, which had set out penalties for the practice of witchcraft and replaced them with a penalty for those who claimed to practise witchcraft and work magic, with a maximum of a year's imprisonment.

The 1944 case was brought against Helen Duncan, a spiritualist, and it was the outrage generated by her subsequent conviction and imprisonment that led to the passing of the Fraudulent Mediums Act. This not only repealed the Witchcraft Act but recognized genuine mediumship by requiring that prosecutions could only be made against those practising mediumship 'with intent to deceive'.

One result of the repeal of the Witchcraft Act was that witches, who had been practising their religion in secret, were able to come out into the open.

Philip Heselton, Hull, East Yorks

In *The Strange Death of Liberal England* (1935), George Dangerfield describes Sylvia Pankhurst's activities in the East End of London's 'sweated and obscure trades'. These include making wooden seeds for raspberry jam. What was going on?

Sylvia Pankhurst did indeed include this as an example of sweated labour in the East End in her 1931 book, *The Suffragette Movement*. The jam was being adulterated, in a similar manner to the 'watering down of the workers' beer'. Sylvia's response was to open a jam-making factory that produced real jam from real fruit at affordable prices. It also offered alternative employment to women who held pacifist beliefs in the First World War and who did not want to work in munitions factories.

Maggie Pearse, Department of Applied Social Sciences, Bradford College

My aunt, a nurse around the time of the First World War, noticed the worn and deformed fingers of a patient. She was told that the patient made seeds for a jam-making firm, whose workers were given minute pieces of seed-shaped wood, which they rubbed continuously between their fingers until they were smooth enough to pass for seeds.

John Youatt Dunning, Walton, Yorks

In the late 1800s and early 1900s, many alien substances were used to bulk out food. I have heard of 50 per cent added water in milk; starch and flour in cocoa; red lead and ochre in cayenne pepper; insects and fungi in sugar; copper contamination in preserved fruits; alum in bread (so that it would hold water and weigh more); and chlorate of lead in confectionery.

Marthe Broadhurst, Twickenham, Middx

In 1952 I was working in the nutrition building at the National Institute for Medical Research, investigating the effects of soft drinks on teeth at a time when fruit 'squashes' had been allowed back on the market after wartime restrictions. None used real fruit – they were all chemical concoctions. A typical formula was 0.5 per cent citric acid, 5 per cent sucrose, flavour (for example, lemongrass oil for 'lemon squash'), starch to give cloudiness, chopped cellulose to imitate pith, and tiny bits of wood to resemble the immature pips you might find in a real fruit squash – the implication being that the large pips had been removed in the straining of the juice.

Citric acid is a weak acid and even when concentrated it has a pH of over 3. We found one lime juice, popular at the time, with a pH of

2.5 and discovered that the enterprising manufacturer had added a slug of sulphuric acid to give it a kick. Happily he went out of business soon afterwards.

Paul Diamond, Woodford Green, Essex

I have heard that at the time of Suez, an RAF Canberra pilot in Cyprus, about to take off, pulled the undercarriage toggle in protest at the bombing of Port Said and the aircraft became a write-off. Is this a myth? If not, what happened to him?

The story is not a myth. The pilot had apparently requested his squadron commander not to send him on the bombing mission, since he had serious doubts about the morality of bombing targets where civilians might be killed due to what he considered to be a misconceived policy by Sir Anthony Eden – a judgement that has now gained considerable support. However, his squadron commander, acting on the principle 'Ours is not to reason why . . .', apparently insisted that the pilot fulfil his role during the engagement.

Whilst lining up for take-off, the pilot retracted the undercarriage, disabling the aircraft. The pilot was subsequently court-martialled and, I believe, given eighteen months' detention, followed by dishonourable discharge from the service. I do not believe the aircraft was damaged beyond repair, although during the Suez crisis two other Canberra bombers were lost.

Dilwyn Hardwidge (former Canberra navigator), Cleethorpes, Lincs

Three years before this, I was standing beside a Canberra in Tripoli with the upper half of my body inside the hatch, talking to the pilot, when the same thing happened, though by accident, because his glove had caught in the undercarriage locking mechanism. I escaped being crushed by inches and emerged with only a sore head from being thumped by the hatch door as the whole thing came down. I was later assured that my suffering would not be in vain because the aircraft's controls would be modified in such a way as to make raising the undercarriage while on the ground impossible: promises, promises!

John Walsh, Swindon

Further to the published replies, I witnessed the following incident at Nicosia airport. I was a corporal (instruments), serving on the pilot's *City of Lincoln*, 61 Squadron; the commanding officer was Squadron Leader Rooke. I don't remember the name of the pilot, but I think he was married to a member of the Guinness family. The aircraft was not a write-off, however; we were told to stand back while it was supported on jacks and the armourers removed the bombs. In January 1957 the aircraft, being flown by Rooke, crashed in Basingbourne (Herts) and he was killed.

Alan Wilson, Crossgates, Leeds

Many of us in the RAF at the time had similar misgivings about the operation – but the pilot's action was entirely wrong. His aircraft was carrying a full bomb-load, and by in effect crashing it on the runway he put at risk not only the lives of his own crew, but those of the other bombers taking off behind him.

Dennis Bird (retired squadron leader), Shoreham-by-Sea, West Sussex

Were famous anniversary dates (such as 5 November) updated when Britain adopted the Gregorian calendar in 1752?

Lord Chesterfield's Act of 1751 stated that saints' days and other church festivals were to continue to be celebrated on the same date; for instance, St George's Day was 23 April both before and after the change.

There were two specific legal exceptions that I know of. A well-known one is the use of 'old quarter days' in connection with the expiry of leases, for instance Old Lady Day, 5 April, instead of 25 March. This was duly changed to 6 April from 1801, but not by a further day in 1901, so that, as all taxpayers know, the Treasury considers the tax year to run from 6 April to 5 April.

The other exception was more esoteric: the 'regnal years' for George II began from 11 June before the change and 22 June after, so that there was no short year. I've never seen any mention of the question of coming-of-age, but imagine that the Act also specified that this should be reckoned by the old calendar for anyone under twenty-one at the change.

Apart from legalities, I suppose observance of birthdays would have been a matter of personal preference. 'Parson Woodforde', born on 16 June 1740, records his thirtieth birthday on 27 June 1770. Boswell gives Dr Johnson's date of birth as 18 September (new style) 1709, that is, 7 September as it would then have been, and this suggests that he observed it on 18 September after the change. He would have had no choice in 1752 as there was no 7 September in that year.

Popular celebrations certainly inclined to favour the 'old' anniversaries. I don't know how long diehards continued singing 'Remember, remember' on 16 November, but there are many allusions to similar persistence. John Byng (*Torrington Diaries*) records on 9 June 1790 there being oaken boughs and bonfires in honour of 'the old 29th May' (Restoration Day). Hone's *Everyday Book* (1826) records 26 September as 'Old Holy Rood day' and 11 October as 'Old Michaelmas Day' (the correct twelve days after the nominal dates).

George Toulmin, Cheltenham, Glos

Further to George Toulmin's reply: Section VI of Lord Chesterfield's 1751 Act listed a series of anniversaries, which were not to be changed when the calendar did. These were mainly financial obligations like paying rents and debts; but it also declared and enacted that 'no person or persons whatsoever shall be deemed or taken to have attained the said age of one and twenty years, or any other such age as aforesaid . . . until the full number of years and days shall be elapsed on which such person or persons respectively would have attained such age . . . in case this act had not been made'.

Eric Thompson, London NW2

Problems relating to the Gregorian changeover persisted into the twentieth century, by which time the discrepancy had increased to thirteen days. Russia continued to use the old Julian calendar until February 1918, and all Russian dates before this time should be defined as 'Old Style' (OS) or 'new style' (NS).

This caused personal problems. My mother was born in Russia on 26 July 1903 (OS), and after the changeover began to celebrate her birthday on 8 August each year, thus keeping her age correct but foregoing the familiar date. Similarly, my father's birthday was shifted from 20 June (OS) to 3 July.

The Russian Orthodox Church still uses the Julian Calendar, so it celebrates Christmas Day on 7 January. Since the date of Easter is defined by complex calculations involving the phases of the moon, the Russian Orthodox Easter sometimes, but not always, coincides with our Easter (as it does this year). I believe the saints' days have remained on the same nominal date.

Mrs H. Davoll, Great Bookham, Surrey

In old spy movies, secret information was transmitted by means of a microdot, perhaps disguised as a full stop on a page. Did such things exist?

Microdots still exist. The microdot is an example of steganography, a system of communication that conceals not only the content of a message, but the very existence of the message itself.

The underlying technology was developed at the Dresden Institute by Emanuel Goldberg and others during the 1930s; from this, the Abwehr, German intelligence, produced the microdot, which J. Edgar Hoover called 'the enemy's masterpiece of espionage'. The process involved reducing a sheet of typewriter paper to the size of a postage stamp, then photographing the image through a reverse microscope, further reducing it to the size of a full stop. When developed and enlarged, it could reproduce an A4 typewritten page with perfect clarity. It had the advantages of being very difficult to detect while permitting the transmission of large amounts of printed data, including technical drawings.

After the Second World War, the microdot was used to great success by Colonel Rudolf Abel, the Soviet KGB spymaster in the United States. He carried the microdots in coins and watches that he, a trained jeweller, had specially altered.

Some years ago, the journal *Nature* reported that a team of genetic engineers in New York had developed a microdot that conceals secret messages in human DNA. The system is doubly steganographic, in that even if the tiny dots were to be discovered, the message, hidden in one of 30 million similar-looking strands of genetic material, would be virtually impossible to find. The delivery system has not similarly evolved, however: the team tested the technique by pasting the tiny dots over the full stops in a typed letter and posting it.

Even though most espionage today appears to rely more heavily on computers and other advanced technology, there is likely to be a niche for the foreseeable future for a device that does not leave electronic trails on a hard disk or across the internet.

Professor William Dunlap, Quinnipiac School of Law, Connecticut, USA

Robert Tronson's 1963 film, *Ring of Spies*, detailed the espionage careers in England of the five Soviet agents of the Portland Spy Ring.

Ethel Gee and Harry Houghton stole top-secret naval papers from the Portland Underwater Research Establishment and gave them to Gordon Lonsdale, a Soviet 'illegal' who passed them on to Peter and Helen Kroger. From their home in Ruislip, the Krogers transferred secret documents into microdots ready for their journey to Moscow Centre. When all five were arrested in January 1961, the police found microdots in Helen Kroger's handbag on a glass slide, and in a search of their house in Ruislip a microdot reader was discovered disguised within a tin of talcum powder.

Simon Wilson, Ampthill, Beds

Was '666' randomly chosen to be the number of the beast, or is there something actually macabre about the number?

The most common conjecture about this is that it is based on the Greek and Hebrew tradition of *gematria*, which assigns to each letter a numeric value and then totals the values in a name to obtain the 'number' of the person.

The then Roman emperor Nero is generally considered the most likely person that John would want to indicate as the Beast, using some code that wouldn't be known to the authorities. However, it is hard to make the name fit. A direct transliteration of Nero's name into Greek or Hebrew doesn't work, but taking the Greek form, Neron Kaisar, and transliterating that into Hebrew does work, if one does a bit of misspelling in the Hebrew. Also, if one takes the Latin form, Nero

Caesar, and transliterates that into Hebrew, one gets the same Hebrew but with one letter missing and a total of 616, which is given in some old texts. All other attempts to associate the number 666 with anything are at least as fanciful.

A different conjecture is based on the fact that the Roman numeral expression for 666 is DCLXVI, the first six Roman numerals in descending order, and might have represented an indefinite, large number, or as we might say, 'a zillion'.

David Singmaster, London SW4

I suggest the questioner looks at the same verse in the Vulgate (Revelation 13: 18) which reads: 'numero bestiae est: Sex, sex, sex.'

George D. Fletcher, Oban, Strathclyde

I recall a Baptist pastor linking the number 666 with an inscription then found on the mitre of the Pope (that is, on his forehead, as St John would have had it). The numerical values of the Latin phrase for 'proxy for the son of god' can be construed to make the phrase add up to 666: Vicarivs (112) Filii (53) Dei (501).

Professor David Corson, Toronto, Canada

George Fletcher has, I suspect, been misled by oral tradition. The end of the verse is 'et numerous eius [sc. bestiae] sescenti sexaginta sex'. Neither the Greeks nor the Romans expressed numbers digit by digit, and their methods of writing numerals would not have encouraged them to do so.

John Trappes-Lomax, Bury St Edmunds, Suffolk

Lord Macaulay, when asked if he thought Napoleon Bonaparte was the Beast, the number 666 having been found in his name, replied: 'The House of Commons contains 658 members. These, with the chaplain, the three clerks, the serjeant-at-arms, the deputy serjeant, the librarian and the doorkeeper, who are the principal officers of the House, make up 666. I hold therefore that the House of Commons is the Beast.'

Stafford Maclennan, Cairns, Australia

The 'number of the beast' is found in the Bible in the Book of

Revelation (13: 18). In the preceding verse it states: '. . . so that no one could buy or sell unless he had the mark, which is the name of the beast or the number of his name'. Thus the mark, or the name, or the number of the beast was associated with financial transaction. Hence the number was probably chosen from the Old Testament (1 Kings 10: 14, or its equivalent, 2 Chronicles 9: 13): 'The weight of the gold that Solomon received yearly was 666 talents.' According to Strong's *Exhaustive Concordance*, this is the only other verse in the Bible where the number appears.

Craig Laferrière, Brussels, Belgium

Robert Graves's convincing conjecture is that this part of Revelation refers to the first-century Roman persecutions of the Christians in that city, either under Nero or Domitian.

In Roman numerals, 666 is DCLXVI, and taking each as the capital letter of a word gives: Domitius or Domitianus; Caesar; Legatos; Xristi (taking X for the Greek *chi*, 'ch'); Violenter or Viliter; Interfecit. This would read: 'Domitius/Domitian Caesar violently/vilely slew the envoys of Christ.'

There is little to choose between Nero or Domitian as worthy recipients of the righteous wrath of the early Christians. The choice of Domitius would have been a sly dig at Nero, who did not like to be reminded that he wasn't a real Caesar – his father was Lucius Domitius Ahenobarbus and his mother was Agrippina, the last wife of the emperor Claudius who had her husband poisoned to hasten her son to the purple. Domitian was a mad blasphemer against all religions who styled himself 'Dominus et Deus', 'Lord and God'.

Ivan Limmer, Barton-upon-Humber, Lincs

Ivan Limmer implies that Nero was not a real Caesar. In fact he had a stronger claim to be a real Caesar than either Tiberius or Claudius, two of his predecessors. Nero's mother, Agrippina the younger (wife of Claudius), was the daughter of another Agrippina, married to Germanicus (brother of Claudius), who was the daughter of Julia, only child of Augustus. The Romans placed great importance on female descent as well as male. Nero's predecessor Caligula had been the son of Agrippina and Germanicus; he was thus also a direct descendant, through the female line, of Augustus. Neither of the two was a great advertisement for the Augustan genes!

Nancy Rowlinson, Headington, Oxford

There is something beastly about the number 666: it makes your bank balance smaller. Since the mid-1980s, all bar-codes have carried a sequence of stripes representing the number 666 to confirm that the bars are being scanned the correct way (left to right). If you attempt to scan right to left, the computer won't be able to read the 666 and will ignore the code. (The reason that the number 666 was chosen remains mysterious, although I suspect that it works out neatly in hexadecimal notation or whatever number base these things are.)

This fact, reported in the *New York Times* and the *Wall Street Journal* in 1992, caused instant conniptions among Christian fundamentalists who saw it as fulfilment of the prophecy in Revelation that no one will be allowed to trade without the number of the beast, as Craig Laferrière relates.

Garrick Alder, Streatham Hill, London

What happened to the brewers and distillers in the United States during the years of Prohibition?

The present-day major American brewers – Anheuser-Busch ('Budweiser' brewers), Millers, Pabst, Schlitz, Coors, etc. – were all large, well-established companies long before the Volstead Act came into force (in January 1920) and they continued in business throughout the thirteen years of Prohibition. They had had a year's warning of the Act's onset, giving them time to change their products; thereafter most produced various soft drinks, 'near beers', root beers and the like. For some reason almost all of these products had strange names ending in 'O'. Bevo, Vivo, Famo, Pablo were some examples; Busch made a chocolate-flavoured Carcho and a coffee-flavoured Kafo. Other diversification included making bakers' yeast (Anheuser is still a giant in this field), or producing ceramics (Coors). A number of brewers went into cereal or malted milk products.

But wine producers suffered – California's Napa Valley was devastated. The distillers were able in some instances to continue making industrial spirits but many of the small 'craft' breweries that existed in 1920 simply closed their doors for good. Prohibition became one of the great forces for consolidation in American brewing.

When repeal of the Act came in 1933, it coincided with the Depression, which hit many brewers just as hard – beer production did not get back to the 1920s level until 1940 and the war years. Just as the Eighteenth Amendment took many years to become law (nine states were already 'dry' by 1912), its repeal left traces that continue until the present day. It was not until 1948 that the last three states (Kansas, Oklahoma and Mississippi) allowed alcohol sales and some Bible-belt counties are still 'dry'.

Pat O'Neill, CAMRA, Eastleigh, Hants

'Avon' is a Celtic word for 'river' (namely, the Welsh afon); 'llama' is the third person singular of the Spanish verb 'to be called or named'; 'kangaroo' (I believe) is an Aborigine term meaning 'I don't know'. What other names have arisen from the apparent misunderstanding of a native's answer to a curious foreigner?

Nyasa, the lake in Malawi (formerly known as Nyasaland), is actually a local word for 'lake'.

Joseph Spooner, London SE14

I read once that the word 'Canada' translates as 'nothing there'. Presumably the discoverer of this new world and those who colonized it were less than impressed.

William Merrin, Leeds

The creature known in Madagascar as the *babakoto* is known in English as the indri, from the Malagasy for 'Look at that!' On the other hand, *ganguru* is the genuine name for a kind of kangaroo in the Guugu-Yimidhirr language of Queensland.

Nicholas Widdows, London NW6

According to Chambers, both Sahara and Gobi mean 'desert'. I also recall a story that the three syllables in Pendle Hill all mean 'hill', so presumably two separate misunderstandings took place, at an interval of several centuries.

Alan Burkitt-Gray, Blackheath, London

The French word for an opening window above a door is *le vasistas* – a simple repetition of the curious German's question, 'Was ist das?'

Nick Tanner, Reigate, Surrey

When the Normans reached Herefordshire after the invasion of 1066, they came across the River Dore and assumed it was the d'Or (meaning 'of gold'). Even today the area is known as the Golden Valley.

S. B. Haynes, Tupsley, Hereford

When the Spanish invaded Belize, their queries about the identity of the indigenous people were met with the reply, 'Maya,' which they took to be the name of the tribe. In fact it means 'I don't understand'.

Anna-Louise Pickering, Matlock, Derby.

There are numerous examples of duplication of place-name elements from different parts of our linguistic ancestry. The Isle of Oxney in Kent is one example – Oxney means literally 'Ox island' but somewhere along the line an understanding of the meaning of '-ey' was lost and we introduced the helpful 'Isle of' affix as an explanation. Sheppey in Kent ('Sheep island') and Osea in Essex ('Ufic's island') have had similar additions.

Phil Back, Bridlington, East Yorks

In the last century the railway line from Portsmouth did not run all the way into Waterloo as it does now, but terminated at Vauxhall. A group of Russians had come to Britain to see the marvellous new method of travel and went back home to build railways in their own country. Ever since, a large railway station in the Russian language has been known as a *voksal*.

Roger Partridge, Surbiton, Surrey

There is a Madagascan lemur called an indri. The OED states that this derives from the Malagasy for 'behold', which was mistaken for its name. I wonder why (as far as I know) there hasn't been an animal that has accidentally been named after an expletive, or the local expression for 'run'.

Paul Ludgate, London N7

Wales derives from the Saxon word *walesi*, meaning 'foreigners'. So much for indigenous peoples!

D. J. Robinson, Paremata, New Zealand

Paul Ludgate wonders why no animal has been accidentally named after an expletive or the local expression for 'run'. The answer is surely obvious: no curious foreigner has survived to relate the experience!

Ray Sefton, Walthamstow, London E17

The last three of the four words in the name Alice Holt Hurst Wood in west Surrey all have the same meaning. Does this reflect the increasing frustration of a local Saxon trying to communicate with a Norman immigrant?

Victor Wyatt, Norwich, Norfolk

To Pendle Hill can be added Torpenhow Hill in Cumbria; similarly 'Hillhillhill Hill' in various languages.

Brian Rolls, Reading, Berks

There must be thousands of place names in Africa where inhabitants, having no names for the places, simply described them; Nairobi, for example, is the Masai language word for 'place of sour water'. In recent times the trend has also been working the other way: a suburb of Nairobi where the British Carrier Corps built their barracks is now called 'Kariakor'.

Jake Kidde-Hansen, Watamu, Kenya

The Russian word for a railway station, *vokzal*, is indeed derived from London's Vauxhall, but it has nothing to do with trains stopping there.

In the eighteenth century the Vauxhall estate in London became famous for its amusement park. This led in time to the name 'Vauxhall' being used generically for such amusement parks. 'Vauxhalls' began to appear all over Europe, eventually reaching Russia. Many Russian country estates had their own Vauxhall; railways there tended to connect country estates and in so doing would connect one Vauxhall to another. Thus the 'Vauxhalls' became railway stations.

John Dingley (Professor of Russian), York University, Toronto, Canada

The Manna story (Exodus 16) states that the Israelites called the substance manna (*mann* in Hebrew meaning 'What is it?'), for they knew not what it was.

Dov Pollak, Jerusalem, Israel

On Jacques Cartier's second voyage to Canada in 1535, he was shown the Iroquois village of Stadacona. He was told that it was *kanata*, Iroquoian for 'village', from which came the country's name.

John Lyng, Toronto, Canada

I'm told that 'Abidjan' is the answer that French colonists in the Ivory Coast were given when they asked the locals, 'Where are we?' The Ivorians thought the question meant: 'Where have you been?' and replied: 'We've been cutting the grass!'

Janet Hazlehurst, Dalton-in-Furness, Cumbria

There is a place in Alaska called Nome because the surveyor did not know what it was called and wrote 'Name?' on his form. This was later misread.

S. H. Lupton, Prestwich, Manchester

Ireland is full of misheard place names. Phoenix Park is a mishearing of the Gaelic *pairc an fionn uisce*, translated as 'field of the clear water'. The name of Dublin itself comes from a mishearing of the Gaelic *dubh linn*, or 'black pool'. Perhaps one on either side of the Irish Sea would have been a bit much.

Gerard Siggins, Sandymount, Dublin

I was told by our classics master that, after the conquests of Alexander the Great, the local inhabitants of conquered nations gradually adopted their own variations of the Greek language. Subsequent travellers in the region, which included the modern Turkey, asked peasants taking produce to market where they were going, and got the reply, 'Eis tan polein', that is, 'Up to the city'. The regional accent was such that they failed to recognize this as Greek and the name of the town thereafter became – Istanbul.

E. N. Martin, Stockton-on-Tees

The city of Buffalo in New York State is not named after the animal that once roamed in huge herds across the Midwest of North America. The city is at least 1,000 miles east of that animal's old habitat.

One story has it that the French were the first European settlers in the area, and they called their settlement 'Beau Fleuve'('beautiful river') after the Niagara River that ran by it. The French abandoned their settlement some years before the English arrived in the area. The English asked the local Seneca Indians what their name was for the place, and the Senecas assumed that the English wanted to know the white man's name for it, which they had heard from the French. The Senecas' attempt to pronounce the French words sounded to the English like 'Buffalo'.

David Apen, London N22

British explorers, wanting to know the Cherokee name for a river in the mountains of what is now North Carolina, pointed towards it and asked, 'What do you call that?' The Cherokees, thinking the river bank to be the subject of the question, answered, 'Egwanulf'ti' ('near the river'). The explorers wrote down what they heard, naming it the 'Oconaluftee' River, leaving us today with the 'Near-the-river River'.

Tommy Shinn, Leicester, North Carolina, USA

In the province of Cordoba, Argentina, is the small town of Fortin. The name comes from the days when, in the late 1800s, British engineers were laying a huge network of railway lines across the country. The branch line that joined two main tracks, and ended at this small town, was line number fourteen!

David Mackintosh, Buenos Aires, Argentina

Excluding hyphens, are there any places in the world that have punctuation in their name?

The humble apostrophe features in many a British place name. Abbot's Langley (Herts) and King's Lynn (Norfolk) are obvious examples of the genitive, although usage often omits the apostrophe, as it does with the saints: St Albans, for example. Some apostrophes indicate an abbreviation or the omission of a letter: Besses o' th' Barn (Greater Manchester), Blo' Norton (Norfolk). John o' Groats in Scotland has both uses of the apostrophe, as its full name is John o' Groat's House.
Michael Smith, Swaffham, Norfolk

Westward Ho! in Devon. According to *The Oxford Dictionary of English Place-Names*, this is a 'modern name commemorating the novel of this name by Charles Kingsley (published in 1855) largely set in this locality'. Perhaps we ought to add Hoo?, Howe?, Ware? and Wye?
David Binney, Tring, Herts

In the Catalan language, 'l.l' equates to the 'll' sound in English. This is to distinguish it from the 'll' without a separating full point, which in Catalan, as in Spanish, is pronounced 'ly' as in paella. Paral.lel exists as both an Avenue and a Metro station in Barcelona. Col.legi (college) and Col.leccio (art collection or gallery) might also be seen as place names.
Martin Cross, Glasgow

Saint-Louis-du-Ha! Ha! is a small town next to Lake Témiscouata in south-eastern Quebec, Canada.
Nick Whitehead, Geneva, Switzerland

Graca Machel Mandela has been married to two heads of state (the late President of Mozambique, Samora Machel, and now former President Mandela of South Africa). Is this a world first?

Cleopatra III of Egypt married three rulers: her two brothers Ptolemy XII Auletes and Ptolemy XIII Auletes, both Pharaohs of Egypt; and Julius Caesar, ruler of Rome.

Berenice, daughter of Herod Agrippa I, King of Judaea, married King Herod of Chalcis and King Polemo II of Cilicia. She was also mistress of Titus, Emperor of Rome.

David Jackson, Coxhoe, Durham

There are at least two examples in English history. Eleanor of Aquitaine (c. 1122–1204) was married first to Louis VII of France, then to Henry II of England. In the previous century Emma of Normandy (d. 1052) was married to Aethelred II ('the Unready'), and after his death to Cnut, King of Denmark and England. Both also lived to see two of their sons become head of state (Richard I and King John in Eleanor's case, Harthacnut and Edward the Confessor in Emma's).

Peter Grant, New Marston, Oxford

In the tenth century AD, Queen Sigrid the Haughty was the wife of Eric the Victorious, King of Sweden. After his death in 995 she married Olaf Tryggvason, King of Norway, who later divorced her. Sigrid vowed revenge and took Sweyn Forkbeard, King of Denmark, as her third husband, whom she compelled to wage a war against Norway in which King Olaf was killed.

Claus Hollenberg, Marburg, Germany

The V&A reports that the Koh-i-noor diamond was brought over to Britain as the State Property of Lahore for the Great Exhibition of 1851. However, there's no explanation of how it then ended up in the state crown as property of the Queen. Did the State of Lahore forget to pick it up after the Exhibition?

The V&A information on the Koh-i-noor is incomplete, possibly because of sensitivities surrounding Britain's imperial past.

The diamond was once owned by the Sikh rulers of the Punjab, until they were defeated by the British in two wars fought in the 1840s. The Punjab was annexed by the British in 1849, but the political situation was complicated by the fact that the East India Company was then responsible for looking after British interests in the subcontinent. This may account for the V&A's assertion that the Koh-i-noor was the 'state property of Lahore'.

Lahore was the chief town in the Punjab, which by 1851 had become an administrative area under East India Company control. At the time of annexation, the Sikhs had been forced to hand over the diamond to the Company, which later presented it to Queen Victoria, through the offices of Lord Dalhousie, the Governor General. It was, in effect, a spoil of war.

The Koh-i-noor, which means 'mountain of light' in Persian, was considered to be unlucky if worn by a man, which is why only female members of the British royal family have subsequently worn it, either as a brooch or set in a crown.

Geoff Clifton, Solihull, West Midlands

Apart from an occasional spy, did an American ever kill a Russian, or vice versa, during the Cold War? Or were both sides content to kill only Vietnamese, Afghans, etc.?

The US and Soviet air forces fought against each other during the Korean War, although this was hushed up by both sides at the time. Stalin sent Soviet aircrews to fight the Americans, but insisted on elaborate precautions being taken to conceal this. For example, their aircraft had Chinese airforce markings; they were instructed not to fly outside North Korean-held territory in case they were shot down; and they also had to conduct radio conversations in Chinese (although this last order was ignored in practice). In spite of this, the Americans realized that they were fighting against Soviet aircrews (they were picking up radio messages in Russian) but kept quiet about it for their own reasons.

Campbell McGregor, Partick, Glasgow

In the United Nations cemetery in Pusan, South Korea, there used to rest the body of a Russian pilot shot down during the Korean War. He was laid to rest in the non-combatants section but, quietly and without notice, the pilot's remains were handed over to the Soviet Union.

Hugh Jones, Victoria, BC, Canada

When was it decided that Christ was born in the year AD 1? And does it matter that Herod had died in 4 BC and that the census of Quirinius mentioned in the story of the Nativity was actually in AD 6?

Luke and Matthew both agree that Jesus was born before the death of Herod the Great (though not long before, according to Matthew 2: 19); this event can be placed confidently in the spring of 4 BC. (According to the first-century Jewish historian, Josephus, a lunar eclipse occurred shortly before Herod's death and this can be dated 12–13 March 4 BC.)

The error that misdated Jesus' birth by at least four years was perpetrated by the monk Dionysius Exiguus, who lived in the sixth century AD and who worked out his chronology without the benefit of sources now at our disposal.

The census held when Quirinius was governor of Syria (mentioned only in Luke 2: 2) is a baffling anomaly, since Quirinius didn't become governor (or legate) of Syria until AD 6. The proposed solutions include the following.

First, Luke confused an earlier census with the one under Quirinius. But Luke gathered his facts with some care and seems to have known that the census in AD 6 was the occasion of the revolt led by Judas the Galilean (Acts 5: 37).

Second, Quirinius was legate of Syria twice, and Luke 2: 2 refers to an earlier governorship. A damaged inscription from Tivoli has been used to support this, but the evidence is weak.

Third, Quirinius may have carried out the census under special imperial commission while someone else was actually legate of Syria (either Sentius Saturninus in 9–7 BC or Quinctilius Varus in 6–4 BC).

And, fourth, Luke actually meant to distinguish the census at the time of Jesus' birth from the better-known one under Quirinius. Hence, Luke 2: 2 should be translated as: 'This registration was before the one when Quirinius was governor of Syria.' There are grammatical problems with this solution, but they are not insuperable and it is probably the best on offer.

Whatever the reason for Luke's reference to Quirinius, a census towards the end of Herod the Great's reign is plausible. Herod had fallen out of favour with Rome and was sick; his sons were squabbling over the succession. It wouldn't be surprising if his overlords wanted a thorough assessment of the situation in and around Judaea.

John Bimson, Stoke Hill, Bristol

With the help of astronomical records going back over thousands of years, the sky above the Middle East 2,000 years ago can readily be displayed. Astronomer P. A. H. Seymour, in *The Birth of Christ* (1998), dates his birth as 15 September 7 BC.

Prior to this research, many theological writers have quoted 7 or 6 BC as likely dates for the birth of Christ. The year zero (or even 1 AD) does not appear to have been taken very seriously by scholars. Was it not odd, therefore, that the Church approached the 2,000-year celebrations with as much enthusiasm as the rest of humanity, whilst many of its leaders were surely aware that the real millennium probably slipped by unnoticed during the autumn of 1993?

K. O. Kemp, Cottingham, East Yorks

John Bimson's solution to the problem of the census at the time of the nativity story is fantastical. A Roman census during the reign of Herod the Great is a contradiction in terms: as King of Judaea, Herod − not Rome − was responsible for collecting taxes. Luke refers to a 'census of all the world' − not the Judaean census at the time of Quirinius, never mind an earlier and even more minor census contrived from a deliberate mistranslation of the Greek. There was no 'census of all the world', either before or after Judaea became part of the Roman Empire, and there was no Roman census of any sort in Judaea during the reign of Herod. These inconsistencies are not 'baffling' if you believe the nativity story is not true.

Peter McKenna, Liverpool

The uncertainty over the date of Jesus' birth need not invalidate his existence (Peter McKenna). The New Testament as a whole puts far more emphasis on his death and resurrection, and it is only these events that the Roman Catholic and Anglican Churches' Creed bothers to date (approximately) by its reference to Pontius Pilate.

Dating was in any case not as exact a science even under the Roman Empire as it is in our day, nor were historical records so carefully kept. Historical uncertainty can occur much nearer our own time. According to *Wellington: The Years of the Sword*, by Elizabeth Longford, the year of the Duke of Wellington's birth is known (1769), but both the day and the place have never been exactly established. (Wellington himself kept his birthday on 1 May; but 6 March and 3, 29 and 30 April are also claimed.) Tradition says he was born at Dangan Castle; he himself believed he was born at Athy; and a Dublin newspaper announced his birth as taking place in the city. I assume that Mr McKenna of Liverpool does not propose that this should invalidate the Duke's existence.

J. A. P. Dutton, Ellesmere Port, Merseyside

Has there ever been a land (or sea) battle fought between three armies, where each simultaneously fought the other two?

At Waterloo on 18 June 1815, Wellington's army was under attack from the French army of the Emperor Napoleon. A Prussian army arrived to support Wellington in the late afternoon and attacked the French. But in the confusion and gathering darkness, there were several casualties from friendly fire between the troops of the two allied armies, at the same time as they both continued to fight the French. The most notable of these tragic incidents occurred on Wellington's far left flank, where a brigade of his German infantry from the Duchy of Nassau fought some Prussian troops for about ten minutes until identities were established. (Source: *On the Fields of Glory: The Battlefields of the 1815 Campaign*, Greenhill Books, 1996.)

Andrew Uffindell, Berkhamsted, Herts

In 1943, north-west of Belgrade in Yugoslavia, the German occupying forces, Tito's Partisans and General Mihailovitch's Chetniks all fought each other in a pitched battle. (Source: *Tito Lifts the Curtain*, Hutchinson, 1953.) The Partisans emerged more successfully than the others and were thereafter regarded as the chief resistance movement by the Western allies.

Hallam Tennyson, London N8

In 1827 the Ottoman Turks brought their powerful Egyptian fleet of eighty-nine ships to Greece in order to defeat Greek naval forces, which were on the verge of winning their country's war of independence. The British, French and Russians, who had established diplomatic relations with the Greek freedom fighters, sent an 'Allied' fleet of twenty-seven vessels to Navarino Bay, nominally under the command of Admiral Codrington, to 'prevent' fighting. During negotiations an Egyptian ship is said to have fired, provoking the battle of 27 October. The French responded by delivering a massive broadside into the Russian fleet because they were still sore about their defeat in 1812 and the subsequent Russian occupation of Paris. Everyone then went on to destroy the Egyptian fleet.

Thus Egyptians died fighting for Turks, killed by British, French and Russians (who were also attacked by the French), ensuring that the Greeks (who took no part in the decisive battle) won their independence. Admiral Codrington got into trouble with his own government for liberating Greece without prior permission.

Ralph Lloyd-Jones, Herne Hill, London

Has religion ever stopped a war?

In the Middle Ages holy men such as St Francis or St Bernard sometimes brokered peace between warring kingdoms, as did Buddhist monks in Japan and Korea. Under Confucianism, China was always nominally pacifist, perhaps because it was never threatened by anyone but nomads and pirates.

Nowadays, no major religion forbids war for a just cause and no nation-state ever admits that its cause is not just. In the Second World War, appeals for negotiation by religious leaders in neutral countries and in Germany, Britain and Japan were ignored. Even so, many disputes that might have developed into wars have been settled peaceably, but history does not record wars that did not happen, nor the part that religion may have played in keeping the peace.

Roger Tennant, Lutterworth, Leics

There is hard evidence that the conversion to Buddhism of the Indian emperor Ashoka stopped all further war during his reign in the third century BC. Ashoka had been deeply shocked at the carnage he had inflicted on the Kalingas when he had conquered them around 262 BC, eight years into his rule. As a result his eyes were opened spiritually, and he devoted the remaining thirty years of his empire to promoting tolerance and the renunciation of war, as detailed on a series of rock edicts that survive to this day. In Edict 13, for example he expresses remorse for the massacre and stresses his belief that 'moral conquest is the principal conquest'. His policies included the construction of hospitals, rest houses and wells, and the introduction of vegetarianism into the royal kitchens.

These principles of non-violence have inspired countless generations of Buddhist leaders ever since, including the current Dalai Lama.

Michael Gold, Twickenham, Middx

In a sense it did in December 1978: Antonio Cardinal Samore, a papal envoy, managed to stop an imminent war between Argentina and Chile. Both countries were governed at that time by military dictatorships (the latter by Augusto Pinochet).

Jorge Grigoriev, Buenos Aires, Argentina

The war against the Amalekites (1 Samuel 15) was stopped, or at least brought to an end, by a massacre that was held to be divinely ordained. The extermination was not, however, immediately completed, and when monotheistic wrath was threatened against the relenting victors, the last of the victims was hacked to pieces, thereby fulfilling God's will.

Jeffry Larson, Hamden, Connecticut, USA

During the siege of Puerto Rico in 1797, the British fleet was anchored in San Juan harbour. One night, led by the bishop, the women of the city marched en masse carrying torches to the cathedral overlooking the harbour. They prayed for the liberation of the capital. Mistaking the women for troop reinforcements, the British withdrew.

Christopher Evans, Viejo San Juan, Puerto Rico

What was the longest single construction project ever successfully carried through by humans?

This is complicated by the fact that there are lots of unfinished or recently finished churches that were started in the thirteenth to fifteenth centuries. For example: the Duomo of Florence (started in 1294, finished in 1887, taking 593 years); Santa Croce in Florence (started in 1294, finished in 1863, taking 569 years); San Petronio in Bologna (started in 1390 and still not finished).

If the church has been built on the foundations of a previous structure, then the beginning of the earlier structure could be taken as the starting date. And, in addition, no church is really 'finished'. Chapels, altars, funeral monuments, porticoes and so forth are often added later, and sections are rebuilt or restored, etc. It is very common to see signs in Italian churches of earlier structures, dating back to early Christian and even imperial Roman times, so these churches have construction periods ranging from 1,000 to 1,500 years or more.

San Pietro (St Peter's) was first started by Constantine in 322 on the graveyard supposed to be the burial place of Peter. It was finished in 1667, taking 1,345 years. But the Vatican continues to be extended and rearranged right up to the present day, giving a time-span of 1,680 years.

David Singmaster, London SW4

Almost everything we eat in this country seems to have originally come from somewhere else (potatoes from South America; wheat from South-West Asia, etc.). What did people in Britain eat before these arrived?

A hundred years ago, they ate family pigs and home-grown vegetables. Flora Thompson's *Lark Rise to Candleford* states:

'In addition to the bacon, all vegetables, including potatoes, were home-grown and grown in abundance ... Fat green peas, broad beans as big as a halfpenny, cauliflowers a child could make an armchair of, runner beans and cabbage and kale, all in their seasons went into the pot with the roly-poly and slip of bacon. Then they ate plenty of green food, all home-grown and freshly pulled; lettuce and radishes and young onions with pearly heads and leaves like fine grass.'

Home-cured bacon was eaten almost daily, supplemented by the occasional chicken or rabbit. Large quantities of vegetables were eaten, and the meal was completed by a suet pudding.

Rodolfo Terragno, Buenos Aires, Argentina

The totals given for those killed by Stalin, Mao or Pol Pot usually include deaths from starvation as a result of social and economic policy. Whilst Britain's Indian Empire was a thriving concern, famines were not unusual – I read of 20 million dead in the nineteenth century – so can any of our imperial figures be counted among history's mass murderers?

Absolutely not. China, which escaped imperial control, suffered even worse famines than India in the nineteenth century and continued to suffer them for the first three decades of the twentieth. By this time India, although still subject to occasional devastating epidemics (of plagues or influenza), had effectively banished famine, at least in peacetime.

Nineteenth-century Indian famines were essentially climatically driven. For much of the year most of India has very little rainfall, but sometimes the intensely wet monsoon season fails, and if there is insufficient stored water this will have a devastating effect on the crops. In a situation where irrigation is inadequate, roads are almost non-existent and the transport of food is dependent on oxen, famine relief is almost impossible.

The British in India, whatever their faults, gave much thought to the problem of preventing drought turning into famine. Although there were occasional horrific examples of the administration finding itself out of its depth (notably the Orissa Famine of 1867), considerable progress was made. By the 1880s, when the rains failed, a programme for dealing with famine relief was well established.

Equally important, the British placed great emphasis on infrastructural development, with railway building and canal construction (for both irrigation and transport) providing physical mechanisms to ensure that large areas did not have to go without food.

Dr Colin Crouch, Harrow Weald, Middx

Most dictionaries define famine as 'an extreme scarcity of food'. We should not concede that there was a famine in either mid-nineteenth-century Ireland, or during Stalin's collectivization programme. Both cases of mass hunger and population exterminations resulted from deliberate government policies to enforce, at bayonet point, the export of huge amounts of local foodstuffs for profitable sale on international markets.

There is no distinction between the two episodes in terms of knowledge of what was going on, intentionality, or the satisfaction of the culprits with the grisly outcomes. If Stalin was a mass murderer, as he surely was, so was Lord John Russell.

Michael Napier, Riyadh

Colin Crouch is absolutely wrong to deny that British rule in India involved mass murder by famine. It can be shown that British policies caused famines in occupied India from the eighteenth century onwards. For example, the Bengal Famine, or 'Man-Made Famine', of 1942–4 killed about 6 million people in eastern India. The famine was caused by British policies, mainly the requisitioning of rice for the war effort and the destruction of all boats – the main mode of transport in Bengal.

Particularly guilty imperial figures must include Churchill himself. When Mountbatten offered for the carriage of relief goods 10 per cent of the space on shipping that was assigned to his military build-up, Churchill reduced his shipping allocation by 10 per cent.

That racism was at the root of British policy towards the Bengal Famine is demonstrated by the successful prevention of starvation among the populations of the defeated white enemy nations at the end of the war. I wonder if that is also the reason that the Bengal Famine is so little known and rarely mentioned in the UK today, and its fiftieth anniversary went unmarked.

John Wilson, London NW3

John Wilson is absolutely wrong to allege that British rule in India was deliberately responsible for the Bengal Famine of 1942. The main cause was the loss of imported Burmese rice following the Japanese invasion of that country (India's indigenous rice production was insufficient for its needs).

The shortage caused a rise in rice prices, which led to hoarding by rice merchants for high profits. The Bengal government tried two tactics: threats of action against hoarders, and the importing of wheat grain from the Punjab as a substitute crop. Neither succeeded.

A. Bailes, Werrington, Stoke-on-Trent

John Wilson rightly raises the question of British responsibility in the 'man-made famine' in Bengal in 1943 and wonders why it constitutes one of the silences of British history. There is a simple answer. The government did order an official inquiry but when proofs of the Famine Inquiry Commission Report (1945) returned from the press, the President of the Commission gave orders that they should be destroyed. Thus, in one act of destruction, history was 'silenced'.

Nevertheless, one Commission member, Sir Manilal Nanavati, kept copies of the five-volume report, which are available to scholars in the National Archives of India. The causes of the famine are complex but the reactions of those who have read the 'silenced' report are unanimous. The British administration was guilty not only of 'incompetence' but also of 'callous disregard of duty'.

Anyone interested in understanding the extent of the suffering should read Bhabani Bhattacharya's historical novel *So Many Hungers* (Victor Gollancz, 1947) to comprehend the devastating effects on the rural poor of Bengal.

Professor Cynthia Carey, University of Paris-Dauphine

Such questions are often muddled by attempting to assess personal responsibility. The late Karl Polanyi noted that the destruction of the Indian village system of distribution, and its replacement by a market system, led inevitably to famine; cash in hand rather than availability of food determined whether one could eat.

Amartya Sen has claimed that there was more food available in Bengal in 1943 – when 3 million died of starvation – than there was in 1942, when the impact of the famine was much less. The difference was that in 1943 wages had not kept up with prices, and the poor did not have cash in hand. As in Ireland in 1846, British rulers could not even imagine that a market system could be anything other than beneficial. Churchill's priority was the war effort, just as Stalin's priorities were feeding urban dwellers and accumulating capital for industrialization. This should not absolve them; Stalin apparently had as little understanding of peasants' needs as Churchill had of the Bengalis'.

American bombing in Cambodia (1970–1975) eliminated 70 per cent of the draft animals on which food production depended, but Pol Pot was blamed for the resulting famine. No doubt he had enough to be blamed for, but some of the starvation was beyond his government's control. In Ireland the British government attempted to do something when they became aware of the problem, but by then it was too late.

The answers are often more complicated than your question.

Jordan Bishop, Ottawa, Canada

Who was the last Western head of state to fight in battle?

The last British monarch to lead troops into battle was George II at the Battle of Dettingen in 1743 during the War of the Austrian Succession. On mainland Europe, Napoleon III commanded at the Battle of Sedan in 1870, and there is a sad vignette of him in Zola's *Le Débâcle*, trying to expose himself to fire so that he might be shot and not survive his defeat. The latest clear example seems to be General Pilsudski, President of Poland 1918–22, who commanded troops during the Russo-Polish War of 1920. In other cases the head of state is usually too remote from the actual conflict to qualify reasonably.

The last European ruler to die in battle seems to have been Charles XII of Sweden in 1718, although one might include F. Solano Lopez, the megalomaniac dictator of Paraguay, in 1870.

Simon Corcoran, Cosham, Portsmouth

Classical literature has many allusions to lions. Were there lions in Europe and when did they become extinct?

References to lions in Greek myths such as 'The Twelve Tasks of Heracles' are not to be taken as good evidence for the existence of lions in Europe; such references would have found their way to Greece through a combination of travel and observation of other civilizations. Lions were not among the creatures found in the Classical Age of Greece (fifth century BC) and any references to them, possibly in Aristotle's *De Anima*, written in the fourth century BC, would have come from extensive foreign research in the Persian Empire, which had links with Africa.

Bibilical and Roman references, such as Daniel in the lion's den, are far more likely to be grounded in fact, as Rome's conquest of Carthage in the third century BC would probably have opened trade routes through parts of Africa, allowing the acquisition of lions.

David Bamford, South Chailey, East Sussex

David Bamford suggests that the lion is uniquely African; it isn't. Nor is the European lion merely legendary; it survived in Thrace even in the second century AD, according to the trustworthy Pausanias, who was alive at the time. There may be later evidence; but, in any case, *The Collins Field Guide to the Mammals of Africa* says that in historical times, lions lived in every country from Greece and the Sinai to India (where a few remain). So, although reluctant to cast Daniel into the den, the Persian emperor Darius could not plead local unavailability of the necessary livestock.

Mike Lyle, Llangynog, Carms

After the establishment of Christianity in the Roman Empire, how long did it take for pagan worship to die out?

When Constantine the Great issued the Edict of Milan of AD 313, Christianity became legal in the Roman Empire. However, pagan worship was still allowed, and Constantine and his successors continued to use the title 'pontifex maximus' – 'guardian of the Roman cults'.

Christianity may have been the religion of the emperors and of many urban populations, but the official calendar of civic ceremonies continued to be largely pagan, even though blood sacrifices were no longer made. Furthermore, as education continued to be conducted entirely through the medium of pagan classics – Homer and Plato – so the literary and academic world remained non-Christian or, indeed, anti-Christian. As for the countryside, the population had scarcely any contact with Christianity at all.

This pattern broadly continued until the catastrophic defeat and death of Valens at the hands of the Goths at Hadrianople in AD 378. Theodosius I, who succeeded Valens in the East, refused the 'pontifex maximus' title – accompanied in this by Gratian, the Western emperor – and effectively proclaimed the Catholic faith (as defined in the Nicene creeds) as the official religion of the empire.

Theodosius followed this by the prohibition of all pagan sacrifices; and when he was established as sole emperor (following Gratian's murder by his own troops) a series of edicts were issued in AD 391 and AD 392, abolishing all pagan cults and ceremonies – including, for instance, the Olympic Games.

This ended explicit civic pagan ceremonial, although the events themselves often continued with a superficial Christianization. Evidence exists for a continued underground existence of paganism among educated people (a series of show-trials of officials accused of covert paganism took place in AD 579–80 in Constantinople). Remoter rural areas, such as Sardinia and parts of Spain, were at that date still said to be unconverted. Paganism appears to have ceased to have any significant foothold only around AD 600.

Tom Hennell, Withington, Cheshire

. As a Pagan, I feel it is important to add that we are still a worldwide network of peace-loving people who practise healing, herbalism and forms of prayer to nature in one form or another. Our festivals celebrate life and love, and we do our best to be grateful and to protect the planet – just as in Roman times.

Catherine Randall, Pagan Federation, London NW3

In England after the fall of the Roman Empire, the Anglo-Saxon invaders brought institutional paganism with them and, despite the return of Christianity with St Augustine, this Germanic paganism continued. In the rest of Britain, and in other areas of the Roman Empire, Roman paganism, combined with older native Celtic paganism, continued underground. It can still be found today.

Admittedly many modern pagan practices are recent imports from the East, or are even made up, but the genuine survival of pre-Christian beliefs – for example, Christmas and May Morning festivals, Easter eggs, superstitions, Hallowe'en, etc. – is not in doubt.

Simon Chadwick, Oxford

The 'Tiananmen Square massacre' is constantly referred to. Why have I never seen film or video footage of a single death? The cameras were there, were they not?

The cameras were indeed there, and showed a peaceful demonstration that went on for a couple of weeks. The government tried to disperse the crowd by the equally peaceful method of persuasion, then by sending in unarmed police. Finally, in exasperation, the army were called in, but the demonstrators chose to instigate violence. Video films clearly show a demonstrator throwing a Molotov cocktail at the first personnel carrier to enter the square. Hand-to-hand fighting broke out and spread to nearby streets, where many people were killed.

The reporting of this tragic episode is yet another example of media manipulation of the news. No one was killed in Tiananmen Square itself; the famous film of the man with the carrier-bag defying a column of tanks shows them stopping and turning aside to avoid crushing him; and the bullet holes that reporters said had riddled the statue in the centre of the square seemed to have suddenly disappeared when we saw workmen cleaning up the following day. The notion that unarmed students had assembled to demonstrate peacefully and were immediately shot down in their hundreds by the People's Liberation Army (like the action of the British army in Amritsar) is a lie.

Michael Short, Hastings, East Sussex

Michael Short states that the reported killing of hundreds of unarmed students 'is a lie'. But there is a mass of photographic and video evidence of the use of firearms by armed forces during and after the night of 4 June 1989, as well as footage showing wounded people being rushed to hospitals on makeshift stretchers. Amnesty International also has many gruesome pictures of dead bodies lying on hospital floors.

There is no doubt that hundreds of unarmed civilians were killed in central Beijing during the night of 4 June and that more were killed in subsequent days. The Chinese government itself said that 200 civilians, including thirty-six college students (and sixteen soldiers), were killed in Beijing in early June. The mother of one of the students killed has gathered a list of nearly 200 names of victims. Through its own research, which included numerous eye-witness testimonies, Amnesty International estimated that at least 1,000 civilians were killed in Beijing as a result of the crackdown.

The Chinese government stated at the time that 'no one' was killed on Tiananmen Square during the students' evacuation of the square between 0430 hours and 0530 hours. This is the extent of the denial made by the authorities. This may be technically correct, to the extent that shooting took place in adjoining streets rather than on the square itself, and that unarmed civilians were killed by armed forces in many other parts of Beijing. But there is no doubt that killings did take place as a direct result of the authorities' decision to use armed forces to clear the square. The pro-democracy movement was overwhelmingly peaceful until the armed forces fired on the crowds.

Mr Short refers to footage of a demonstrator throwing a Molotov cocktail at the 'first' personnel carrier to enter the square. To our knowledge, that incident did not occur on Tiananmen Square, and did not concern the 'first' personnel carrier.

Pierre Robert, The China Team, Amnesty International, London WC1

Pierre Robert (China Team, Amnesty International) uses the same wordplay tactics of which he accuses the Chinese government. China never said that 'no one was killed in Tiananmen Square during the students' evacuation between 0430 and 0530'. Mr Robert's implication is that the killings might have taken place other than between those hours.

The pro-democracy movement was not 'overwhelmingly peaceful until armed forces fired on crowds'. I have masses of video evidence from the TV (including some that was suppressed after a first showing), plus reports appearing in the *Guardian* at the time.

And has the mother's list of 200 victims been proved authentic?

Lawrence Sutton, Orpington, Kent

'Look at it this way,' a British diplomat who was in Beijing at the time told me. 'Those in the square were not peasants, factory- or mine-workers. They were, by and large, the offspring of those who would have ordered any firing. Draw all your own conclusions.'

D. R. Johnson, Andover, Hants

What became of Black, Asian and Arabic people in Nazi-occupied Europe during the war?

All were rounded up and transported to the United States in October and November 1941. In response, Congress declared on 11 December that a state of war existed between Germany and the United States. Plans to ship all the Pennsylvania Dutch back to Germany were never finalized.

James G. Baird, Woodstock, USA

Black people were virtually non-existent in Europe. France had a small population of Africans, mostly active in the entertainment field but, before the German invasion, most returned to the French-African territories from which they had come. While the Germans espoused their Aryan master-race theories, they had to be careful not to offend Asians, as the Japanese were their allies. A small number of Indians were recruited from prisoner-of-war camps to form an Indian brigade fighting the British. As for the Arabs, the Germans courted a faction of Palestinians in the hope of instigating an uprising against the British. The head of the Palestinian Muslims, known as the Grand Mufti of Jerusalem, lived in Berlin during the war and incited Arabs to rise in support of the Germans.

Peter Terry, Bridgehampton, NY, USA

Peter Terry is wrong in saying that Indian soldiers from prisoner-of-war camps in Europe were recruited to form an Indian brigade to fight the Allies. It was in South-East Asia that some Indian POWs were prevailed upon by Subhas Chandra Bose – one of the most popular political leaders of Indian freedom movement – to desert their units after the fall of Singapore and join the so-called Indian National Army. They marched with the Japanese army and were annihilated in the Battle of

Kohima. However, most Indian soldiers preferred to remain loyal to their regiments and suffer imprisonment. In Europe, the Indian prisoners of war met with the same fate as their British and American counterparts.

Capt. Narendra Phanse (Retired), Elstree, Herts

There were Africans from Germany's former colonies such as Cameroon living in Europe during the Nazi period. Also a number of mixed-race children were born during the occupation of the Rhineland by French troops after the First World War. About 40,000 black French soldiers are believed to have been based in Germany.

In 1927, the commissioners for the Palatinate informed the Imperial Bureau of Health that considerable cause for concern would arise as these black children matured. He enquired whether it was possible to render them infertile. By 1937, 400 mandatory sterilizations of African-Germans had been recorded.

Some black people were used for propaganda purposes and others were engaged in films such as *Hans Albers Quax in Africa* or *Water for Canitoga*.

Several died in concentration camps but those who survived were excluded from compensation payments. However, the Swiss Embassy in London recently stated that black people who were victims of Nazi persecution may be eligible to benefit from the Special Fund for Victims of the Holocaust, which was approved in February this year by the Swiss Federal Council.

David Sparks, Race Equality Consultant, London E6

Africans presenting a political threat were liquidated immediately. The Chadian nationalist, Tiemoho Kouyate, was executed in Paris by the Gestapo in 1940.

Etienne Ofori, Camden, London

Military expediency forced some strange twists in Nazi armed-forces recruitment. Professor A. J. Gregor, in his book, *The Ideology of Fascism*, noted that by 1945 the 'Aryan' Waffen SS was among the most multi-racial armies in history, having within its ranks black Africans and Americans, Arabs, Indians, North Africans, central Asians and whole divisions of Slavic Russians and Poles.

Even more bizarre is a reference in the book, *The Iron Wall: Zionist Revisionism from Jaboltinsky to Begin* (1984), which claims that in 1941 a fringe element of the Jewish Irgun in Palestine made an approach to the German Embassy in Turkey, offering to form a pro-German SS unit.

Dave Merrett, Canberra, Australia

In May 1944 all the Chinese in Hamburg were rounded up and transported first to the concentration camp at Fuhlsbuettel and then to a labour camp.

Viola Braunburg, Hamburg, Germany

Captain Phanse oversimplifies rather. Subhas Chandra Bose went first to Nazi Germany in 1941, where he did recruit a small number of Indian POWs as the Free Indian Legion. The Indian National Army in South-East Asia was first raised by captured Indian officers and nationalists in exile in Japan. However, they soon fell out with the Japanese and Bose was sent to take over, leaving the Indian Legion behind. The legionaries spent a peaceful war in the South of France until the Liberation, when they were brought back to Berlin. The Nazis made them mess with a handful of British POWs who had been persuaded to go over to the German side by the British fascist, John Amery. At the fall of Berlin, the Indian legionaries offered their services to the Russians, who then handed them over to the British.

None of this answers the original question, as the Nazis were always opportunists and had no problem accepting the services of *Untermenschen* while maintaining their racist principles. At least one African-American, working in Europe as an entertainer while the USA was neutral, died in a German concentration camp, partly due to the racism of US diplomats.

John Wilson, London NW3

The name Jerusalem means 'city of peace' and Benidorm means 'sleep well'. Are there other similarly ironic place names?

I grew up in Buenos Aires, which means 'good air'; it was true, perhaps,

in the 1500s when it was named, but not quite the grimy, humid air I remember.
Alex Laidlow, London E2

Passengers flying in to Kai Tak airport might question the fact that Hong Kong means 'fragrant harbour' in Cantonese.
Dan Coulcher, London W2

Greenland?
Neil Croll, Allestree, Derby.

Philadelphia, PA, is the 'City of Brotherly Love', but you have a one-in-five chance of being the victim of a violent crime in any given year.
P. Sanderson, Glenloch, Philadelphia, USA

'Benidorm' doesn't mean 'dormir bien'. It comes from the arabic word *beni* (meaning 'songs of'), like a lot of others villages in Valencia (Benitachell, Benimuslin, Beniarres). They are all old Spanish-Musulman sites.
Angel Ocon Gimenez, Valencia, Spain

In reply to Alex Laidlaw: the name Buenos Aires, literally 'good airs', has nothing to do with the quality of the air we breathe – which isn't bad as big cities go because the flat pampas and the River Plate, the widest river in the world, help the winds to get rid of pollution.

Before self-propelled ships, sailors had to depend on the right winds to reach their destination safely. So it was only fitting that, when the first Spaniards reached this (for them) remote place, they thanked the patron saint of seamen, Santa Maria de los Buenos Aires, or St Mary of the good winds, by baptizing this city after her.
Roberto Asseo de Choch, Buenos Aires, Argentina

Although there are mountains just outside Los Angeles, the cities of El Monte, Monterey Park and Montebello are all securely in the flatlands, while the names of their neighbours, Claremont and Montclair, are doubly ironic in that they are both in the flatlands too and subject to the worst smog in the area.
Tom Schneidermann, Washington DC, USA

Beni in Arabic does not mean 'songs of'. It means: 'children of', 'sons of', 'family of' or 'offspring of'. It reflects the fact that people lived a tribal lifestyle at that time.

M. Al-Ahmad, London W3

The source of the name Jerusalem is disputed. While it certainly came to be interpreted as 'City of Peace' (from Hebrew *yrv* 'to found' and *shalom* 'peace'), the name probably originally meant 'city of Shalem', the latter being an ancient West Semitic god.

Peter Bently, London N6

Is there any town in Britain that doesn't have at least some claim to fame: about which no superlative can be said, which has never had any famous resident, which has no celebrated architecture or which hasn't even a well-known derogatory association?

The questioner could consider Slammanan, near Cumbernauld, in central Scotland; Harthill, halfway between Edinburgh and Glasgow on the M8; or Whitburn, again situated on the M8. I am sure at least one of these three would satisfy his criteria.

Greg Russell, Edinburgh

Melksham, in Wiltshire, must be a strong candidate. Almost all its notable houses have long ago been demolished. Its history occupies one slim volume; it tried to be a spa town, emulating Bath, with no success; and it has no famous residents, past or present. I'm quite fond of the place, but what can you say about a town when the talking point for months is the opening of a branch of Sainsbury's?

Pat Thomas, Chippenham, Wilts

My nomination: No Man's Land, near Looe, Cornwall. What can there possibly be to say about that place?

Richard Webber, Bristol

A railway bridge over the main road into Oldham welcomes you to 'The home of the tubular bandage'. They must be struggling to get into

any of the questioner's categories.
Paul Cruthers, Chorlton-cum-Hardy, Manchester

In response to Pat Thomas, Melksham is recorded in the Domesday Book, 1086. When it was a village, the early kings of England used to hunt in what was then a forest, stretching from Chippenham to Calne in the north and from Semington to Rowde in the south. We can boast that we still have the Kings Arms Hotel; in the early nineteenth century the stage coaches stopped there en route from London to Bristol and changed horses.

Rachel Fowler – sister to John Fowler, who invented the steam plough and revolutionized the cultivation of heavy soil – was a great benefactor to the town. The beautiful parish church, St Michael and All Angels, is about 900 years old, and in the churchyard a 700-year-old yew tree still stands. We can claim two Roundhouses in the town – one in Church Street dates from the seventeenth century. Surely it must be agreed we have some history?
Sheila Wilkinson, Mayor of Melksham, Wilts

Yes. Somewhere in the borders between England and Wales (or is it Scotland?) there is a small village whose name I forget at the moment.
Steve Ellison, Walsall Wood, West Midlands

Greg Russell is wrong. Slammanan, Harthill and Whitburn have all been mentioned in a national newspaper.
Lawrence Cairns-Smith, King's Norton, Birmingham

Lord Horne (of Slammanan) adopted his title after a political career as a Tory politician during the inter-war period and as a cabinet officer during the General Strike, also accruing various other honours. I can, however, vouch for the blandness of the two other towns!
C. Imrie, Balham, London

If the search is extended to Ireland, there are numerous examples. Craigavon (Co. Armagh) is famous only for its roundabouts. Strabane (Co. Tyrone) has a tourist information centre, but no tourist attractions. Even its famous ex-sons don't actually come from the town itself, but a place a few miles up the road. And for years, Letterkenny's sole claim to fame was having the only set of traffic lights in the whole of Co. Donegal. Now that the town has two sets, even this claim has evaporated.

Nick Brown, Belfast

Melksham, as named by Pat Thomas, is famed as the birthplace of the Quaker naturalist Dr John Rutty, whose name is perpetuated throughout Africa by handsome shrubs called ruttya. He was the author of several books: *An Essay Towards the Natural History of the County of Dublin* published in 1772; a work on mineral waters of Ireland; and, most famously, an extraordinary spiritual diary, published posthumously.

Charles Nelson, Wisbech, Cambs

Hannibal of Carthage crossed the Alps with his elephants. Where did he get them, and how were they trained? Carthage is in North Africa, but the African elephant today is regarded as untrainable.

The Carthaginians regularly made use in war of the North African forest elephant, a breed now extinct. This elephant species was much smaller than its bush elephant cousins, measuring on average about 2.5 metres at the shoulder. There is, however, evidence from coins that the Carthaginians also imported Indian elephants.

Hannibal apparently took thirty-seven elephants with him to Italy from his headquarters in Spain, where he was governor of Carthage's empire there. Most died en route and perhaps a dozen survived to fight in his first major Italian battle, at Trebia, in 218 BC. Despite the fame of Hannibal's exploit, the role of the elephants in his campaign was short lived and very minor. A larger number was brought to Italy by his brother Hasdrubal a few years later, but he and his army were defeated by the Romans before they could link up with Hannibal.

Jonathan Drake, Clapham, London SW12

It is a widespread fallacy that African elephants are untrainable. The largest working group in Africa, to my knowledge at least, was in the then Belgian Congo earlier this century. These were undoubtedly working, trained African elephants that were used to move wood and other articles. In its prime, the herd numbered over a hundred. A further example of working African elephants comes from Zimbabwe, where there is a herd of around five animals, which are being trained to carry game scouts during anti-poaching operations.

Graeme Cumming, Oxford

What is the origin of the crescent moon symbol seen throughout Islamic cultures?

Islam emerged in Arabia, where travel along the desert trade routes was largely by night, and navigation depended upon the position of the moon and stars. The moon thus represents the guidance of God on the path through life. The new moon also represents the Muslim calendar, which has twelve months each of twenty-nine or thirty days. So in Islam the lunar month and the calendar month coincide, and the new moon is eagerly awaited, especially at the end of the month of Ramadan when its sighting means that the celebrations of 'Id al-Fitr can begin.

Linda and Phil Holmes, Cottingham, North Humberside

The use of the so-called crescent moon in many Islamic symbols cannot be related to the importance attached to the new moon in Islam. The moon depicted on, for example, many Islamic flags, is the old moon, the reverse shape of the new moon, which is like a letter 'C' backwards.

Again the word 'crescent', implying 'increasing', is properly applicable only to the young moon; the old moon is diminishing in phase. Presumably the moon is depicted as a crescent in Islamic, and many other, contexts as that shape is unambiguously lunar.

A. A. Davis, London SW7

Although the crescent is indeed a very widespread motif in Islamic iconography, it is not Islamic in origin nor is it exclusive to that religion.

The emblem has been used in Christian art for many centuries in depictions of the Virgin Mary, for example. It is in fact one of the oldest icons in human history, having been known in graphic depictions since at least as early as the Babylonian period in Mesopotamia. The stele of

Ur Namu, for example, dating from 2100 BC, includes the crescent moon to symbolize the god Sin, along with a star representing Shamash, the sun god. Later the moon became a female deity, typified by the goddess Artemis and her many counterparts, including Diana, who was celebrated as the moon-goddess in Roman times and who was depicted with a crescent on her brow.

The device seems to have entered Islam via the Seljuk Turks who dominated Anatolia in the twelfth century. It was widely used by their successors, the Ottoman Turks, who eventually became the principal Islamic nation, and whose Sultan held the title of Caliph until 1922. The story that the Ottomans adopted the crescent to symbolize their conquest of Constantinople must be dismissed as mere legend, since the device considerably pre-dates 1453. In the late nineteenth century the Pan-Islamic movement, sponsored by the Sultan Abdul Hamid II, used the crescent and star on a green flag as part of its propaganda, and from this were derived the flags of Egypt and Pakistan as well as those of many other Islamic states.

William G. Crampton, Director of the Flag Institute, Chester

A detailed answer will be found in the entry for 'Hilal' in *The Encyclopaedia of Islam* (second edition, Brill, Leiden, 1960).

Professor Richard Ettinghausen, writer of the entry, notes that the crescent moon (*hilal*) motif is featured with a five- or six-pointed star (the latter is known as Solomon's shield in the Islamic world), seen on early Islamic coins c. AD 695, but it carried no distinct Islamic connotation. Some 500 years later, it appears in association with various astrological/astronomical symbols on twelfth-century Islamic metalwork, but when depicted in manuscript painting, held by a seated man, it is thought to represent the authority of a high court official: 'the sun [is] to the king and the moon [is] to the vizier . . .' Its use as a roof finial on Islamic buildings also dates from this medieval period but the motif still had no specific religious meaning as it decorated all types of architecture, secular as well as religious.

In fact Ettinghausen argues that it was the European assumption — that this was a religious and national emblem — that led to several Muslim governments adopting it officially during the nineteenth century.

(Dr) Patricia Baker, Farnham, Surrey

Can anyone confirm that somewhere in a field in the North of England there used to be a sign saying: 'Please do not throw stones at this notice'? Are there other examples of this kind of helpful public information?

There is a sign at the back entrance to the botanical gardens in this town that says: 'Slow Down – You are entering a work zone.'
Paul Mestitz, Geelong, Victoria, Australia

In a coffee-bar in Sincelejo, northern Colombia, the following is displayed: 'Bread with butter: 100 pesos. Bread with margarine: 80 pesos. Bread without butter: 60 pesos. Bread without margarine: 40 pesos.'
Bernardo Recamán, Bogotá, Colombia

The strictures against 'throwing stones at this notice' seem positively tame compared to the list of prohibitions posted at a beach called Wilderness, Cape Province. They read:
'The following are prohibited:
'No: picnic between sunset and sunrise; bad language; firearms; singing; playing of musical instruments; use of loudspeakers; dumping of rubbish; camping; animals; damage of vegitation [sic]; washing of crockery or laundry; gatherings; alcohol. Thank you.'
Beverley Roos, Cape Town, South Africa

Seen in a field in West Yorkshire: 'Beware of the Bull. Entry Free. Bull Will Charge Later.'
Mrs Ray Tantram, Great Bookham, Surrey

Printed on toilet-paper tissues at the Harwell Laboratories in the 1970s: 'Not for resale.'
Dr J. G. Booth, Department of Physics, University of Salford

In the Raemoir House Hotel near Aberdeen there used to be a sign on a door which read: 'Room for shooting guests only.' The room is now the manager's office.
Colin Millar, Oyne, Aber.

The NSW Public Works Department had a portable toilet with a sign: 'Please do not place your handbag in the urinal.'
B. Kesteven, Hurstville, NSW, Australia

Seen at the tip of Great Camanoe Island in the British Virgin Islands (1962–4): 'No trespassing without permission.'
A. S. Batham, Taupo, New Zealand

I am told that in Belize, in a place called 'The Dump', there was a football field with a sign saying: 'Anyone throwing stones will be persecuted.'
R. E. G. Smith, Maseru, Lesotho

Out in the wilds of Connemara there is a gaunt granite monolithic monument, with a plaque reading: 'On this spot in 1897 nothing happened.'
Ruth Smith, Cambridge

Outside Shap Abbey in Cumbria stands this notice: 'Admission Free. Special terms for parties.'
Marcus Cousterdine, Blackpool

A notice that reflected the spirit of the question was written in chalk on a wall in Cambridge not long ago. It read: 'This graffito is biodegradable.'
Bernard Cashman, Biddenham, Beds

In recent years there was a blue Heritage plaque on a house in Zinzan Street in Reading, which stated: 'William Hogarth (1697–1764) never lived here.' It has since disappeared. Maybe they found out it wasn't true?
Maxine Wicks, Bishopston, Bristol

My favourite road sign is in Chesham, Bucks, where the highway authorities – having spent large sums of taxpayers' money to build a relief road with two lanes in each direction – now instruct motorists: 'Use Both Lanes.'
Geoffrey Allen, Pavia, Italy

There is a sign at the edge of a pasture in Belgrade, Maine, which states: 'If you can't cross this field in 9.9 seconds or less, DON'T TRY IT. The bull can make it in ten.'
E. A. Mayer, Belgrade Lakes, Maine, USA

When we lived in Massachusetts in the 1960s, I distinctly remember a sign on a high-tension electricity pylon saying: 'To climb this structure means instant death. Anyone found doing so will be prosecuted.'
Nicholas O'Dell, Phoenixville, Pennsylvania, USA

At a seminary in Ibadan, Nigeria, a sign posted over a telephone on a landing of the staircase in the staff residence read: 'This telephone is to not be used for either incoming or outgoing calls.' (Subsequently, the phone was stolen, but the sign remained.)
Calvin H. Poulin, Nairobi, Kenya

This notice was posted at the Dunbar (Vancouver) Post Office: 'For your added convenience, this Post Office will be closed on Saturdays.'
Hulbert Silver, Vancouver, Canada

Written around the edge of my son's 'I am two' badge taken from a birthday card are the words: 'Unsuitable for children under three years of age.'
Jane Fallows, Gordonvale, Queensland, Australia

Outside Stafford prison there is a sign that reads: 'Long Stay Car Park.'
Frank Nowikowski, Buenos Aires, Argentina

Roadsign in the former Transkei homeland: 'When this sign is under water, this bridge is impassable.'
Laura Yeatman, Johannesburg, South Africa

While crossing Quito, Ecuador, by bus, I noted the following message written in Spanish on a wall at the side of a busy thoroughfare. 'Warning to Motorists: Reading graffiti is a frequent cause of traffic accidents.'
Raymond Denson, Ontario, Canada

In a village hall in Kent there is a notice: 'In the event of fire, evacuate the hall and call the Fire Service.' The nearest public telephone box to this hall is opposite the fire station.

Tony McColgan, Hull, North Humberside

Some time ago I received some junk mail that was addressed to 'The Occupier, 33 Easton House', etc. Above the address was the instruction: 'If addressee has moved, please return to sender, giving new address.'

Richard Phillips, Bath

There is a sign in a lion park in Australia (normally viewed from the safety of a motor car), which reads:

'Adults: $5
'Children: $2
'Poms on bicycles: Free.'

J. G. Shelley, Vaucluse, Australia

Seen on a motorway in Vermont, USA: 'Rest area ahead. No rest rooms.'

Guy Johnston, Kirchhundem, Germany

Sign on a farm gate new Oyen, Alberta: 'We shoot every third salesman.'

J. C. Haigh, Saskatchewan, Canada

Noted at a service station along the main highway between Sydney and Melbourne: 'Due to unavoidable delays, this service station will not be closing until 1 August.'

Rob Wetselaar, Canberra, Australia

Standing in the water, twenty feet away from the beach in a state park in southern Florida, is a row of signs, each carrying the same message: 'No Wading or Swimming. Do Not Feed the Alligators.'

David G. Onn, Newark, Delaware, USA

How did the ancient Romans calculate with their Roman numerals? Am I right in thinking that they could neither multiply nor divide?

Addition and subtraction are fairly straightforward, but multiplication and division are more difficult, and I can only find one author who addresses the problem: Lancelot Hogben, in his book for children, *Man Must Measure: The Wonderful World of Mathematics*.

He says: 'We rightly think of the Romans as a nation of conquerors, but they were never able to conquer the art of calculating as we know it today. Even simple multiplication was a slow and space-consuming process. The Roman merchant might use numerals for recording, but calculating was still a task for the slave working with an abacus.'

Hogben then gives an illustration of the sum, 123 × 165, in Roman numerals, which is too space-consuming for these columns.
Bill Williams, Life Fellow, University of Leeds

The Romans surmounted their problems in calculation with the aid of the abacus, which appears to have been in use in Egypt by about 500 BC. The symbol for zero, essential to modern numerical notation, seems to have been suggested by an Indian mathematician in about AD 500 and was picked up by the Arabs about 200 years later. The first book, by an Arab, that used positional notation appeared in about AD 810. (Source: I. Asimov, *Chronology of Science and Discovery*.)

I have seen shopkeepers in the central Asian republics of the old Soviet Union using an abacus at a similar speed to that of some of our own shop assistants using a pocket calculator.
Bryn Giles, Henleaze, Bristol

Why is Saint George the patron saint of England? And why is he the patron saint of Catalonia?

In his *Oxford Dictionary of Saints*, David Hugh Farmer explains that St George was adopted as patron saint in the Middle Ages by England and Catalonia, as well as by Venice, Genoa and Portugal, because he was the personification of the ideals of Christian chivalry.

St George had been known in England since the seventh or eighth centuries but his cult gained new impetus in England during the Crusades. A vision of George and Demetrius at the siege of Antioch preceded the defeat of the Saracens and the fall of the town on the first Crusade. Richard I placed himself and his army under the saint's protection, and St George was subsequently regarded as the special patron of soldiers. Edward III founded the Order of the Garter under St George's patronage in 1348. In 1415 – after the Battle of Agincourt, when Henry V invoked the saint as England's patron – St George's feast was raised in rank to one of the principal feasts of the year.

St George remained popular in the post-medieval period, but as there is considerable doubt about the historical veracity of his legend, his cult was reduced to a local one in the reform of the Roman calendar in 1969.

Katherine Lewis, York

By the time George took over from Edward the Confessor as patron saint of England – at the founding of the Order of the Garter – he had already been guarding Doncaster for over 400 years. In the East he was generally held to protect the armies of Byzantium, and he is claimed as national saint by both Georgia and Ethiopia. In Germany he is one of the 'Fourteen Saints' who are considered particularly receptive to prayers for help, and in this century he was to become the favourite national image of Nazi propaganda.

George's attraction was originally as a martyr in the persecution of Christians in AD 303. Tradition elaborated his death into a highly imaginative and varied list of tortures, offering church artists a complete iconographic programme – as at St Neots in Cornwall. At the time of the Crusades he also begins to be shown as a mounted dragon-slayer, a depiction probably borrowed from late Egyptian carvings of the god Horus.

Tom Hennell, Withington, Manchester

4

Lifestyle and Society

After forty years' addiction I have not smoked for two months. How long must I persevere before I can describe myself as a non-smoker?

When, standing at a bar, you no longer scratch your ear, bite your nails nor tap your jacket pocket.
Ken Softly, Harpenden, Herts

Until you find yourself persecuting smokers as nastily as non-smokers used to persecute you.
Barbara Murphy, Wallingford, Oxon

Till you're on your deathbed.
Quentin Burrell, Ballabeg, Isle of Man

All you were ever doing by smoking a cigarette was scratching an itch and thus ensuring its return. Your mind interpreted that experience as pleasure, or relief, whereas it was simply feeding the addiction. You are a non-smoker the moment you realize that smoking does nothing for you and is thus completely pointless.
Jim Trimmer, Isleworth, Middx

From the moment the very last cigarette is stubbed out, it is essential to regard yourself as a 'non-smoker'. Otherwise, there is always the possibility that having only 'stopped' you might start up again. It also prevents friends trying to encourage you to resume the habit. A firm 'I don't' is far less likely to be ignored than a lame 'I've given up . . .' It does work!

Andrew Pache, Croydon, Surrey

I gave up twenty-five years ago and still smoke in my dreams, sometimes a whole packet in one night.

Bruce Hunter, London NW1

I started smoking in my early teens and kept it up for thirty years. It has now been almost eleven years since I gave up. After about six months the vivid, almost orgasmic, smoking dreams stopped (they were better than any cigarette I had ever had) and after a year or so the violent urge to smoke became reasonably infrequent. I now like to stand downwind of outdoor smokers and breathe deeply but I can't stand smoke if I'm confined indoors nor the smell of stale smoke. At the first sign of serious stress, I still start to reach for a cigarette and I hope to be with it enough on my deathbed to light up for a final drag.

Kathie Stove, Adelaide, South Australia

When you can no longer say 'I haven't smoked since . . .' because you can't remember when.

John McLeod, Saskatoon, Canada

Who is responsible for today's blame culture?

Margaret Thatcher, who is culpable for everything.

David Sharpe, Beeston, Notts

Anyone but me.

Margaret Downing, Cambridge

Parents of naughty children who, at a loss to know what to do but feeling guilty about it, refuse to accept their responsibility for their

child's behaviour, and teach their children in turn that if they have a problem it must be someone else's fault.
Michael Draper, Sandbach, Cheshire

I don't know, but when I find out . . .
Mike Cooper, Kirkbymoorside, North Yorks

Does anyone share my phobia of cotton wool?

What a relief to find that I am not alone! But what causes the shuddering, the dry mouth and feeling of revulsion? And why do cornflour and compacted snow cause the same reaction?
Brenda Burrows, Upper Layham, Ipswich

Both of my sons hated having their nappies changed, and I've always felt their phobia stems from the use of cotton wool during this process. One son recently had minor surgery, which in itself held no fear, but the thought that they might mop up the blood with cotton wool sent him into a panic.
Mrs E. Jannson, London N13

I can hardly bear to touch it because it makes me feel as though my tongue is too big for my mouth. I think the worst part is tearing cotton wool. It just goes straight through me, putting my nerves on edge. My dad's reactions are the same as mine when it comes to the touch, or even sight, of cotton wool.
James Aldred, Darwen, Lancs

Only when it's in my mouth. Even to think of those little rolls of the stuff that the dentist shoves between my gum and my cheek . . . uuuuurrrrggghhhhh!
Jo Griffiths, Rhiwbina, Cardiff

Satan invented cotton wool when he found out I didn't mind the sound of fingernails scraping down a blackboard.
Ben Griffin, Roundhay, Leeds

Worse than the phobia itself is the fact that it receives scant concern from friends and colleagues. I frequently find cotton wool stuffed into my pockets or strapped to the mouthpiece of my phone at work. I'm glad to hear there is someone else afflicted with this phobia and wonder if there may be mileage in starting a support group. Polystyrene also fills me with dread.

Michael Ventella, Prestwich, Manchester

I blame the TB jabs when I was a child; the swab, the jab, the swab!

Roger Murrow, West Bridgford, Notts

I share this phobia. I have always attributed it to having had the stuff put into my ears when I suffered from earache in early childhood.

Tony Wilmott, Fareham, Hants

We hear a lot of different job titles for Islamic clergy. What are the ranks, and how are they attained?

Clergy do not exist in Islam. There are no intermediaries between God and men. The person who leads the congregational prayer is called *imam*. He can be anybody from the community, usually the one who knows most of the Quran by heart, although many mosques employ paid *imams* to lead the five daily prayers. There are different titles, however, for experts in religious law.

The term *mulla* (from Arabic *mawla*, 'master') is used in Iran and central Asia and is roughly the same as the *faqih* in the Middle East and North Africa: that is, an expert of *fiqh* or jurisprudence, the science that deals with the observance of the religious laws. There are different schools, based on different interpretations of the same sources, namely the Quran and the example of the Prophet Muhammad.

A *qadi* is a judge appointed by a ruler or government. A *mufti* is a *qadi* who gives general rulings, or *fatawa*. *Shaykh* means literally 'old man', but he can be a leader of a tribe, a spiritual leader, a holy man or just someone who through age and wisdom has earned the respect of his community.

There are ranks within the *mullas* and *qadis*, not dissimilar to the ranks within our legal profession.
Fatima Martin, Woking, Surrey

When did prudery arrive, when man decided that clothes should be worn other than for warmth?

'Then the eyes of both of them were opened and they realised that they were naked. So they sewed fig-leaves together to make themselves loin-clothes' (Genesis 3: 7).
Ania Plank, Chesham Bois, Bucks

When having a P was considered 'rudery'.
Syd Cunliffe, Kenilworth, Warwicks

According to the *Concise Oxford Dictionary* (fifth edition), a prude is a 'woman of extreme propriety in conduct or speech'; hence one might assume that prudery is a quality unique to woman – despite Ania Plank's quotation from the Bible.

In her book *A Return to Modesty*, Wendy Shalit argues that women are naturally modest, men less so. She does not believe that so-called prudery is the result of humans covering up for warmth, but rather that covering up is the way in which certain religions and cultures have protected society's requirements for modesty. In our society, modesty is often regarded as a craze of the Victorians. Shame is not something we identify with, hence modesty became prudery, with a whole set of negative connotations.
Duggi Zarum, Mill Hill, London NW7

Do 'twin-towned' areas have to have anything in common? I recently saw that Denham, near Slough, is twin-towned with Shark Bay, Western Australia. Is it all just an excuse to give town councillors a freebie trip?

Denham has been twinned with the town of Denham in the shire of

Shark Bay, Western Australia, since 1994. It was the idea of local resident Andrew Shaw – who planned it to mark the centenary of parish councils in England – and it has been extremely successful. Schoolchildren in both communities exchange letters, and visitors to their twin town find that people across the world are ready to welcome them and extend the hand of friendship.

Denham in Shark Bay has no historical link with us, although we are pleased to have forged a friendship with the great-great-grandson of Admiral Sir Henry Mangles Denham, who as a captain in the Royal Navy charted the coast of Western Australia in 1858. No council tax money is spent on visits, or indeed anything connected with the twinning, other than postage when exchanging newsletters.

Paul Graham, Denham Parish Council, Bucks

Keighley and Poix du Nord are the oldest twinning towns in the country and possibly in Europe, and this is certainly not about freebie trips for councillors. Early commercial contacts were made before the First World War but the official twinning in 1920 was a recognition of the devastation that the community of Poix du Nord had experienced in the war years. Keighley people contributed to building a community hall in Poix, which was named Keighley Hall. It is still well used and in its foundation stone is a parchment that records Keighley's 'compassion for the sufferings borne by the commune during the German occupation of 1914–1918'. Our annual exchanges are not for councillors but for families whose friendships are lasting.

Michael Scarborough, chair, Keighley and District Twin Links Association, West Yorks

Several years ago, on a driving holiday in south-west Germany, I came across the semi-industrial town of Idar-Oberstein, which has a reputation for mining and processing semi-precious stones. I imagine that the burghers asked: 'Is there somewhere in England also famous for its rock?' Idar-Oberstein is twinned with Margate.

Fred Batten, Cheshunt, Herts

Well over a thousand towns and villages in Britain display their twinning signs. My home city, Bristol, has twinned with no less than six places worldwide: Bordeaux, Oporto, Beira (Mozambique), Hanover,

Tbilisi (Georgia) and Puerto Morazan (Nicaragua). Whereas the first three named are trading ports like ourselves, only the first two actually traded directly with us.

Hanover is of a similar size and their people are grateful to Bristolians for help given after the war, but apparently with Beira and Puerto Morazan we have 'friendship agreements' as opposed to 'formal twinning arrangements'. They are deemed places with difficult histories: Beira has its battles against apartheid; Puerto Morazan is in war-torn Nicaragua; Tbilisi earlier had a civil war. For these reasons, Bristol would like to show them its support.

The European Commission has actually produced a twinning booklet, which instructs the respective mayors to sign an oath promising that the two communities will 'join forces to help secure, to the utmost of our abilities, a successful outcome to this vital venture of peace and prosperity – European Union'.

After I saw a sign go up in my local suburb of Bishopston, saying that it was now twinned with the Indian village of Kuppam, I set about trying to create what I saw as a truer twinning. I found another Bishopston on the Gower, South Wales, with the same origin as our name, that is, 'the Bishop's town', and I forged links with their local history society members. The project continues to this day. I have linked with an Ashley Down in Hampshire and have just found a 'Horfield' in South Australia, but whether anyone will pay for me to go on a freebie down under remains in serious doubt!

Richard Webber, Bristol

A friend of mine who lives in Denham, near Slough, was on a world tour last year and visited Denham, Shark Bay. He was surprised at the lack of a road sign indicating a reciprocal twinning arrangement, and local people seemed unaware of the relationship. Even when he asked about the twinning arrangement in the local community office, there were blank faces.

Bernard Taylor, Wootton Bassett, Wilts

After gaining office, how long does it take for politicians to go bonkers?

The *Washington Post* columnist David Broder said in 1973: 'Anybody that wants the presidency so much that he'll spend two years organizing and campaigning for it is not to be trusted with the office.' The answer would appear to be: two years prior to the election.
Brian Robinson, Brentwood, Essex

About twenty years ago I saw a memorable television drama, *The Year of the Sex Olympics*, which anticipated the impact of 'reality TV'. Is the programme still available?

The play depicted a future society divided into two groups. The elite were known as 'high-drive' and spent their time making TV shows; they all spoke with a mid-Atlantic twang and were the 'beautiful people' of the time. The rest of the population were known as 'low-drive' and all they did was sit in front of the TV eating junk food.

After several incidents that made him question the status quo, a high-drive man discovers that his natural daughter is destined to become low-drive. He, along with his daughter and a woman, agree to take part in *The Live Life Show*, in which they are marooned on an island and have to fend for themselves under the gaze of automatic television cameras. They do not know that there is already someone else marooned on the island – a psychotic old man and his female companion. There is a shocking finale, with three deaths, including those of the daughter and the old man, following which the former high-drive man destroys all the cameras he can find – but he does not find them all! In the last scene the other high-drives laugh as they continue to televise the ruins of his life.

There is a wonderful irony to the play, throughout which the TV station announces the 'Olympics' with a harsh, a cappella fanfare: 'This is the Year of the Sex Olympics – Sex Olympics Year.' At the end it is repeated over and over again, while the final credits roll. Eventually the viewers realize that *this* is the year of the Sex Olympics, and they have been glued to their screens like low-drives!
Paul Thompson, Scone, Scotland

The 103-minute play, starring Leonard Rossiter, was written by Nigel

Kneale – who is best remembered as the author of the *Quatermass* serials, although more recently a writer of feature-length episodes of *Sharpe* and *Kavanagh QC*.

His play was first broadcast by BBC2 in July 1968 as part of the 'Theatre 625' series and was then repeated on BBC1 in March 1970. It was collected with two other scripts of his (*The Road* and *The Stone Tape*, soon to be released on DVD) and was published in book form in 1976. It isn't available on video, but can be viewed, by appointment, at the British Film Institute in central London (tel: 020-7255 1444).
Sergio Angelini, British Universities Film and Video Council, London W1

Maybe it's time to start a campaign to get plays like this back on TV where they belong.
Philip Leach, Nottingham

It is not possible to buy a video of the play, though it is one of over 600 classic British programmes available for viewing free of charge in TV Heaven, a gallery of our museum in Bradford.
Sheena Vigors, National Museum of Photography, Film and Television

How can I bring down the forces of global capitalism without losing my well-paid job?

If real socialism replaced capitalism, you could then be 'well paid' in kind rather than money. Instead of an income, there would be permanent free access to whatever goods and services you needed. There would also be many other rewards from living in a moneyless cooperative society based upon direct collective ownership and democratic control of all productive assets, such as an end to property crimes, unemployment, poverty, homelessness, inequality, profit-driven environmental destruction and pollution, wars over resources, and money-hampered essential services like health care and public transport.
Max Hess, Folkestone, Kent

1. Give wildly untruthful answers to market researchers. Through

lying about both your income and your shopping habits, aim to give the impression that your average trip to Sainsbury's costs more than you earn in a year.

2. Never give to the poor and needy. Doing so will only sap their will to riot.

3. Indulge in any gratuitously pointless behaviour that might be deemed 'irrational' by the global capitalist. Examples include switching banks on the basis of your favourite colour, ordering a Fillet O'Fish in MacDonalds, voting LibDem, etc.

4. Deliberately frustrate any desires that may be the result of an advertising campaign. Be particularly wary of supposedly 'normal' desires, such as playing sport, maintaining personal hygiene and communicating over long distances.

Will Davies, London E1

Change your career to economic regeneration bureaucrat. Most areas of the UK outside the South-East are now under the rule of these people. The job is well paid; here in Liverpool we have dozens paying between £50,000 and £100,000 per annum. These bureaucrats destroy capitalism: income per head has gone down 2 per cent per year over the twenty years of Liverpool's 'regeneration'.

Sean McHugh, Liverpool

If I were to win big money on *Who Wants to Be a Millionaire* having phoned a friend, what proportion of my winnings would I be morally obliged to give him or her?

I believe that half of the amount won on the question answered by the friend should be given. So, if the question was to get you from the £8,000 level to £16,000, you should give your friend £4,000. The reasoning is they would not have had an opportunity to win anything without your participation up to that point, and you would not have the opportunity to go on to a possible greater reward without theirs.

Of course, if one is explaining this to friends before going on the show, it would be sensible to include it as part of the deal that, were

you to get a subsequent answer wrong and return to the £1,000 level, your morals go out of the window!
Peter Willis, Hackney, London E9

Perhaps the fairest way would be to divide the total prize money by the number of the question that the friend was phoned to help with. So if 'phone a friend' was used to answer the £1 million question, then the total would be divided by fifteen. So the friend would get £66,666. An answer to question ten would divide the prize money by ten; if the contestant then went on to get £1 million, this would give the friend £100,000 and so on. Using this method, though, would mean that phoning a friend for question one would give the friend 100 per cent of the winnings. But then if you need help with question one, you don't deserve to be there in the first place!
Cris Haldenby, Newport, Isle of Wight

Surely, as you would not have won anything other than the prize offered for the answer to the previous question, morally all subsequent amounts should go to the friend. It is perhaps for them to solve the dilemma of how much they should give back to you.
Bert Fletcher, Broad Oak, East Sussex

I really don't know. Can I ask the audience on this one?
Mark Griffiths, Nottingham

I disagree with the previous replies. You would not be morally obliged to give your friend any money, unless you had agreed a deal beforehand. You have paid for the original stake in the form of a £2 telephone call. You have asked your friend for a tip, so he/she can choose to respond or not. You can then choose to take that tip or disregard it.

If the *Guardian* horse race expert fancied a few bob on a named nag and published such a tip in the paper, you would not be morally obliged to hand over the readies if the horse came up trumps – although you might buy him a pint if you bumped into him afterwards.
Danny McEvoy, Brighton, East Sussex

Is there any benefit to the contemplation of one hand clapping?

A Zen koan (such as the sound of one hand clapping) is, as I understand it, a way of accessing one of the basic (and most difficult) aspects of Buddhist philosophy: the idea of 'emptiness'. This, briefly, means that objects do not exist inherently 'out there' but that consciousness is a player in shaping 'reality'. For a Buddhist the benefit of understanding this is to be on the path to Buddhahood: the end of suffering and the ability to help all sentient beings.
L. G. Roberts, Ripon, North Yorks

The benefits are at least threefold, all related to the attainment of nirvana.

First, such koans help to stun the mind so that the aspirant can experience his/her true self as supra-mind.

Second, one can realize that life in the world is always dualistic; opposites, such as happiness and unhappiness, exist in a relative and interdependent state, and one cannot be experienced without the other.

Third, one can realize that there is only one entity here: that is, pure undifferentiated consciousness. The ego, the one hand, can produce nothing at all.
Michael Dillon, Sheerness, Kent

Clap your hands and you have noisy dynamism. Now take one hand away and keep the other clapping. What do you have? Silent dynamism. One represents the active level of universal life, the other the silent level that underlies all this activity. In physics at school I learned that the 'vacuum state' underlies and gives rise to the whole of creation. One hand clapping is just a graphic example of this quiet but eternally active level.
Paul Davis, Kinver, Staffs

The master asks the pupil: 'What is the sound of one hand clapping?' The pupil doesn't know, so the master slaps his face. Violence can be an aid to enlightenment.
Luce Gilmore, Cambridge

If life is what occurs between the moment of birth and the moment of death, am I right in concluding that the essence of life is time?

The essence of life is eternity. Since I am not conscious of anything before I became a self-conscious being, and will be conscious of nothing after I cease to be so, my life is eternal. I know that I shall die, and others will know that I am dead; but I shall never know, or be conscious of, death: it is a contradiction in terms. History in fact began at my birth (or a little later) and will end at my death (or a little before). All I will ever know is being; so I am experiencing eternity now. This is what philosophers know as ontology, and it is the way to remove the sting from death. The sorrows of death are the sorrows of the living, not of the dead. I may mourn for others; I shall never have to do so for myself.
Ray Billington, Battersea, London SW11

If I had a life I wouldn't have time to answer this question.
Adair Broughton, Childer Thornton, Merseyside

Ray Billington is wrong in saying 'the essence of life is eternity'. Human beings are the only creatures to know that they will die. To that extent, I am capable of mourning my eventual death and all that I shall miss thereby. Mahler's Ninth Symphony is a paean not only to (his) life but also to what he will miss being dead. The essence of life is the time we spend being 'aware' – which is far too short for many!
Philip Lee, London SW18

Surely if before and after birth we are nowhere, the essence of life is not time but space.
Nicholas Blomley, Burnaby, Canada

The answer that the essence of life is space, not time, is unsatisfactory. Space and time cannot be conceived as if they inhabited hermetically sealed domains. According to Einstein's theory of general relativity, the universe that all life occupies is a four-dimensional continuum in which the one dimension of time cannot be separated from the three of space. More useful to the purpose is the distinction between time as such and our consciousness of it.

Baffling as it appears to almost everyone not versed in contemporary theoretical physics, it is far from unorthodox for scientists categorically to deny any meaning or reality whatever to time (for an up-to-date extreme statement, see Julian Barbour's *The End of Time: The Next Revolution in Our Understanding of the Universe*). Our subjective sense of 'nows', 'thens' and 'futures' is revealed as precisely that – solipsism and illusion with no place in the scheme of things. Accordingly, there is no 'moment' of birth or death.

So how does that square with our compelling perception that a succession of moments in time, however elusive or refractory to definition, is what frames our existence and makes it uniquely meaningful to us? What of the the common metaphor – reflected in the literature of all human societies – of time as an arrow or winged chariot that ineluctably drives our lives onward? There is no resolution of this deepest of mysteries. Physics may have banished time for ever, but our consciousness of time remains the essence of life and one of the principal factors that make us human.

Dr Paul Underhill (Open University), Swindon, Wilts

Ray Billington wrote an interesting answer. What puzzles me, however, is that his acceptance of total annihilation at death is presented as an assumption rather than a belief. In our ongoing debate between Christians and atheists, it is always the Christians who are having to defend their position, while non-belief is allowed to stand. If theism cannot be proven, neither can atheism.

Rodney Knock, Newcastle, NSW, Australia

Rodney Knock states that if theism cannot be proven neither can atheism. However, this is a false comparison. Atheists simply seek to describe the world the way they see it, and they see no evidence of God or gods. Of course this absence of evidence is not a proof; nor is there any need for atheists to seek a proof. Atheism is simply a response to a lack of evidence. It is for this reason that theists feel that they are always on the defensive – we keep asking for the evidence.

Peter Martindale, Grantham, Lincs

Dr Underhill's answer showed a common misunderstanding – that 'time is the fourth dimension'. Time is only used as the fourth dimension in a coordinate system; in other words, you would locate someone on a street corner in three physical dimensions and the specific time that they would be there. There is otherwise no reason that time would be considered the 'fourth dimension', especially since physical dimensions are not limited to three. The fourth dimension is actually the third dimension squared. And just because we're not aware of it in everyday life doesn't mean that it doesn't exist.

Einstein's special theory of relativity, which has to do specifically with the interrelationship of space and time, can be expressed thus: time cannot exist without change. Change is the essence of time; if everything is absolutely static, then there is quite literally no time. Without some form of change, even if that is simply the constant movement of quantum and atomic particles, the very concept of time is meaningless. Things, by their nature and all the evidence that we have so far collected, change constantly; quantum particles are constantly on the move, atoms are never still. Therefore, since time = change, and things can't exist without change, and change cannot exist without things, time and things are inextricably dependent on each other. And from this we can also conclude: the essence of life is change. This is also why physicists are so passionately interested in what would happen at 0° Kelvin; at this temperature, as far as we can work out, all atomic motion ceases; essentially, time stands still.

Lynne Batik, Aberdeen

Several times, on the Metropolitan Line platform at London King's Cross, I've heard a recorded announcement: 'Would Inspector Sands please report to the Operations Room immediately.' Is this some kind of code? Why not just make a live announcement? And was there ever a real Inspector Sands?

This message is almost certainly a coded warning for underground staff that they may have to evacuate passengers from the station, possibly as a result of a bomb scare or a fire. Most buildings that have large numbers of the public on their premises – for example, theatres, stations, some department stores – have a coded message (known in the theatre as a 'fireword'), which can be given to staff without alarming the public and causing panic. It doesn't necessarily mean that there is a fire or other hazard on the premises, just that staff should know that an incident is being investigated and be ready for a possible emergency evacuation. The word or phrase is generally something that would seem innocuous to the public but be easily recognizable to front-of-house staff or managers.

Attention needs to be paid to choosing the right phrase, however. I was told a (possibly apocryphal) story from the 1970s about a theatre in southern England which, for easy recognition, had 'Paul Temple' as its fireword – as in 'Paul Temple is in the foyer' – only for the actor Francis Matthews, who played the character in the TV series, to turn up one night to see the show. When someone backstage spotted this as the audience was coming in and casually said, 'I see Paul Temple's in the stalls,' a number of technical staff immediately ran out through the stage door.

Don Keller, Haringey, London N15

When I worked at the old Cumberland Royal Infirmary in Carlisle, announcements would be made for porters to transfer a patient from one ward to another. However, when the message was, for example, 'Transfer the patient from Ward 6 to Ward 13,' only the staff knew that 'Ward 13' didn't exist. It was in fact the morgue. But I somehow think it was more reassuring to the patients to announce it in code.

Tony Myers, Erdington, Birmingham

In a library that I used a few years ago, the announcement, 'Will Mr Sands report to the office,' was broadcast to alert staff to the fact that there was a security problem, such as a suspect package. Customers were even more baffled by the alternative announcement used for this purposes, which was: 'There is a magpie in the library.'

Chris Willis, London WC1

Prior to the rebuilding of Euston Station in the late 1950s, a request over the tannoy for the 'Horsebox Inspector to report to the forecourt' would result in the arrival of a maroon-painted, windowless 'wendy house' on a four-wheeled trolley. This would be used to transport a coffin from a waiting hearse to the guard's van of a Scotland-bound train.

Roger Boa, Ware, Herts

On my first day at work for a high-street bank in the 1980s, I was greeted by the doorman with the puzzling words: 'Late again? Good morning.' Only later was it explained that this was my employer's idea of a sophisticated security measure. In the event that the greeting was not given, staff were to assume that a robbery was under way and should walk away from the building.

Name supplied, Liverpool

In the early 1990s, I worked in a nightclub in Caerphilly where announcements concerning a 'Mr Peters' meant that a ruckus was developing at the given location. For example, the DJ would announce: 'Mr Peters to the bar', or 'Mr Peters to the dance floor'. Particularly good was 'Mr Peters to the DJ booth', which was always delivered with a hurried and high-pitched hint of panic. Eventually, regulars cracked this code, and Mr Peters was reborn as Casanova.

Julian Moruzzi, Cardiff

If an election crisis similar to the Bush–Gore stand-off in 2000 were to occur in the UK, would our lack of a written constitution help or hinder us in resolving it?

It is not correct to say that we do not have a written constitution. The UK constitution is spread over several Acts of Parliament, as well as the 'Bill of Rights', drawn up after James II's abdication.

The difference from the USA is that in the UK there is no single document that acts as a definitive source and, more significantly, there is no equivalent to the US Supreme Court, which can use such a document to override executive actions and Acts of Congress. In the UK, Parliament itself is the highest authority and can enact any legislation it thinks fit. The EU treaties don't fundamentally affect this, because treaties that allow EU decisions and directives to take precedence over domestic law have the consent and authority of the UK Parliament.

The Bush–Gore stand-off couldn't take place under the UK constitution. It only happened in the USA because of the electoral college system, which means that there is not, in fact, a direct popular election; voters were electing the electors within each sovereign state.

The other key difference is that the US President is head of state and chief executive. In the UK, the constitutional position is that the Queen, as head of state, chooses (with the assistance of her constitutional advisers) whoever she thinks is best able to form a government with the Parliament that has been elected. Conventionally, that is the leader of the largest party, but as long as the leader can convince the Queen (and his or her fellow MPs) that he or she can form a government and put through a legislative programme, it doesn't have to be a majority party. Strictly speaking, such a leader doesn't even have to be a Member of Parliament, although this would hardly be practical, given the need for the Queen's ministers to be accountable to Parliament.

If there is no one willing or able to form a government, the Queen can dissolve Parliament and have a new election. This is not an option in the USA, because Americans are constrained by the dictates of their Constitution; a new president had to be elected (by the electoral college) before Clinton's term expired.

Robert Ward, Leeds

Is it wrong to be wealthy?

If you came across a child drowning in a pond, then it would be indefensible not to act – wet clothes and a sniffle being less important than the saving of a life. Similarly, it is indefensible to be inactive in the face of third world poverty and famine. The fact that those dying are thousands of miles away and that there are millions of other people who could also help but remain inactive is insignificant. The only justifiable course of action is to give away your wealth to help these people, until the marginal loss for yourself is equivalent to the marginal gain of the recipient.

John Hampson, Chester

It is good to be wealthy. Wealth should not be confused with money – it means having plenty of everything. Plenty of money is good to have if used usefully and creatively; it is undoubtedly a wonderful aspiration to be wealthy, healthy and wise.

Margaret Percy, Kempton Town, Surrey

To someone on the breadline, most of us are wealthy. However, if we say to be wealthy means having capital of more than a couple of million pounds, then it depends on how you came by it.

If you earned it by bringing to fruition a brilliant idea with a lot of hard work, and provided good employment to lots of people – like the inventor of the Dyson vacuum cleaner or the founder of the Body Shop – people can only admire and not envy you.

If you inherited it from a forebear who made millions out of munitions in the Great War, or was the bastard child of a former monarch, it should be handled with humility and circumspection.

If you won it in the Lottery, remember that it came from millions of other people like yourself, so spread it around a bit – perform 'random acts of kindness and senseless acts of beauty'.

A. F. Bennett, Chichester, West Sussex

Only if it's right to be poor.

Paul Wiseman, Rio de Janeiro, Brazil

Yes, for two reasons. First, it creates an unhealthy imbalance in the mind of the wealthy individual; second, it creates an unhealthy imbalance in the society.

Overemphasis on wealth can lead to a desperate obsession to accumulate more. The resources of our planet are limited and ought to be utilized for the welfare of all. It cannot be considered acceptable for one member of a family to eat excessively and hoard food, leaving the other members to live on the verge of starvation.

John Garrido, Stamford Hill, London N16

Of course not, but while some are wealthy and others poor, we must look further. Three hundred years ago, Gerrard Winstanley the Digger said: 'No man can be rich but he must be rich by his own labour, or by the labours of other men helping him. If other men help him to work, then are those riches his neighbour's as well as his; for they may be the fruit of other men's labours as well as his own. But all rich men live at ease, feeding and clothing themselves by the labours of other men, not by their own, which is their shame and not their nobility.'

Is this applicable today? I believe so, even in our complex middle-class economy. A wealthy wage-earner must still ask: 'How are my wages calibrated? How much reflects my own labour, and how much that of others? Is what I get for my work fair?' The answers are harder to reach today and the questions themselves are normally ignored, but they remain compelling. It is good to prosper, but not at others' expense.

Paul im Thurn, Forest Hill, London SE23

Where can I find peace of mind?

Alone, in the Grand Canyon at sundown.
Lissu Niemi, London NW4

Classical mysticism in general, Eastern philosophy in particular, and yoga philosophy even more specifically, have all suggested that peace of mind can be found in experiencing the fact that the real you (the true 'I') is in the mind. The mind, which by its nature is not capable of peace, is seen as a bundle of thoughts that usurps its position (as problem solver) and assumes the position of 'I' in the body.

Many ancient myths symbolize this process with an unworthy imposter ousting the true ruler. The mythic story then involves the true ruler regaining the throne, with harmony being restored in the kingdom.

Finding peace, which is a natural characteristic of the true 'I', is a matter of exposing the mind for what it is. Many methods are employed to do this, such as various meditation techniques; koans in Zen; dancing in Sufism; chanting mantras; and self-surrender in devotional religion. Eternal peace of mind can only be found by understanding and experiencing the fact that you, in your essential nature, are not the mind.

Michael Dillon, Sheerness, Kent

Philippians 4: 4–7: 'Rejoice in the Lord always. I will say it again: Rejoice! Let your gentleness be evident to all. The Lord is near. Do not be anxious about anything, but in everything, by prayer and petition, with thanksgiving, present your requests to God. And the peace of God, which transcends all understanding, will guard your hearts and your minds in Christ Jesus.'

Stuart Stoner, Shoeburyness, Essex

Try the M4 westbound, with London disappearing in the rear-view mirror. It always works for me.

Jeff Williams, Ystrad Mynach, Mid-Glamorgan

Several foreign parliaments sit in a crescent-moon or head-table shape. Do any other countries adopt the Westminster style with opposing factions facing each other?

The Royal Chapel of St Stephen was part of the Palace of Westminster, principal residence of British monarchs from Edward the Confessor to Henry VIII. In 1547 Edward VI gave it to the Commons, which was then without a proper home and had been meeting in the octagonal chapter house of Westminster Abbey, a gothic building from the thirteenth or fourteenth centuries. There, the members faced each other because of its 'choir' layout. The latter survived substantial alterations that were made over the centuries to accommodate larger numbers of members as the kingdom expanded.

In 1834, fire destroyed the chapel/chamber together with the entire palace, apart from Westminster Hall. By this time the layout of the chamber was presumably so much a part of our parliamentary tradition that it was preserved in the Barry/Pugin rebuilding of 1840–52, and in the post-war reconstruction. A circular arrangement, as some radical parliamentarians have pointed out, would be much more efficient. But perhaps not very British.

Liz du Parcq, London SW16

In the Netherlands and Luxembourg, opposing parties sit facing each other. However, it is sometimes an awkward situation, as proportional voting laws give seats to smaller parties and produce coalition governments that do not fit easily into this seating. A lot of local councils in Europe sit around a Westminster-style 'table'.

Tom Krieps, Luxembourg

Canada's Parliament building was built in the mid-nineteenth century and is a hybrid gothic style modelled on Westminster. Canada, of course, was a British Empire dominion and its House of Commons is almost a spitting image of Westminster's.

Michael Lewis, Dublin

I was brought up to believe that British subjects had certain freedoms – freedom of movement, assembly, speech, etc., as well as trial by jury, presumption of innocence, habeas corpus and so on. Do any of those rights still exist in full, or have they all been curtailed by legislation?

Rights in the UK are traditionally residual rights; that is, whatever is left when other actions have been made illegal. However, in the United States and some European countries there are positive rights, where freedom of expression, movement, etc., are enacted in a Bill of Rights or similar legislation. In these countries, extra criteria have to be met in order for these laws to be repealed or amended, making it difficult for governments to change them. Without this safeguard, such legislation is pointless, as any future government that wanted to undermine these rights could simply repeal the legislation that granted them.

However, the idea of entrenched legislation goes against the principle of parliamentary sovereignty, which is a major part of the British constitution: if a future Parliament cannot change laws made by a past Parliament, the Parliament is not sovereign. So past laws granting freedoms of movement, habeas corpus, trial by jury, etc., can be removed as long as a majority in Parliament agrees to the change – as can be seen in the passing of the Prevention of Terrorism Act.

Despite this, Britain does have certain obligations regarding rights, derived from the Universal Declaration on Human Rights and the European Convention on Human Rights. It is not compulsory for

Britain to adhere to the rights in these documents, but there would be major international outcry if they were greatly infringed. It is planned for the European Convention on Human Rights to be incorporated shortly into British law (it has already been incorporated into Scottish). However, this is just ordinary statute law and could be repealed in future as any other law could.

Matthew Gee, Disley, Cheshire

Why do church and cathedral lecterns take the shape of an eagle?

The eagle is a symbol of the fourth evangelist, John, and it presumably became associated with his gospel because of the many links between 'the Word of God' of which he writes (made flesh in Christ, made real in preaching) and the Bible as being, almost literally, God's word. The eagle soars upwards; it is strong, direct in its flight and inspiring in its overarching majesty. Just like good public reading of scripture or oratory!

There are thirty-two references to eagles in the Bible, all but four of them in the Old Testament, and most of them are very positive. According to Isaiah: 'those who wait for the Lord shall renew their strength [and] mount up with wings like eagles'; and Psalm 103 blesses the Lord 'who satisfies you with good ... so that your youth is renewed like the eagle's'.

Symbols of Church Seasons and Days, by John Bradner, states: 'The eagle is depicted on some old fonts. In some cases this may be intended to show that the eagle, like the Spirit, renews the life of the baptised Christian, just as, according to legend, this bird was supposed to renew its youth by flying near the sun and then plunging into water.'

The eagle is also one of the four 'living creatures' around God's throne, according to Revelation 4:7, the other three being 'like a lion ... like an ox ... [and] with a face like a human face'. As early as the second century (CE), these four creatures had been linked to the four gospels (the other three gospels being, respectively, Mark, Luke and Matthew), whilst also becoming symbols of four events in the life of Christ: the Nativity (man), his sacrificial death (the ox), the Resurrection (the lion) and the Ascension (represented by a flying eagle).

Occasionally, an eagle is used as a symbol for the Holy Spirit, but usually the more gentle dove is employed. St Irenaeus (c. CE 130–200), in writing about the four living creatures, likens the eagle to 'the Spirit hovering with his wings over the Church' – an image obviously mirroring the 'dove from above' at the baptism of Jesus (see Matthew 3: 16).

For lectern purposes, however, an eagle certainly has bigger wings than a dove on which to rest large books!

Revd Alec Mitchell, Mossley, Lancs

There are exceptions, the most notable being Wednesbury parish church in Staffordshire. The lectern, reputedly older than the Reformation, is in the form of a gilded fighting cock. It is perhaps not surprising that Wednesbury, together with Walsall and Bloxwich, were famous in the Black Country for cockfighting.

Derek Warner, Chorley, Lancs

Because the eagle is a bird of pray.

Sean Connor, Beckenham, Kent

All TV weather forecasters seem to have the same choreographed hand movements. Are they taught by the same person?

I've been irritated for years by their habit of making a clockwise circular motion when indicating a low pressure area. Winds in this hemisphere circulate anticlockwise round low pressure. Michael Fish is the prime offender.

Another annoying habit some of them have when delivering the 5 a.m. forecast is calling today 'tomorrow'. The impression given is that they make their up-to-the-minute forecast at about 10 p.m. and then go off for a good night's kip.

Patrick George, Cullompton, Devon

It's my job to train TV weather presenters, and hand movements are initially one of their main worries. The job is harder than it looks, since the map doesn't physically exist — it's wholly computer-generated and is superimposed on a blank blue or green background. The presenters watch a composite TV picture to see where to point.

No, they're not taught the choreography, but they copy others. Until a few years ago, everyone just pointed vaguely; then 'stroking' gestures were invented by Francis 'Fluffy Bits' Wilson. Sian Lloyd at ITV went on to develop graceful 'Balinese dancer' wrist movements, and now everyone else is having a go.

Mart Gottschalk, Sutton Coldfield, West Midlands

Did 'rag and bone' men really collect bones?

Until local authorities were made responsible for the task, the collection and disposal of all household wastes in big cities was in the hands of men who regularly toured the streets with their horses and carts. In those days, lavatory paper and sanitary towels did not exist, so old rags were used instead. The main residue from meals was bones. Rags and bones were naturally rich in plant nutrients, and when mixed up with the contents of the cesspools and the sweepings of horse dung from the streets, the whole concoction could be sold to farmers in the surrounding countryside as manure. Charles Dickens's Uriah Heap was one such rag and bone man.

Michael Carmine, Buckingham, Bucks

In the days before Superglue, the 'bones', left over from meals, were boiled down to make glue to repair furniture, which could also be resold.

Joe Callaghan, Stockport, Cheshire

Yes, bones were a valuable raw material in the nineteenth and early twentieth centuries. Bonemeal was used in making steel and, after calcining and grinding, it was an essential constituent of the raw material for 'bone china'. The demand was so great that bones were imported from all parts of the world.

Even the most mundane materials could have value. One of the most surprising is 'pure', the collection of which was documented by Henry Mayhew. 'Pure' is dog faeces, which were used until the mid-twentieth century in the tanning of the finest kid leathers. Mayhew reports that the white ones were more sought after than the brown and that the collectors used to roll the brown in lime to enhance their value.

Stanley Graham, Barnoldswick, Lancs

Bones remained an important commodity for rag and bone men much later than suggested in the previous replies. In the summer of 1968 I worked in a Hereford scrapyard where we bought bones from several dealers who collected bones from butchers. There was a large pile of bones in the yard, going green with mould, which were eventually sent for processing. I was assured that they would be used to make cosmetics.

Roger Backhouse, Ilford, Essex

Rags were not a waste problem at all. As early as 1585 there was a petition for the prohibition of the export of rags from England. This was to protect the paper industry, whose staple raw material was rags right up to the nineteenth century. This splendid example of recycling ended when wood pulp came into use. And the bones? These were used to make glue for the sizing of the paper. The paper industry depended on rags and bones, plus much water, for more than four centuries.

Russell Jones, Penryn, Cornwall

If fish could scream, would people still go angling?

If grass could scream, would you still mow the lawn? If insects, worms and snails could scream, would you still light that bonfire?

Find an amoeba in a drop of pondwater on a microscope slide. Place a little acid on one side and the amoeba will ooze away from the negative stimulus. Prod it with a fine wire and it will also seek to 'escape', because it's programmed to do so. The fact that an organism behaves in a manner which, translated into human terms, seems to indicate pain or distress does not necessarily mean that the organism itself has any awareness of the experience. I doubt if fish have any self-awareness, and if they do I would guess that it is but a faint glimmer. Which has the greater self-awareness, a fish or a four-month-old foetus? Would people find abortion acceptable if a foetus could scream?

Glenn Baron, Leigh-on-Mendip, Bath

For a fish to scream they would need to feel pain and they don't have the same pain system as humans. Anti-anglers cite the RSPCA-commissioned Medway Report as saying fish feel pain, but the argument relies on only one professor who gave fish the benefit of the doubt. There is no evidence at all that the nerve endings near the brains of fish can transmit pain.

Moreover the so-called emotional centre of the brains in animals, the cerebral cortex, is tiny in fish while in mammals it is huge. Put another way, if a human was hooked in the mouth, they would feel pain and would not fight against the pull. Fish fight to get away, which they wouldn't do if they were feeling the pain associated with mammals. And as all coarse fish in the UK are looked after carefully and released without harm, there is no way angling is going to stop.

Thomas Petch, Angler's Mail, London

Glenn Baron doubts whether fish have any self-awareness, but he offers no evidence for this and I would argue that their possession of a brain and a nervous system is fairly convincing evidence that they are self-aware and can feel pain. Thomas Petch of the *Angler's Mail* says that if a fish could feel pain it would not struggle to get away when hooked. In fact the survival urge can force animals to endure immense pain; for example, animals caught in leg-hold traps will sometimes chew off a limb in order to escape.

Both correspondents show how some anglers are determined to convince themselves that fish cannot feel pain. However, the authoritative Medway Report (which did not rely on only one professor, as Mr Petch claimed) made it very clear that they can. I wish fish could scream. Angling would then be about as popular as other types of hunting.

Toni Vernelli, People for the Ethical Treatment of Animals, London SW18

Surely the pain reflex is one of the most fundamental components of life – if you don't feel hurt by damage, why avoid it? – and so you get bitten, then eaten, then become extinct. Of course fish and even more primitive creatures must feel pain. How, otherwise, could even an amoeba be 'programmed'? If 'it has no awareness of the experience' why would it react?

John MacKinnon, Kirkcaldy, Fife

Researchers at the University of Utrecht in the Netherlands concluded that fish feel pain and fear comparable to the human experience were a fish-hook to pierce our upper palates. Elsewhere, in the article 'The Moral Standing of Insects and the Ethics of Extinction' (*Florida Etymologist*, 1987), the authors reported that insects can feel pain. These conclusions supported those arrived at by C. H. Eisemann et al., in 'Do Insects Feel Pain? A Biological Review' (*Experientia*, 1984).

Buddhists say that we cannot live without hurting other sentient beings, but that the aspiration to hurt them as little – and help them as much – as possible is the source of all individual and social happiness. The real question surely is: if our consciences screamed, would we be so willing to hurt vulnerable creatures?

David Edwards, Bournemouth

Angling is a largely working-class hobby, which preserves lake and river ecosystems in general, and fish in particular. Fish-eaters may write to newspapers objecting to angling; but they financially support companies that vandalize the marine environment and nearly wipe out entire stocks while suffocating fish under tons of their fellows, hooking them for hours on a long line, or disembowelling them alive. A hook in the mouth is a horrible idea, but few non-vegans have the moral standing to criticize amateur fishing.

Michael Lyle, Llangynog, Carms

How does a citizen's arrest work? Is it a crime to resist such an arrest? Can anyone perform one on anyone – for any crime?

The really significant difference is that the police can arrest a person on suspicion of committing an arrestable offence, while anyone else can only arrest someone whom they have actually witnessed committing such an offence.

Both the police and others can only arrest a person for an arrestable offence; many crimes do not qualify. Resisting lawful arrest is a crime whether the arrest is made by the police or by others. Anyone who unlawfully detains another person (for example, 'arresting' them for a crime that is not an arrestable offence) may be sued. A citizen who arrests anyone should hand the arrestee over to the police as soon as is practical.

Jonathan Gurney, Saltburn, Cleveland

In 1977 I was in central London outside the Bulgarian tourist office, on a picket called in solidarity with dissidents facing state repression of protests. The police chief ordered his officers to try to force us away from the venue. I asked: 'What law says we can't stand there?' and he replied: 'My law.' As his behaviour was likely to cause a breach of the peace, I made a citizen's arrest on him, and I said to his sergeant: 'Arrest this man.' After a short stunned silence the suspect (the police chief) was not apprehended, but instead the conscientious citizen (me) was arrested. I got fined for 'obstruction'.

Dave Morris, Tottenham, London N17

The burglar I attempted to apprehend, when I found him breaking into my house, was not so well acquainted with the law and, after pushing me forcefully out of his way, made good his escape whilst offering me explicit advice as to what I could do with my citizen's arrest.

Mary Fisher, Norwich

Is there a record kept of the length of sumo bouts? If so, how long is the longest?

Times have been published since 1955. The longest (excluding break time) took place in that year, taking seventeen minutes and fifteen seconds, between Chiyonoyama (Grand Champion) and Wakanohana. Two break times (*mizuiri*, literally 'water supply') did not decide the issue and the bout was resumed after two other bouts, only to repeat *mizuiri* and finally end in a draw. Both contestants were totally exhausted but never relented. It was the spectators who effectively stopped the bout, shouting and screaming 'Stop it!', 'Break them!' or 'It's a draw!' Compared to the present standards, where the average weight of the first division sumo-tori is well above 150 kilos, the Grand Champion weighed just 115 kilos and Wakanohana only 94 kilos.

The longest bout in the past ten years, between Naminohana and Kotobeppu in 1995, took eight minutes – five and a half minutes before and two and a half minutes after a break. But in 1931 there was reportedly a bout that had to be resumed the following day.

Shoji Oshima, Kunitachi, Japan

Why does the City of London still have its own police force? Is London the only major city to have two forces, and have there ever been plans for them to merge?

The City of London Police came into existence in 1839, although organized policing, usually by uniformed policemen, has existed throughout much of the City's history since Roman times.

At one period, the majority of cities and boroughs had their own police force: for example, Leicester (until 1967), Leeds (until 1974) and Colchester (until 1947). A number of cities had two or more police forces operating within their area. However, the 'second' force normally policed a specific area or building and did not have full Home Office police powers. One example was to be found in York where the city police worked alongside the York Minster Police. The latter still exists.

All the city and borough forces, with the exception of the City of London Police, have been incorporated into county or metropolitan area constabularies. The City of London Police is a Home Office police force like any other, offering the full range of policing services. It is acknowledged as a world leader in areas such as investigating fraud and preventing terrorism, and is seen as vital to keeping the financial 'City' secure. There are, of course, other police forces operating in London as well as the City and Metropolitan; for example, the British Transport Police and the Royal Parks Police.

Roger Appleby, Curator, Museum of the City of London Police, London EC2

Brussels is made up of nineteen communes, each with its own separate police force. The state police have authority over all of them. As I understand it, if a traffic accident occurs on the boundary of two communes, three separate forces may be involved.

Patrick Kirby, Brussels, Belgium

Why is it that attractive women become even more attractive when wearing glasses?

I would have thought it was because you could see them more clearly.

Vicki Bean, Garton-on-the-Wolds, East Yorks

Not everyone would agree. Dorothy Parker said: 'Men seldom make passes at girls who wear glasses.'

Roger Tennant, Ullesthorpe, Leics

I think this is because, when wearing them, they appear to be more thoughtful, intelligent and less intimidating – showing another more delicate, refined side to their personalities. Also, glasses draw attention to the eyes, increasing eye-to-eye contact.

P. J. Dunne, Crawley, West Sussex

Hemingway was a brilliant writer because he used crumbs of precise and understated language to describe dramatic and brutal events. P. G. Wodehouse was brilliant because he used extremely sophisticated language to describe extremely silly events. Pretty women (and men) wearing harsh-looking glasses benefit from the same pleasurable cognitive dissonance; as do 'he-men' wearing ponytails; as do dogs sitting upright in the passenger seats of cars.

By responding to this ostensibly trivial question with disproportionately serious but (crucially) plausible arguments, this answer is itself an example of this device!

David Edwards, Bournemouth

Don't be fooled. They are just making spectacles of themselves.

Gary Cornford, London SW12

In terms of body language, eyes are our most expressive feature by far. Modern glasses, after years of improved styling and promotion, are seen as fashion accessories. They frame the eyes, thus concentrating the observer's attention. They add form and shape to the area, also colour – as does eye make-up, but a bold frame can beat that hands down; they partly mask the eye area, thus imparting a suggestion of mystery. Whilst our subconscious still relates glasses to books and learning, we now treat informed intellect as an asset, not a dull handicap. So we appear to get beauty, mystery and brains all in the one package.

A. K. Cragg, Plympton St Maurice, Plymouth

I read that gephyrophobia is a fear of bridges. What is it exactly that scares those suffering from this phobia?

I am gephyrophobic, but only when the bridge is narrow enough for me to see the chasm underneath (I suffer from vertigo) or when it sways in the wind. (The footbridge over the river in Inverness is particularly fearsome.) I also want to throw up when I see some of the graffiti-covered monstrosities on the motorway, but I'm not sure that counts.

Helena Newton, Ilford, Essex

Once when I was a child at a party, someone held me over the stairwell and threatened to let go if I didn't stop screaming. Later, I was bribed with a bag of sweets not to tell my parents. The next time I crossed a bridge, the railings reminded me of the banisters. The flowing water underneath seemed to pull me in. I started to refuse crossing bridges and instead would crouch down, crying. My parents questioned this strange behaviour, but not enough to my mind to make me break the promise I'd given not to tell. In the end, they lost patience with me and I gradually grew out of it.

Ursula Light, Ashford, Kent

I used to suffer from gephyrophobia, but it's all bridge over the water now.

Garry Chambers, London N3

Your correspondents seem to be afraid of going over bridges. When I was a small child my fear, especially on the railway, was of going under a bridge. The looming shadow of even the slenderest footbridge made me cower and cover my eyes. I later learned that my mother had a long, hard labour and it was touch and go whether I would survive. I have since attributed my fear to this experience.

A. Adcock, Oxford

The potential phobias associated with bridges are multitude and in recent years Australians have seen some of them realized at their expense.

There is sub-gephyrophobia, the fear of a bridge falling on to one, as occurred in the Granville disaster in Sydney in the late 1970s; there is supra-gephyrophobia, the fear of a bridge collapsing beneath one, as occurred to many Australians in the Maccabean Games disaster in Israel in 1997.

Extra-gephyrophobia is the fear of being hit by something falling or being thrown from a bridge; degephyrophobia (as with defenestration) is the fear of being thrown from a bridge. There are a whole raft of possibilities involving being trapped under a bridge in a raging torrent; being caught by a draw- or swing-bridge as it closes; or rushing headlong off a draw- or swing-bridge as it opens.

All in all, bridges are pretty fearsome creatures and it is a little surprising that they have not yet been banned or restricted to consenting adults who are suitably trained.

Robert Keogh, Claremont, Western Australia

Has anyone ever sold their car by leaving it outside their house with the asking price stuck on the windscreen?

I sold my daughter's 1974 Morris Marina this way within a few days (genuine 12,000 miles only, after being locked in a garage from 1978 to 1994). It had previously been advertised in a trade magazine and on the internet without success.

R. S. Medley, Weston-super-Mare, Somerset

I used to own a red Citroën 2CV painted with yellow-bordered green spots. Despite my conviction that such a car was was unsaleable, within hours of my displaying a sign a very nice couple called in and bought it. The next day, a neighbour called by to say that they had some friends in Belgium who also wanted to buy it. Maybe I should have asked for more money.

Nick Holden-Sim, Chorlton-cum-Hardy, Manchester

My father-in-law sold his car just as he was sticking the price on to his side window. A passer-by on his street in Greenwich stopped and said, 'I'll have that.' He turned up an hour later with the £400 in cash and drove off in it – surely the fastest sale ever.

Andrew Sangster, Berkhamsted, Herts

Yes, twice and both times within a fortnight. Both were somewhat specialist vehicles – a Reliant Robin and a Fiat Caravelle mini-camper van – which may have had something to do with it. The advantages are: it's almost certainly a private sale; the vehicle's on its own as opposed to being in a long line at a dealer's; prospective buyers see it as opposed to reading a written description in an ad; and there's no need for a specially arranged visit.

Martin Lewis, Chelmondiston, Suffolk

A friend was once flagged down on the M6 by a driver of a white van who tried to strike a deal on the hard shoulder.

Don Burnett, Lancaster

Is there any sport or activity that I could take up in my late twenties and still have a chance of representing England competitively?

I started playing Ultimate, a team game played with a frisbee, in 1995 when I was twenty-six. This month I will be competing in the World Ultimate Club Championships at St Andrews, Scotland. Over 1,600 players from eighty-nine teams around the world will take part; I will be playing for Overflow, the Great Britain team in the over-thirties division. The age range of the team is between thirty and forty-nine, the oldest of whom didn't start playing until the age of thirty-seven!

Wayne Ziants, Clapham, London SW4

Archery is much cheaper than golf; in addition, it does not demand either a high fitness level or exceptional strength or stamina. Archers continue to compete into their eighties and many types of disability are no barrier. Our national teams perform well and it is an Olympic sport.
Colin Ledsome, Cranford Archery Club, Middx

I took up orienteering aged forty-one, and got my England call-up aged seventy-one.
Maurice Collett, South Ribble Orienteering Club, Kendal, Cumbria

The questioner should have no problems representing the England cricket team at international level. In fact, if he rings a mate they could open the batting and possibly the bowling.
George Mathews, Sheffield

I learned to drink for England in my late twenties. And I'm Irish.
Aine Duffy, London E5

Golf croquet is considered the poor relation of Association Croquet, but someone in their late twenties would have a great chance of representing England. It is a wonderful sport for oldies, but younger players attain the skills much more quickly. England does not yet have a player in the world's top ten, so you have a good chance.
Jennet Blake, Witney, Oxon

I hope Maurice Collett's description of getting his call-up for the English orienteering team at the age of seventy-one doesn't reinforce the common misconception that orienteering is a bit of a ramble in the countryside. This week's World Orienteering Championships involved high-speed racing through sixteen kilometres of steep, rocky, boggy, heather-strewn Scottish forests – a bit much even for the most spritely seventy-year-old. When Maurice competes for England he does so in the over-seventies age class.
Steven Hale, British Team, World Orienteering Championships, Inverness

Success is easier to come by in certain sports simply because the competition for places is less intense. For instance, it's more likely that one could represent England in a sport like baseball, which has about a hundred clubs nationally, than it would be to represent England in football, which has over 40,000 clubs affiliated to the FA.

Where sports are largely confined to specific social classes (for example, polo or skiing – remember Eddie 'the Eagle' Edwards?) or specific minority ethnic groups (for example, kabaddi), the differences in competitiveness are particularly pronounced. Even in a small nation such as the UK, the popularity of sports can be regionally specific. As curling is mainly played in Scotland and Gaelic football in Ireland, the England national side for these two sports might prove relatively easy to break into.

However, perhaps the single most relevant factor for the questioner to consider is gender. All but a few sports (for example, equestrianism) are rigidly partitioned along these lines. Furthermore, some sports are rarely played by women (for example, rugby union, boxing) and some are rarely if ever played by men (for example, lacrosse, netball).

Dominic Malcolm, Centre for Research into Sport and Society, University of Leicester

A friend of ours, Yvonne Danson, started running for fun and exercise in her late twenties, while living in the Far East. She found that she had the necessary speed and stamina, and took up marathon running seriously. After good results in the Beijing and Boston marathons, she was selected to represent England in the Vancouver Commonwealth Games, where she won the bronze medal.

Peter White, Formby, Liverpool

Is it true that beer is 'watered down' in some pubs, as many people believe is the case with poor-tasting beer, or is this just an urban myth?

Unscrupulous landlords have often 'watered' their beer in the past, to increase profit at the expense of the poor drinker. This was more prevalent in the days before sealed metal kegs, when not only water but the contents of drip trays etc. could be returned to the beer. However, the practice is still possible, and I know of at least one court case in recent years. Needless to say, this is not a practice I have ever indulged in!

Nick Wakeling, Jack Beards at the Grosvenor, Islington, London N5

I used to work in a pub and restaurant owned by one of the larger brewers, where we were actively encouraged to pour back into the barrel the mixture of beer and water that was the by-product of cleaning the lines once a week. All the lagers went back into one particular brand of lager (commonly the one that the managers didn't like) and likewise with the bitters. This resulted in that particular lager tasting not at all as it was supposed to and numerous adverse comments from the punters.

In the defence of the industry, it must be said that many people complain of poor-tasting beer when there is nothing at all wrong with the barrel – for example, greasy lips will affect the beer. Others just like pretending they know what they are talking about when it comes to beer – especially real ale drinkers – and insist the barrel is 'off' when you know that it has been treated correctly and is fresh.

Simon Gant, address supplied

Who was the least deserving person to win a Nobel prize?

Henry Kissinger, President Nixon's Secretary of State, was co-winner of the peace prize for a peace that was not secured. But as he is one of the prime architects of the USA's 'dirty wars' and its illegal actions in Cambodia, there is also at least a prima facie case to be made for an indictment against him as a war criminal.

Terry Philpot, Oxted, Surrey

The American comic songwriter Tom Lehrer, when asked why he had retired, said that political satire became redundant the day that Kissinger was awarded the prize. There's also a case to be made against Winston Churchill's prize for literature, though with that, as with Judi Dench's Oscar, there may have been other considerations.

David Cottis, Putney, London SW15

Any economist. Alfred Nobel left money for prizes in physics, chemistry, physiology or medicine, literature and peace. In 1968 the Swedish Central Bank began to award the Swedish Central Bank Prize for Econometrics in Memorial of Alfred Nobel. Now the prize has been smuggled into the sequence of genuine awards.

Of all the worthless economists in a stiff competition, the wooden spoon must go to Scholes and Black in 1997 whose gambling system for playing the world markets was demonstrated to be faulty in 1997 by two Californian physicists, and it blew away a rumoured $300 billion from Long Term Capital Management (LTCM) in 1998. This precipitated a world financial crisis. Previous distinguished economists have only managed to destabilize individual economies.

Sean McHugh, Liverpool

Egas Moniz won the Nobel prize for medicine in 1949 for the lobotomy – an operation that put an end to most psychiatric problems, including personality.

Athar Yawar Chyang, Oxford

Most of my contemporaries who grew up under the Soviet regime would agree that it is Mikhail Sholokhov in 1965 for the epic *And Quiet Flows the Don*. He did not write it at all; the author was anti-Bolshevik Fyodor Kryukov – Don Cossak – who died during the Civil War. The prize was awarded clearly to pacify Moscow, which was deeply offended by the choice of Boris Pasternak and, earlier, Ivan Bunin.

Margaret Loeffler, Fremantle, Western Australia

After the Israeli Premier Menachem Begin received a Nobel prize for peace, an Israeli academic wrote to the Nobel Committee, nominating him for a Nobel prize in physics. He argued that Mr Begin's contribution to physics was at least as great as his contribution to peace.

Dipak Ghosh, Bridge of Allan, Stirling

In nominating Mikhail Sholokhov, Margaret Loeffler trots out an old canard that his novel *The Quiet Don* was actually written by someone else, namely Fyodor Kryukov. *The Handbook of Russian Literature* published by Yale University Press (1985) calls this hypothesis untenable, and cites historical, stylistic and biographical reasons for doing so. Computer-assisted investigation by Scandinavian scholars of passages by the two authors has reinforced this judgement. Finally, in 1991 the rough manuscript of the novel was recovered; it had been

missing since Sholokhov's house on the Don was bombed during the Second World War. Handwriting tests by graphologists have proved its authenticity. It is full of insertions, corrections and comments.
Dr H. A. Meek, Southport, Merseyside

The work on insulin, for which the 1923 Nobel prize for medicine was awarded to Fred Banting and John Macleod, was actually performed by Banting, Charles Best and J. B. Collip. The contribution of John Macleod, Professor of Physiology at Toronto, was to give the other, junior researchers the run of his lab while he went on a long fishing trip. Best and Collip received no recognition whatever.
Tom McGlynn, Launceston, Tasmania

David Trimble?
Brian Carty, Sheffield

The maligning of J. J. R. Macleod by Tom McGlynn cannot remain unchallenged. For years following the awarding of the prize (for insulin research) there was extraordinary recrimination and backbiting in academic circles, especially in Canada. This was due largely to fellow award-winner Fred Banting, a young rural Canadian surgeon, and to Canadian chauvinism – Macleod was a Scotsman from Aberdeen and an established expert in the field of carbohydrate metabolism.

In 1982 Professor M. Bliss, a historian at the University of Toronto, published a book, *The Discovery of Insulin*, which has definitively resolved the whole controversy in Macleod's favour. Macleod, incidentally, divided his share with researcher J. B. Collip; Banting then divided his with Charles Best.
D. F. Magee, Castlebellingham, Co. Louth, Ireland

Why is the UK possibly the only country in the world where most bathrooms have two separate taps? Since the late 1940s, everywhere else has introduced the miraculous mixer tap.

Historically, in Britain when domestic hot water came mostly from back boilers and electric immersion heaters, and mixer taps did their mixing with the taps themselves, water-supply authorities prohibited these taps because of a risk of cold water being siphoned back into the hot supply and exploding the cistern or boiler. The modern 'mixer' tap solves the problem by having separate hot- and cold-water tubes within the tap right down to the nozzle outlet. The water, therefore, now actually mixes outside the tap – less efficiently but more safely.

John Lisle, Llanfyllin, Powys

I believe that the answer lies in the fact that the British idea of washing something (or somebody) consists in immersing the item (or body) in a receptacle of (static) water and soap, rather than using running water (for example, the use of baths rather than showers to wash oneself). It is obvious that separate taps can do the job quite well in this case. However, for those of us who do prefer running water, washing is a rather painful process of scalding or freezing oneself.

Katerina Ananiadou, Department of Psychology, University of Warwick

John Lisle's answer is misleading. Mixer fittings were introduced into Victorian bathrooms when few houses had domestic hot water systems and even fewer a reliable mains source of water. To provide adequate volumes and flow rates, both hot (via a boiler and storage cylinder) and cold supplies to the bathroom were gravity-fed by a cold water storage cistern, usually in the roof space. With the wider availability of reliable mains supplies, it became common but bad practice to connect the cold side of the mixer fitting directly to the mains, thus reducing the amount of pipework and the size of cistern required. With unbalanced pressures at the mixer fitting, a sudden drop in mains pressure could result in contamination of the mains (and hence drinking) water by the ingress of lead, copper and/or iron particles that had accumulated in the boiler and storage cylinder. (Siphonage of cold mains water into the domestic hot water system would not cause an explosion but merely cool the water.)

Such practices were prohibited until the introduction of new water by-laws in 1989, which allowed the connection of mixer fittings to unbalanced supplies as long as single check valves are fitted.

Mixer fittings are uncommon in UK bathrooms because most domestic hot water systems still rely on gravity feed from a storage cistern, whereas all other developed countries have moved to using mains pressure to distribute hot and cold water, which eliminates the problem of unbalanced pressures.

Nigel Hankin (architectural design consultant), Brockenhurst, Hants

Living in the USA, I've come to the conclusion that mixer taps are a step backwards. The taps in an old-fashioned two-tap set-up are simple devices that last a hundred years. They contain a single washer and are easily fixed should it deteriorate and need to be replaced. The mixer taps in my house are less than twenty years old and have all had to be fixed; each contains at least nine tiny washers and O-rings, all of which must be perfectly clean and properly seated for the tap to work without leaking. As they deteriorate it becomes hard to find a position that will turn the tap off. The taps are designed to be operated without much force (a noble goal for the benefit of the old and less strong) but this causes them to leak at the bottom when others turn them with force. After I repaired all of mine two years ago, they are all leaking again. I'll probably replace them with simple non-mixing types.

Michael Scott Flynn, Mountain View, California, USA

At what age these days would it be accurate to say one is 'old'?

One's age plus twenty years.

Owain Greenwood, Bristol

It is not a simple case of defining oneself. According to the *Annual Abstract of Statistics* and recent health studies literature, there are three categories. The 'young old' are between the ages of sixty-five and seventy-four; the 'old' are between the ages of seventy-five and eighty-four; and the 'very old' are eighty-five years and over.

Joanne Ashmore, Finsbury Park, London

Shortly after the Second World War, my grandfather was sent the following poem scribbled on a scrap of card:

Age is a quality of mind.

If you have left your dreams behind

If Hope is lost
If you no longer look ahead
If your ambition's fires are dead
Then you are old!
But if from life you take the Best
And if in life you keep the jest
If Love you hold
No matter how the years go by
No matter how the birthdays fly
You are not old!

The letter was posted in the House of Commons, but neither author nor sender were established.

Christopher Lambton, Broughton, Peeb.

At any age when addressing people younger than oneself.

Matthew Scott, London EC1

When you find yourself writing to a newspaper to pass the time away.

Michael Dagley, Stockport, Cheshire

The poem that Christopher Lambton quotes is by Sir Archibald Flower. It is reprinted in an old Birthday Book in my possession with an acknowledgement to 'The Country Man'.

Mrs B. B. Simmonds, Croydon

Ogden Nash, in 'Crossing the Border', wrote:

Senescence begins
and middle-age ends,
the day your descendants
outnumber your friends.

Ian Sewell, London SW4

My answer, as a near-octogenarian, is that growing old comes in two stages. The first is when your children start to give you advice. The second is when you ask for it.

Graham Gifford, Balcolyn, NSW, Australia

On TV news, press photographers are often seen running alongside prison vans firing flashguns through blackened windows. Has a photograph ever been produced by this means?

As pointless as it may seem, firing a flashgun at the blackened window of a van can work. If the prisoner or person being protected sits close to the window inside the van, the power of the flash will be strong enough to illuminate them. Sometimes the light bounces straight back into the camera and you get nothing, but once in a while it pays off, as in the case of Rosemary West (and there were very few pictures of her during her trial).

Eamonn McCabe (Picture Editor, Guardian), London EC1

Surveys that correlate population growth, thus increasing the production of consumable goods, pollution and the depletion of non-renewable resources, all point to the inevitable destruction of civilization as we know it. Despite these predictions, economists, company executives and politicians continue to measure success in terms of increasing growth. Why are these supposedly responsible creatures urging us 'lemming-like' to the edge of the abyss?

Corporate capitalism is a system of economic evolution, selecting for maximum revenue in minimum time at minimum cost. Individuals and corporations attempting to place other considerations – say, human rights and environmental sustainability – above short-term profits tend to lose their jobs, their market share and their capital investment, or be taken over, and so on. In this world, the notion that we might be approaching 'the edge of the abyss' is perceived merely as a threat to consumer confidence, which must be overcome through public relations.

Essentially the same is true for politics, which, as John Dewey wrote, is 'the shadow cast on society by big business'. It is important to remember that politicians are where they are because they have been passed as 'fit' by the corporate (including the corporate media) system. The moment they go 'off message', by offending investors, advertisers and corporate interests generally, they are undermined and disappear from public view.

In the land of the blind, the one-eyed man is 'uncompetitive'.
David Edwards, Bournemouth

An employer will hire labour only when s/he can sell the product that the labour has produced. For example, if we all decide today to stop consuming petroleum, all employment on North Sea oil rigs and in national car plants will disappear tomorrow. Further, technological advancements cause labour productivity to increase over time so that, to produce the same amount of product, we gradually need fewer and fewer people. Those being made redundant can only re-enter the labour market if additional demand for consumables is created.

Whatever we think, if we are made redundant today we will seek employment, so that somebody somewhere will have to consume the product we would produce. There have been some primitive societies that learned to live within the constraint of their natural habitat. In these societies they had, for example, a specified season to catch a certain kind of fish, giving the species time to recover. But in a modern industrialized society that is not possible.
Dipak Ghosh, Bridge of Allan, Stirling

It is not true that all economists or all company executives are leading us to the edge of the abyss. On the MSc degree in Responsibility and Business Practice at the University of Bath, graduates in key positions in business, governmental and non-governmental organizations have been studying the many ways in which businesses are beginning to respond to the challenges of sustainability and social justice: more ecologically sound products, 'triple bottom line accounting', stakeholder dialogue, fair trade and so on. There is much to be done, but a start is being made.
Dr Peter Reason, School of Management, University of Bath

We have been through all this before. A *Blueprint for Survival* was first published in 1972. It was a brilliant study of how all the world's raw materials were running down. 'If current trends are allowed to persist, the breakdown of society and the irreversible breakdown of the life-support systems on this planet, possibly by the end of the century, certainly within the lifetimes of our children, are inevitable.'

This is still true; only the time-span has lengthened due to human ingenuity. In a way it turned out to be crying wolf, so it is more difficult to make the crisis apparent to those who do not want to know. The West will continue to thrive for some time, but it is getting harder for the third world all the time, and Armageddon may come from unrest in the South before raw materials actually run out.

Margaret Curtis, Helsby, Warrington

Dipak Ghosh writes: 'There have been some primitive societies that learned to live within the constraint of their natural habitat.' Indeed. Some of them have survived for thousands of years in fragile and marginal ecosystems. Some of them (the American Chief Sealth, Aborigines and Maoris) have gone on record as critical of our contemptuous mistreatment of the environment.

By contrast, resource depletion and environmental destruction date from the dawn of farming and have been implicated in the destruction of a number of civilizations. The pace has quickened since the introduction of machine power and today we can map the universe or explain the first moments of time but not, apparently, adapt to meet the real and present danger of environmental changes that could destroy our civilization within the next century. Would that be 'primitive' or 'highly sophisticated'?

Roger Crosskey, London W10

The non-profit organization, Redefining Progress, developed the Genuine Progress Indicator (GPI) as an alternative measure of economic activity. The GPI takes into account the costs of growth as well as the benefits, and it measures facets of the economy that the traditional 'gross national product' (GNP) ignores, such as environmental degradation, loss of leisure time, housework as 'labour', etc., to give a clearer picture of 'growth'. Examples are personal medical or automobile repair bills, which the GNP portrays as 'consumption' or 'growth' but which real people experience as 'costs'.

While the United States' GNP has roughly doubled in the last forty years, the GPI, which rose in the 1950s and 1960s, has fallen steadily since the 1970s, losing almost 50 per cent of its value in the last thirty years. This reflects the intuition of many people that the quality of their lives has not improved substantially despite the sterling performance of 'the economy'.

Redefining Progress provides GPI kits to community groups so they can evaluate the real social benefits and costs of the projects proposed for their communities by private developers.

Ken Kopp, San Francisco, USA

Why do even 'smart' people take a pride in the fact that 'they were never any good at maths', while they would never confess to having problems reading? Why is innumeracy acceptable?

Several years ago I went for a run with a girlfriend along a lakeshore. As my mind was turning to fractals as we jogged along, I said that it was a good thing that we couldn't follow the shoreline exactly since we would then have an infinite distance to run. Not only was she unimpressed, but I was put down in no uncertain terms.

The moral is that if you want to get on in life and pass on your genes, you have to have a good line of chat. Hence a high degree of literacy is an advantage. However, if your partner gets a hint that you are numerate, this can only work against you.

Terence Hollingworth, Blagnac, France

The good and bad in art are subjective, transient and determined wholly by people, placing humans at the pinnacle of creation.

Logic, mathematics, and physics involve facts that are objectively determined, independently of human wishes. Emphasis on these subjects places humans in a minor role, struggling and often failing to understand the complexities. To cast down knowledge of these subjects avoids recognizing this uncomfortable fact, which is why people so frequently do it.

William Allen, Oxshott, Surrey

Numeracy is a skill required in some junior trades – humble clerks and oily-handed engineers – and you can always employ such people to undertake these dull tasks for you. To be cultured and so converse in polite society, you need to have read noble literature. This is the usual elitist argument for the lack of social stigma associated with being innumerate; but for me it just doesn't seem to add up.

Professor Nigel Allinson, Department of Electrical Engineering, UMIST, Manchester

A. J. Ayer, in his *Language, Truth and Logic* (1936), argued that mathematics is merely a huge tautology. It is a system built on the fact that the expression '1 + 1' is synonymous with the expression '2', and '2+2' with '= 4', etc.

Ayer did believe that maths had an intellectual value as we do not know how this system progresses beyond a certain point without calculation, but he admits that 'a being whose intellect was infinitely powerful would take no interest in logic and mathematics'. Hence 'smart' people have every reason to disparage a system that is only of interest to lower intellects.

William Merrin, Derby

Does anyone know of an effective cure (ancient or modern) for morning sickness in early pregnancy?

Each individual woman experiences sickness differently, and a remedy that works for one pregnancy may not be effective in a subsequent one. However, you may find some relief by drinking ginger tea and/or wearing a seasickness ('acupressure') bracelet. A light snack can be helpful in averting an impending nausea attack (I always carried a supply of bananas). Also, don't clean your teeth very soon after eating, or whilst you are feeling nauseous.

If all else fails, you could emigrate to New Guinea, where I am told that morning sickness is virtually unknown – there, boils are symptomatic of early pregnancy.

Sue Brearley, London SW18

A former colleague living in Washington told me that friends recommended a spoonful of the syrup, then available in US pharmacies, from which Coca-Cola is made. His wife found it very effective. You can't buy the syrup here but a friend who drank a bottle of Coke found it helped.

Mike Broadbent, Luton, Beds

Sickness is a remedial effort on the part of the body, which constantly produces metabolic waste that is eliminated by the kidneys etc. During pregnancy the mother has the extra waste from the foetus and placenta to eliminate.

In early pregnancy, when there are feelings of excitement, apprehension, etc., the mother's body may need a temporary rest from the work of digestion, in order to cope with this elimination. Hence, she vomits.

Do not try to cure your morning sickness. Stop all food and drink only water for a few days, and the sickness will soon be over. Contrary to popular opinion, this will not harm you or your baby. When you can face the thought of food again, have a day when you only eat fresh, uncooked, ripe fruit. Introduce other foods gradually, beginning with salads, then lightly cooked fresh vegetables.

Alan Ashley, Bramford, Ipswich

Alan Ashley was dangerously misleading. Morning sickness occurs primarily in the first twelve weeks of pregnancy as a normal, but unpleasant, physiological response to the production of pregnancy-protecting hormones in the maturing placenta. It is not the body's way of coping with the elimination of waste products, as the kidneys perform this function perfectly adequately throughout pregnancy.

Nor is there a need for a 'temporary rest from the work of digestion'. Unlike most causes of vomiting, morning sickness often responds positively to food intake and many pregnant women report that eating one or two dry biscuits immediately on waking helps considerably. It would be dangerous to both the mother and the foetus to 'stop all food for a few days', as the problem can last many weeks.

The higher calorie demands of pregnancy should be met by taking frequent small snacks and plenty of fluids until the problem eventually subsides.

Dr J. M. England (General Practitioner), Tonbridge, Kent

From my experience of three pregnancies, the more exercise taken the better – particularly walking, swimming and cycling. It focuses the mind, thus taking attention away from the nausea; and it enables the body to

produce more endorphins, a natural painkiller and antiseptic.
Anne Carpenter (reflexologist), Clevedon, Somerset

What is meant by 'the economic cycle'? Is economics unique among modern sciences in adhering to a medieval 'cyclic' view of history, or is the term simply gobbledegook used to justify politicians' economic incompetence?

The trade cycle of boom, slump, recession and recovery was observed early in the history of capitalism. The Scotsman, Abram Combe, described it in his *Parable of the Cistern* in 1823.

He correctly diagnosed periodical overproduction as the cause, as profit was derived from the exploitation of workers whose purchasing power was therefore insufficient to buy back the goods that they had produced.

Pro-capitalist economists were unwilling to accept this, and some looked for external causes. In 1876 Professor Stanley Jevons proposed that the trade cycle was caused by the eleven-year sunspot cycle affecting agriculture. Henry D. Moore blamed the planet Venus for getting between the earth and the sun. Others, like Pigou, looked for psychological causes, such as loss of confidence, but did not explain how this could be cyclical.

Marx alone produced the only valid explanation. Capital, accumulated during the 'boom' phase, becomes too great for profitable sales. Artificially created scarcity, or 'reduction of inventories', is necessary until the reduced volume of capitalism can become profitable again. Hence the paradox of poverty side by side with idle resources and 'food mountains'.

Karl Heath, Coventry

What would be the constitutional consequences if the heir to the throne declared that he/she was an atheist?

The legalist would say that a non-Protestant cannot be monarch under the 1688 Bill of Rights. However, the Bill of Rights was basically a package of measures created by the ruling class of the day to nail a monarch who could use such ideas as the Divine Right of Kings to rule in an absolute fashion. The requirement that the monarch be a Protestant was so that he/she could not become a Catholic and ally him- or herself with absolute monarchs of the day, who tended to be Catholic.

These days, if the heir to the throne became an atheist, this would not entail an abrogation of British freedoms and there could be a case for amending the Bill of Rights by an Act of Parliament to make provision for an atheist monarch. This, of course, would have an impact on relations with the Church of England but Parliament could simply pass an Act declaring that the monarch is no longer the Supreme Governor of the Church in England.

Patrick White, London N19

As an atheist, the new monarch could not take the oath, created by the Coronation Oaths Act (1688), by which he/she promises to maintain 'the Protestant reformed religion established by law'. And the Accession Declaration Act (1910) requires the new monarch to swear before Parliament that he/she is a 'faithful Protestant' and will maintain 'the enactments which secure the Protestant succession to the Throne'.

Parliament could try to repeal these Acts before the atheist heir succeeded, but the existing monarch would have sworn the oath and declaration, and so could not assent to their repeal. These are the only two Acts in British law designed to prevent their own repeal.

The first way round this conundrum is the Baudouin device. In 1992 the king of the Belgians abdicated for a day to enable a designated successor to assent to an abortion law that the king found morally unacceptable. In principle, a British monarch could do the same.

The second is to have the repeal bill ready for the monarch's death. In common law, the monarchy is never vacant. The lawful heir inherits all the monarch's powers immediately on his/her death, before being crowned or making the Accession Declaration. So the atheist heir could immediately assent to the repeal bill and lawfully become an atheist monarch.

Laurie Smith, Carshalton, Surrey

By the Act of Settlement of 1701, the lawful heir to the throne is the first in the line of succession of Sophia, Electress of Hanover, who is also a 'faithful Protestant'. When the monarch dies, the proclamation of a successor must, therefore, pass over any declared atheists (or Catholics) in favour of their God-fearing offspring.

Patrick White and Laurie Smith have correctly pointed out that this law could itself be repealed, but they overlook the fact that the British monarch is also the head of state of other Commonwealth member countries – and, under the Statute of Westminster of 1931, no alteration can come into effect governing the British succession until equivalent laws have been passed in all affected legislatures. This was last done on the abdication of Edward VIII – when it took several months – and the Commonwealth is both bigger now and less inclined to defer to British prejudices.

In any case, there could be no point to the change. It is inherent in the monarchy's claim to rule that they embody the principle that the government acts 'by the grace of God' – which is stated so explicitly in all royal titles, proclamations and commissions. It would certainly be possible to re-express the fundamental basis of government on entirely secular principles, but there would then be neither need nor justification for continuing to support a monarchy.

Tom Hennell, Withington, Cheshire

Why does the wedding ring go on the third finger of the left hand? I am left-handed. Is it socially acceptable to have the wedding band on my right hand?

Brewer's Dictionary of Phrase and Fable states: 'Aulus Gellius tells us that Appianus asserts in his Egyptian books that a very delicate nerve runs from the fourth finger of the left hand to the heart, on which account this finger is used for the marriage ring.'

And further, in the Roman Catholic Church, the thumb and first two fingers represent the Trinity, and the next finger 'is the husband's, to whom the woman owes allegiance next to God. The left hand is chosen to show that the woman is to be subject to the man.'

One could therefore assume that it was socially acceptable for a man to wear this ring on the right hand, but not a woman.

Bob Harper, Gateshead, Tyne and Wear

My wife and I have worn our matching wedding rings on the third finger of the right hand for thirty years and no one has remarked upon it.

Peter Shield, Woodthorpe, Notts

What is the difference between erotica and pornography?

The height of the bookshelf.

Terry Victor, Caerwent, Mon.

As a former bookseller, I would suggest that the term 'erotica' is used by bookstores to disguise the fact that they are selling what most people perceive to be 'pornography'. The distinction lies in the psyche of the purchaser (or retailer): if you feel guilty about what you buy (or sell), then you call it 'erotica'. I once had a colleague who claimed that a book full of pictures of naked bodies is art, so long as it is available only in hardcover.

Vincent Finney, Edinburgh

Pornography is erotica that is not to the taste of the person describing it. Usually, pornography is 'stronger' than that which the person considers erotic, although it is not hard to conceive of homophobes considering a man having sex with a woman as merely erotic, whilst finding two gays kissing pornographic.

Tony Green, Ipswich, Suffolk

It's one of these irregular nouns: 'they' read pornography, 'you' read erotica, 'I' read stimulating adult narratives.

Jane Carnall, Edinburgh

When does a cult become a religion?

When it is granted a tax-free status by the government.

Anthony Breckner, London W4

When it progresses from killing its members to killing non-members.
David Lewin, Oxford

The essential difference is openness. Religions publish their beliefs openly in the Bible, Koran, Bhagavadgita, etc., and seek to persuade the public of their truth. Anyone who accepts these beliefs and the accompanying rituals is recognized as a member of the religion. There is a priesthood, which is open to any (normally male) person with the necessary commitment. Religions therefore seek a mass following.

Cults, however, rely on secret or special knowledge, which is revealed only to initiates by the cult's founder or his/her chosen representatives. Beliefs aren't normally published. Everything depends on a personal relationship between the founder and followers, who are required to separate themselves from the rest of the world. This enables the founder and his associates to dominate and exploit the members.

All religions begin as cults. Christianity began as one of several competing messianic sects and became a religion when Paul and his followers began proselytizing outside Judaea. Cults fade away when those who knew the founder die. Who remembers the Ranters, the Sandemanians or the Muggletonians now?
Laurie Smith, Carshalton, Surrey

Are there any names that I am not allowed to use if I want to change my name by deed poll? Could I, for instance, call myself Coca-Cola? Would anyone object to me being called Her Majesty Queen Elizabeth II?

You can't change your name by deed poll (or by statutory declaration, which is cheaper), whatever your solicitor and others may lead you to believe. In law your name is what you are known by (legitimately including aliases – for example, pen-names, stage names, women using both married and maiden names). A deed poll is only a formal declaration of intent, but it has no relevance if you use a different name in practice.

Say your name is John Smith. You go into a solicitor's office and execute a deed poll, 'changing' your name to Elvis Presley (it has happened). If, on coming out of the office, you continue to sign your cheques 'John Smith', your name is still 'John Smith'; if you start signing them 'Cliff Richard', then your name is Cliff Richard. Of course, you need to be consistent, and the bank and the Inland Revenue will require evidence that you really are the person known as what you say you are (which is why deeds poll are taken, for practical purposes, as 'evidence').

There is no legal restriction on the name you are known by, but the use of that name is subject to all the obvious restrictions on the use of language generally: obscenity, fraudulent impersonation, electoral malpractice, racism, blasphemy, libel and slander. So you can call yourself 'Her Majesty the Queen' as long as you don't pretend to be the Queen. You could probably get away with calling yourself Coca-Cola (after all, you can't really be prevented from calling yourself W. H. Smith, F. W. Woolworth or Ronald McDonald), provided that you didn't do it by way of trade or affecting anyone else's, although I wouldn't vouch for the response of courts in the United States.

Dr J. B. Post, Axbridge, Somerset

The titles of the ancient bishoprics and deaneries of the Church of England are protected by the criminal law. Under the Ecclesiastical Titles Act – which is mainly directed at preventing a rival establishment of the English hierarchy by the Catholic Church – misappropriating one of these titles would be an offence.

Tom Hennell, Withington, Manchester

A few years ago I read of a man who wanted to change his name to his favourite chatline number. However, his bank refused to accept it as a signature for his chequebook on the basis that it was too easily forged.

Mark Wilkinson, Uxbridge, Middx

A few years ago I read of a man who wanted to change his name to F731 HDB, claiming that it was cheaper than buying a personalized number plate for his car.

Bob Morton, Hale, Cheshire

It's (almost) officially admitted that MI5 and MI6 exist. During the Second World War there was, I believe, an MI9 and an MI14. But what did MIs 1–4, 7, 8, 10, 11, 12 and 13 do?

This question shouldn't really be asked – or answered – but basically it seems probable that they did nothing, but drew pay for it.

It is believed that MI1 and MI11 were eliminated long ago because of confusion between Is and 1s in the accounts department. As to the rest, it is said that out of the huge sums voted as 'contingencies', modest amounts are transferred to MI2 and MI3. These are then allocated to the Prime Minister and the Home Secretary to reward their alleged responsibilities for the non-existing MI5 and MI6. Further amounts, charged to the MI4 account, may be offered either to the Chancellor of the Exchequer or to the Foreign Secretary, to compensate for the loss of tied weekend cottages – and the like.

The large balance (charged to MIs 7, 8, 10, 12 and 13, which are 'notional' only) is used as necessary to bump up 'invisibles' in specially bad months to keep balance-of-payment deficits below the £2 billion mark, where possible. But please note, this is off the record.

A. I. Pottinger, Edgbaston, Birmingham

Why are dusters yellow?

As an office and industrial cleaner for many years, I offer these suggestions.

One of the duster's great attributes is its use for polishing. In the past, before the advent of pressurized canisters and the dreaded CFCs, this was done with beeswax. Manufacturers may have decided to make and sell the necessary complementary dusters. Wishing to keep an identification with their main product, they would naturally have dyed them yellow. Early dusters were not the bright colour of today, but a more ochre shade – indeed, some were pastel green.

Alternatively: an enterprising marketing director of yesteryear may have attempted to corner the market by using most people's association of the colour yellow with springtime, with its increase in sunshine and daylight hours. He would have realized that sales of dusters would be increased enormously by using the appropriate colour, especially during the annual spring-cleaning season. There are many examples of how the colour has become connected with spring, such as daffodils and the expression 'to be as busy as a (yellow) bee'. Spring-cleaning with (yellow) wax and duster is an almost symbolic gesture of spreading sunlight around the home.

P. Millard, Bristol, Avon

If, as P. Millard suggests, dusters were originally coloured yellow in order to work upon the public's association of the colour with the season of spring, then the ploy has probably been unsuccessful.

Despite the increase in sunshine hours and various other yellow connotations, green and not yellow has been shown to be more commonly linked with this particular season. This was proved in 1976 by the psychologist, P. H. K. Seymour. In order to test a phenomenon of perceptual confusion known as the Stroop effect, Seymour's version of the phenomenon involved the linking of seasons and colours. In order to lay the groundwork for such an experiment, extensive testing found that the majority of people link yellow with summer, brown with autumn, white with winter, and green with spring.

So if, in a few months' time, you find yourself automatically reaching for some green dusters, beware the mind-games played by *Guardian*-reading marketing directors.

Michael A. Martin, London SW20

I have despaired of reading a sensible explanation for why dusters are yellow. Here is my theory instead.

In the first half of the nineteenth century a large quantity of bright yellow cotton cloth was imported from Nanking in China. It was subsequently imitated and produced in Britain, where it was used to make highly fashionable trousers (known as 'nankeens'). After the garments wore out, the remaining cloth was recycled as polishing rags in the hands of the thrifty. Yellow buckskin breeches had been fashionable earlier and they were made of leather, cotton or wool. White linen and cotton rag was usually recycled for high-quality paper, and there was never enough.

I do not know if the two sense of 'buff', that is: (1) yellow ox-leather; and (2) to polish with a piece of the same, have anything to do with the matter, but see OED. The traditional association between a yellow material and polishing may have reinforced the use of nankeen cloth for dusting and cleaning after the fashion for the trousers ceased.

Charles Newton, London N22

If trapped in a plummeting lift, what is the best position to assume to minimize injury?

The safest position is one where the legs are slightly bent, rather than braced. Survival depends on the length of drop, of course, but at least this position ensures that the thigh bones are not driven upwards into the abdominal cavity.

Jumping upwards to reduce damage is not recommended, for three reasons. First, it is very difficult to time and could worsen the situation if you land on the floor of the lift in an uncontrolled way. Second, by the time you have thought about this tactic, you will already have impacted. Third, if you have time to think about this and act on it, you have already fallen too far to survive.

As a survivor of a drop in an ancient goods lift back in 1962 (three and a half floors with a load of two tons of chewing gum), I have to warn your readers that all is not over after the first impact. Close inspection of the bottom of lift shafts reveals a series of springs designed to absorb energy. This energy has to be expressed in some way, and in the case of a plummeting lift, it has the effect of propelling the lift back up the shaft. You will return up the shaft with a slightly reduced velocity to that with which you descended only a few seconds ago. At the top of your rise you will experience an instant of déjà vu as you descend again. After approximately five repetitions of this experience, you will come to rest. Thus you will have plenty of time to practise any position that comes to mind, consider the nature of human existence, or just let blind terror take over. After this you can consider the next problem: how to get out of the wreckage. I am happy to say that I emerged uninjured but shaken. Others have not been so lucky.

Stephen Lutman, Faversham, Kent

Any position that you adopt depends on the early recognition that the lift is in free fall. For this reason you should always carry a set of bathroom scales, which you can stand on in the lift. You should of course ignore the initial drop in weight as the lift begins a normal descent, but you should then watch avidly in case the reading approaches zero for more than a second. Having established that all is not well, your safest position is on top of the other occupants of the lift. One should therefore never travel in a lift less than half full, and if the choice exists one should choose fellow passengers who are overweight. They not only offer the greatest cushion on impact but generally they are less mobile when fighting for position.

Peter Jackson, Prees, Shropshire

What is the meaning of life?

In Douglas Adams's book, *The Hitch Hiker's Guide to the Galaxy*, we are informed that the computer, Deep Thought, ponders over a period of 7.5 million years the question of the meaning of Life, the Universe and Everything. It is widely understood that this machine calculated the total answer to these three separate concepts as forty-two. Thus dividing forty-two by three, it can be deduced that the meaning of life alone is fourteen. This, however, can only be assumed if the ratio of Life to both the Universe and Everything is 1: 1: 1.

Khairoun Abji (student at Luton VI Form College), Luton, Beds

What we do know with certainty is that we were not once, are now, and will not be again.

Brian Mendes, Bromley, Kent

Life is a sexually transmitted condition with a 100 per cent mortality rate.

P. Mellor, Centre for Software Reliability, City University, London EC1

Life is not a linguistic item and hence has no meaning. The question makes as much sense as: 'What is the meaning of lumbago?'

Graham Bryant, Nottingham

My old pal Plotinus has it thus: 'If a man were to enquire of Nature the reason of her creative activity, and she were willing to give ear and answer, she would say, "Ask not, but understand in silence, even as I am silent and am not wont to speak."'

N. J. Crofton-Sleigh, Norwich

The *Concise Oxford Dictionary* states that life is a 'state of functional activity and continual change peculiar to organized matter and especially to the portion of it constituting an animal or plant before death'. God knows (sic).

Jeff Thirburn, Nuneaton, Warks

Life has no meaning related to an external frame of reference, only the meaning that you decide to give it. It follows that any such meaning given is as valid as any other for you, and any change is also up to you. Have fun being Cesare Borgia on Wednesdays and St Francis on Thursdays.

Brian Cattermole, Stevington, Beds

Before directing the questioner to the nearest dictionary or his local priest, I would strongly advise that this is a question not to be asked, unless rhetorically. History shows that individuals who asked this of themselves or others are prone to insanity, alcoholism or other addictions, even visions of religious ecstasy. None of these help in the least with an answer, only offering a temporary palliative for the passing of life while it is being experienced, or in providing hope for the hopeless. Matters such as destiny, happiness and other connected issues only complicate the question and should not be dragged on to the stage of reasoning.

The greatest minds that have ever lived have not come near to answering this question; choose what eschatology you will for now. The chances are that whichever one you adhere to, we have all got it wrong (if only fundamentalists knew as much). This is a great mystery and long may it remain so. There is something a little dull about the prospect of knowing everything and our humble brains are not wired for that prospect. Life is for living, surely.

James A. Oliver, London WC2

According to a BBC2 *Horizon* programme screened some months ago (not on 1 April), the meaning of life may have something to do with the notion that the most important living entity on this planet, the earth itself, may regulate various life forms within its confines in order to ensure its own survival. Thus, for example, although the sun is now very much hotter than it was at the dawn of life, the proportion of oxygen in the atmosphere has remained more or less constant at 21 per cent, any greater or lesser amount being catastrophic. This suggests some kind of self-regulating mechanism, which may be provided by the gases, particularly from manure, of all living things. That would also explain various epidemics and natural disasters, as Mother Earth controls the number of living creatures and thus the level and mixture of atmospheric gases. What the meaning of life is for planet earth is another matter.

D. Fisher, Maidenhead, Berks

Has anyone ever died of boredom?

On the face of it, George Sanders, the suave film actor, would seem a likely candidate.

When in 1972 he did away with himself with a lethal cocktail of nembutal and vodka, the most publicized of his three suicide notes declared: 'Dear World. I am leaving because I am bored. I feel I have lived long enough. I am leaving you with your worries in this sweet cesspool. Good luck.' But Sanders had been suffering for some time from a screwed-up private life, feelings of rootlessness, severe financial problems and deteriorating health. The give-away word is 'cesspool'. However stylish the form of his farewell note, 'boredom' is scarcely the word to summarize his sad decline.

Since chronic boredom is closely linked with depression — it is, in fact, a form of depression — it's doubtful that anyone ever died of boredom in the relatively trivial everyday sense of the word. However, when human beings are subjected to solitary confinement and sensory deprivation, they are often brought to the brink of despair and self-destruction.

Neil Hornick, London NW11

Dean W. R. Inge was accurate in his contention (see *The End of an Age*, 1948) that: 'The effect of boredom on a large scale in history is underestimated. It is a main cause of revolutions ...' The answer has to be yes, lots.

(Revd) Clifford Warren, Machen Rectory, Gwent

Boredom has certainly been responsible for a number of deaths, often by mistake.

Louis XIV regularly started wars out of sheer boredom. In Chicago in 1923 Nathan Leopold and Michael Loeb plotted the murder of a schoolboy, just as a relief for their interminable ennui. Death has also been caused in trivial moments of tedium: on 2 November 1973, a passenger was killed on a DC10 because an engine exploded after a bored flight engineer had meddled with a few of the buttons in the cockpit.

Although Samuel Beckett's two tramps in *Waiting for Godot* might be suffering a terminal boredom when they whine 'We are bored to death', and NASA is worried that boredom may well cause serious problems on the manned mission to Mars, it's unlikely that boredom leads to the final decision to die rather than to continue a life of bland indifference. In the words of Morrissey, that guru of bedsit boredom: 'I think about life and I think about death, but neither one particularly appeals to me.'

John Dutton and Chris Horrocks, London N4

My family is convinced that an actor cousin, who sadly died while in the cast of *The Mousetrap*, must indeed have died of boredom.

S. Marking, Toller Whelme, Dorset

On 31 July 1861, whichever of the Goncourt brothers was on *Journal des Goncourts* duty that day asked whether their lack of success might actually mean that they were failures. He then adds: 'One thing reassures me as to our value: the boredom that afflicts us. It is the hallmark of quality in modern men. Châteaubriand died of it, long before his death. Byron was stillborn with it.'

Richard Boston, Reading, Berks

What is art?

The definitive answer was provided thirty years ago by Marshall McLuhan: 'Art is anything you can get away with.'
John Whiting, London NW11

Tolstoy offers the following definition: 'To evoke in oneself a feeling one has once experienced, and having evoked it in oneself, then, by means of movements, lines, colours, sounds or forms expressed in words, so to transmit that feeling that others may experience the same feeling – that is the activity of art. Art is a human activity, consisting in this, that one man consciously, by means of certain external signs, hands on to others feelings he has lived through, and that other people are infected by these feelings, and also experience them.' (From L. Tolstoy, *What is Art?*, translated by A. Maude.)
George Crossley, Bradford

The best definition I have come across is by James Joyce: 'Art is the human disposition of sensible or intelligible matter for an aesthetic end.'
Wolf Suschitzky, London W2

'A work of art is a corner of creation seen through a temperament' (Emile Zola).
C. Heritage-Tilley, Winchester, Hants

'Art is a stuffed crocodile' (Alfred Jarry, 1873–1907, author of *Ubu Roi*).
Titus Alexander, London E17

Art is 'pattern informed by sensibility' (Sir Herbert Read, *The Meaning of Art*).
Henry Burns Elliot, Colchester

Life is serious but art is fun (source unknown).
Nathan Wood, Birmingham

I like Tolstoy's definition of art as the ability to transmit a feeling one has experienced to others through 'movements, lines, colours', etc. But surely pornography does this very effectively. Did Tolstoy consider pornography to be art?

Frank Miles, Beckenham, Kent

None of the answers offered so far is satisfactory. McLuhan's 'Art is anything you can get away with' might admit undetected shoplifting or terrorism, neither of which would normally be considered art.

Tolstoy's definitions suggest that the essential property of art is its ability to communicate the expression of emotion to a perceiver. Although art often embodies this characteristic, the definition doesn't account for emotional communication, which most people would recognize as 'outside art' in, for example, common expressions of anger or sadness.

James Joyce's definition highlights the use of materials for aesthetic ends. This is quite convincing in the implication that a work of art must have been intended to be a work of art by the artist. The problem is that many works that are now widely accepted as art (such as cave paintings, ritual masks) were not made for aesthetic or artistic reasons.

The hundreds of thought-provoking attempts to define art all hold true for some art but not for all art, and often are equally valid for things that are not generally understood to be art. Those who become exhausted by their attempts to answer the question with a single definition might take up the advice of the American philosopher Nelson Goodman and rephrase the question: 'When is an object a work of art?'

The dynamic character of much of the most interesting art was, I think, well expressed by the artist Jeff Nuttall, who wrote in 1980, in an article entitled 'Art, Politics and Everything Else':

'Art is the skill of examining the range of our perceptions by the making of artefacts . . . Often the last place you're likely to find the perceptions being extended is in the compartment marked Art, which may have been frozen into stasis by devices like the Standards of Good Taste, Proven Criteria, the Maintaining of Tradition. In the drawer marked Art there may well be no art at all.'

David Ainley, Matlock, Derby.

As Rock Hudson said in *Magnificent Obssession:*'Art is just a boy's name.'
Hugh Raffles, London W14

Are there any valid arguments, other than religious ones, as to why it would be better for the planet for the human race to continue rather than to become extinct?

The questioner asks whether or not it would be better for 'the planet'. This is a problem of values. The planet, in so far as it is a material object, clearly has no values of its own, since values are a product of consciousness. The planet could no more experience pleasure in the continued existence of life than it would lament its passing. It therefore follows that any positive attributes that the planet is thought to possess only exist because of their presence in the mind of a living being capable of experiencing them.

So far as we know, humans are able to experience more complex and varied responses to the world than any other animal. This opinion may be no more than 'speciesist' vanity, but the existence of anything approaching human levels of creative thought in other animals is so far unproven. In any case, whatever other animals think, we can only answer this question from within our own value system.

To this extent it answers itself. The beauties and pleasures of the natural world that we experience are only recognized as such because we are here to do the recognizing. If we didn't exist, neither would these experiences. The planet is only valuable as long as someone is here to value it. Our existence is thus a necessary condition for the continuation of the planet itself as something that is meaningful.
(Dr) P. Barlow, Sunderland University, Tyne and Wear

Dr Barlow's answer is based on the assumption that 'better' necessarily means 'morally superior'; this makes no sense in the context.

In the English language the word 'better' can also mean 'in a superior physical condition', as when we say that someone is better after an illness. In this sense the planet would obviously be better without the human race. In these days of efficient contraception and when there are few family businesses left to keep going, the main motives for perpetuating the human race must be to satisfy the parental instinct, to attempt to achieve some sort of immortality, or to keep *Debrett's Peerage* in business.

However, it may surprise the questioner to know that two Christian sects, the Albigenses and the Cathari, who lived in the eleventh to thirteenth centuries in southern France and elsewhere, condemned procreation on the grounds that it increased the amount of evil in the world, which they saw as a battleground between spiritual good and material evil. They were condemned as heretics and became the victims of a crusade led by our Simon de Montfort.

Robert Sephton, Oxford

It was not our Simon de Montfort, Earl of Leicester, born in 1208, who led the merciless crusade against the Albigenses and Cathars in south-west France. It was Simon IV le Fort, Sire de Montfort, who was appointed to lead the crusade in 1209, following the assassination of the papal envoy, Pierre de Castelnau, near St Gilles. Meanwhile, our Simon de Montfort was a babe in arms.

F. Paul Taylor, Frodsham, Cheshire

I wonder if Robert Sephton realizes that by introducing the Albigenses and Cathars into the debate, he undermines his own argument. These sects, like other forms of Manicheism, believed that all matter was evil. For them, the world would be a better place if all biological life was extinguished. By this logic, a healthy planet is a dead planet. So keep up the good work, all you polluters out there!

Flavia Dunford-Trodd, Liverpool

If it is acceptable and rational for a parent to step in front of a speeding bullet to save a child, which most people would agree on, then it is also acceptable and rational to wish for my/our extinction in order to save the planet. All one needs to do is give a plausible defence of what one is trying to save.

If there are two alternatives – the complete extinction of all life on earth or the extinction of all human life – which do we choose? According to Dr Barlow, who says that 'the planet is only valuable as long as someone is there to value it', one might as well make the decision with a pin. This I cannot accept. The second alternative leaves the planet intact and with a wealth of biological diversity, whereas the first leaves just another dead planet. There is a difference. The real question is: is this the alternative that faces us?

Giles Radford, Ashford, Kent

By what right can the British State require me to observe its laws and accept its institutions, given that I have never been asked to signify my assent to arrangements that include ones negotiated in previous generations by tiny elites?

If you have ever made use of the provisions of British law yourself, it could be argued that you have implicitly consented to comply with the entire body of it. But it is easier to argue that you imply consent when you participate in the democratic process by voting. This may also be the principle that leads opposition parties to withdraw from elections when they think they will be rigged. By not putting up candidates and by asking their supporters to abstain, they presumably hope to invalidate the government's claims on them for compliance, freeing them and their supporters to oppose the government both within and outside the law.

But even this latter argument for compliance seems rather stretched; many people comply but don't vote; and many people who vote are nonetheless outraged at some of the legislation they are asked to comply with.

Rights are things you get when they are granted to you. You have no rights (in law) other than those granted to you, and conversely the State's rights over you can only be the rights you have granted to it.

John Cleaver, London

John Cleaver's answer is not entirely satisfactory. If the state has no rights over an individual without their consent, then it can have no right to control the actions of most people under the age of eighteen, since it does not allow such people to vote, nor does it ensure that they have the opportunity to consent in any other way. This would imply, for instance, that the only reasonable way to remove a twelve-year-old playing on a railway line would be through impact with a train.

Any answer to the question should take into account that a state is not only an abstract entity: it also impacts on huge numbers of individuals, in part through the existence of consensus. For example, when police officers restrict an individual's liberty by preventing him or her from driving the wrong way up a motorway, their action frequently draws the approbation of the majority of onlookers. These onlookers wish this aspect of state activity to continue. There does not seem to be any reason why their wishes should not be accorded at least as much respect as the wishes of dissidents who would prefer to be free to drive on the right if they want to, like other Europeans.

Readers might conclude that whilst the majority of people are perhaps not always right, doing what they want – obeying the state, for example – does violate the wishes of fewer people.

Hudson Pace, Teddington, Middx

Tom Paine, in his *Rights of Man* (1791), supplied an answer to this question:

> There never did, there never will, and there never can exist a parliament, or any description of men, or any generation of men, in any country, possessed of the right or the power of binding and controlling posterity to the 'end of time', or of commanding for ever how the world shall be governed, or who shall govern it; and therefore, all such clauses, acts or declarations, by which the makers of them attempt to do what they have neither the right nor the power to do, nor the power to execute, are in themselves null and void. Every age and generation must be as free to act for itself, in all cases, as the ages and generations which preceded it. The vanity and presumption of governing beyond the grave, is the most ridiculous and insolent of all tyrannies. Man has no property in man; neither has any generation a property in the generations which are to follow.

John Davies, History Department, Liverpool Institute of Higher Education

Questions on the nature of the individual, their moral fibre and their rights were argued about at length during the eighteenth and nineteenth centuries. John Stuart Mill argued for utilitarianism, of which the founding principle was that 'society' was more important than any one person or group of individuals. So individuals had the right to do as they pleased, provided they did not impinge upon the rights of others.

There was also a theory that just and otherwise law-abiding people, of suitable moral rectitude, were within their rights to disregard laws that they considered inherently unjust. This presupposes that 'good' citizens do not need laws to keep them in check. Thus, individuals are not going to object to a directive or law which prohibits something that they would never dream of doing anyway.

All the theories on law and moral development were developed when the law was so draconian that society was effectively lawless – if you are going to hang, you might as well commit a big crime.

Today we may consider that some laws that exist from those times are petty, but they rarely result in conviction. And we may think that some sentences passed by judges are ridiculous, or that their comments show a lack of understanding, but this does not necessarily undermine the authority of the law or our obligation to obey it.

Graham R. Jones, Withington, Manchester

Many are the political philosophers who have tried to turn the fact that humans are social animals into some ethical or pseudo-scientific basis for the injunction to observe laws. But as any good anarchist knows, by the right of might is the true answer to this question.

The fact that it is sensible or desirable to have some rules and to obey them, such as traffic rules, does not give generalized grounds for observing all laws. Each of us has the right, even the duty, to question the laws imposed on us.

In some forms of direct democracy, individuals have the chance to acquiesce deliberately in the rules that are generated to govern the society to which they belong, and to argue for changes or new ones. In the so-called representative so-called democracies, we are powerless and allow institutions to frighten us into obedience. Their 'right' is our 'duty'.

Whilst the sanction of punishment for breaking laws is undoubtedly one reason that many people are law-abiding, the really clever part is the fear that is conditioned into us — a fear that makes us delegate our power as individuals to the state and lets us duck the moral responsibility for our actions.

Maurice Herson, Oxford

5

Life, the Universe and Everything

Is there any truth in the claim that warm or hot water freezes faster than cold water?

Yes, boiling water will freeze faster than room-temperature water if evaporation is allowed (for example, with open containers) because sufficient mass is lost from the increased evaporation to compensate for the higher starting temperature. For further information, see http://www.urbanlegends.com/science.

Dr Richard Balthazor, Upper Atmosphere Modelling Group, University of Sheffield

I heard the following explanation given by Jearl Walker in a spectacular demonstration lecture at an American Association of Physics Teachers Annual Conference in the late 1970s.

Ignoring the effect of evaporation, and starting with two buckets of water with equal volume, one at 100°C and the other at 0°C, the hotter one has less mass (because of the thermal expansion of water). The dominant factor is not the cooling but the freezing process, because the 'latent heat of fusion' of water – the energy required to freeze it – per unit mass is so great. So the full hot bucket has sufficiently less mass to overcome the energy loss in cooling the hot bucket from 100°C to 0°C, and the hot bucket will freeze sooner.

Ian Fairweather, Budapest, Hungary

This belief is a classic old-wives' tale: previous correspondents have been deceived by pseudo-scientific explanations.

The maximum density of water occurs at 4°C, when it is 1.000. The density of water at 100°C is 0.9584. On this basis a litre of water at 100°C would give up a total of 173,000 calories in cooling to 0°C and freezing. The 1,000 grams of water at 4°C would give up 84,000 calories. On this basis the hot water would take approximately twice as long to freeze as the cold water.

In fact there are a whole lot of other factors to take into account, but all are minor in relation to the huge difference in calories required. During recent cold weather the local tapwater was about 5°C. I put out water for the birds on a regular basis, and I also put out hot water at about 60°C. It consistently remained liquid several hours longer than the cold water.

Lawrie Brown, Denbighshire, Wales

Assuming a bucket of water is at 100°C and another at room temperature, the hot one will freeze first because eddy currents are set up in the hot bucket and not in the cold one. The hot water near the sides of the bucket cools rapidly and, being more dense, sinks. Hot water in the centre of the bucket rises and these thermals are maintained almost to freezing point. Hence, the hot bucket overtakes the one at room temperature.

Bryan White, Hemlington, Cleveland

There are two examples in the solar system (moon/earth and mercury/sun) of a body whose period of rotation is exactly the same as its period of orbit, so that it always presents the same face to its mother body. Surely this cannot be coincidence?

The answer is friction. The gravitational effect of the moon, for example, pulls the oceans on the earth (which of course creates the tides) and energy is dissipated due to the heat generated. The earth has a similar effect on the (more solid) moon. Essentially this means that in any system where one body orbits another, their rotations will be slowed. The effect is greater on smaller bodies, and thus almost every satellite in the solar system (not just the moon) keeps the same face towards its parent planet.

In the Mercury/sun system, Mercury in fact makes three rotations on its axis for every two revolutions of the sun. This situation is stable. The sun/Venus system is also slightly complicated in that it appears that Venus has slowed down too much. This means that, unusually, Venus is now rotating in the opposite direction to its orbit. There are several possible explanations for this, the most obvious being that perhaps it always rotated in that way.

Satellites can also lock into synchronous orbits and produce important effects. For example, three of the satellites of Jupiter (Io, Europa and Ganymede) have orbits that are simple multiples of each other. The gravitational forces exerted by the satellites and the planet are directly responsible for the volcanoes on Io.

Alan Craig, Shadforth, Durham

The same thing is happening to the earth. The length of the year has not changed, but the day used to be much shorter; in the Middle Cambrian Period 50 million years ago a year lasted for 400 days. Eventually tidal forces will slow down the earth until it too shows only one face to the sun (provided the solar system lasts that long).

David Godfrey, London WC1

During Captain Bligh's 4,000 mile voyage with nineteen people crowded into an open launch, it rained almost non-stop. To avoid hypothermia Bligh had everyone soak his or her clothing in sea water, wring it out and put it on. For the rest of his life he maintained that this strategy saved their lives. What, if anything, was happening to protect them?

In 1951 I took part in the trials in the Johore Straits of the tented, automatically inflated life-rafts developed by the Royal Navy. Over most of the world's seas, cold is the most urgent threat to a castaway's survival but in the tropics (where virtually all long voyages took place) the problem is loss of fluids. This is greatly increased by sweating. We found that instructing the volunteers in the rafts to keep their clothes continuously wet with sea water during the daytime, together with the other aspects of the raft drill, was totally effective in countering sweating: that is, it reduced loss of water from the body by evaporation to exactly the level seen in the same subjects in an ideal environment in the laboratory.

As compared with the worst case − survivors in an open craft exposed to the tropical sun and with no fresh water − expected survival time would be increased from two to three days to two to three weeks. Some rain is usually available in the tropics but unless there are effective means of collecting it (such as the life-raft provides) it is likely to sustain only a small number of survivors for really long voyages.

Romaine Hervey, Wells, Avon

Albert Einstein received a Nobel prize for his 1905 explanation of the photoelectric effect but no such recognition for his work on special and general relativity, the theories on which his fame is based. Why not?

Einstein was nominated for the Nobel prize in physics every year from 1910 to 1922 except for 1911 and 1915. In most cases he was nominated for his work on both special and general relativity.

Historians of science have given two reasons why Einstein never received the prize for special and general relativity.

First, these theories were so revolutionary that the scientists on the awarding committee simply didn't understand them well enough at the time to pass judgement; also they were concerned that not all his predictions had been experimentally verified.

Second, it is said that certain anti-Semitic members of the Swedish Academy of Sciences awarding committee were influenced by the lobbying of the German physicist, Philipp Lenard, later to become a Nazi, who claimed that relativity was a counterintuitive, non-Aryan and Jewish theory.

However, the spectacular confirmation of Einstein's general theory in 1919, when light from distant stars was shown to be deflected by the gravitational influence of the sun, made him the first scientific superstar and the Swedish Academy could no longer ignore him. His 1922 Nobel prize citation read: 'For his services to theoretical physics and especially for his discovery of the law of the photoelectric effect.' The letter to Einstein from the Secretary of the Academy added, 'but without taking into account the value which will be accorded your relativity and gravitation theories after these are confirmed in the future'.

Einstein was awarded the prize for his quantum theory explanation of the photoelectric effect, published in 1905. The irony is that this phenomenon was discovered by Lenard, for which he was awarded the 1905 Nobel physics prize. Lenard's virulent anti-Semitism prevented him from ever accepting Einstein's quantum explanation for the effect.

Reg Dennick, Nottingham

How did delicate creatures like jellyfish, or soft-skinned vertebrates such as amphibians, survive the environmental catastrophe said to have caused the mass extinctions at the time the dinosaurs died out?

Whatever the manner of the extinction mechanism, it is not a question of soft skin that determined survival. What seems to have been crucial was being able to survive cooling temperatures and, perhaps, also to exploit unusual food resources.

Amphibians may have survived because of their ability to hibernate or to enter states of torpor. When the temperature drops they become dormant but remain alive. Dinosaurs would not have had this ability. Of course the small mammals alive at this time did not hibernate, but they had insulating fur and could burrow underground.

Much still remains to be understood about this mass extinction, but most of the creatures that perished were large bodied; none survived beyond the Cretaceous Period.

Mark Swindale, Brodick, Isle of Arran

Recent studies of the catastrophic event that caused the extinction of the dinosaurs and other species at the end of the Cretaceous Period have shown that the consequential environmental fallout was, in fact, very selective. The fate of animals and plants was determined by their place in the food chain, rather than their robustness. Herbivorous animals and their predators became extinct because green plant production was temporarily stopped, whilst the detritus feeders, insectivorous animals and their predators were relatively little affected.

This would concur with the theoretical consequences of the impact of an extraterrestrial body on earth, causing an injection of dust into the atmosphere, leading to the darkness and gloom that in turn would stop photosynthesis.

Jellyfish and frogs are both very fragile animals; but both are carnivores feeding on insects, small worms or fishes, and are not directly dependent on green plant production. Moreover, jellyfish and amphibians, as well as some other survivors of this catastrophe, possess larval stages resistant to starvation and cold, whilst dinosaurs and other large-size vertebrates would have been of a much more delicate constitution.

Lionel Cavin, Musée des dinosaures, Espéraza, France

How many inches of snow would be the equivalent of one inch of rain?

The general rule of thumb is twelve. This, however, is a bit like asking: 'How long is a piece of string?'

Skiers will know that the powder snow high on a mountain-top has a consistency not unlike feathers – even with skis on, you can sink in up to your waist. But at the bottom of the slopes, particularly if the snow doesn't melt for a long period, it will progressively recrystallize and pack down, turning into solid ice in time. Ice just at the point of melting has a density that is 92 per cent that of water at room temperature; in other words, ten inches of rain would give eleven inches of ice. Snow, depending upon where you find it, is somewhere between the two extremes.

Terence Hollingworth, Blagnac, France

A TV programme once stated that there are more stars in the universe than there are grains of sand on every beach on the planet. Can anyone prove this?

This may well be true. Estimates suggest that there could be up to 100 billion galaxies in the universe, each with 100 billion stars. However, some galaxies are much smaller than this, so let's say the universe has a total of 1,000 million million million stars. A grain of sand typically has a volume of 0.01 cubic millimetres. If an average sandy beach is fifty metres wide and has sand to a depth of two metres, 1,000 million million million sand grains would form a sandy beach some 100,000 kilometres long, which is about two and a half times the circumference of the earth. So even with huge coastal sand dunes like those at Culbin or Porthcawl, I would guess that the number of stars in the universe exceeds the number of sand grains on the earth's beaches by at least a factor of ten.

Hillary Shaw, School of Geography, University of Leeds

Is there any proof that homeopathic medicine works?

No, but the less proof there is, the more effectively it works.
Les Killip, Newton-le-Willows, Merseyside

There are several levels of evidence for the effectiveness of homeopathy, which has the best research profile of the alternative medical systems.

Thoughtlessly disregarded by the scientific community is so-called 'anecdotal evidence'. Whilst much of this is flimsy, the best carries no small weight. This would include reports of clinical experience by homeopathic doctors who have used conventional methods with less success. Taken together, this material (which is vast) suggests to a fair-minded observer that something interesting is taking place.

Second, there is some good-quality historical evidence, particularly the experience of the American and European homeopathic hospitals in the nineteenth century, where mortality from infectious diseases like cholera was markedly lower than in conventional hospitals. In the modern period, the Society of Homeopaths has published reports on the work of members within primary-care groups in the UK.

Most importantly, a significant body of scientific literature representing, in the main, reports of clinical trials, has accumulated over the past twenty years or so. Four meta-analyses have been published, and the broad agreement is that homeopathic medicines work; indeed, that they work very well.

Where there is still a lack of clarity is the question of how they work. Not that a lack of understanding of a mechanism has ever stopped drugs and therapies being introduced into orthodox medicine.

Dr Denis MacEoin, chairman, The Natural Medicines Society, Newcastle upon Tyne

No properly conducted study has yet produced convincing evidence that it has any more value than a placebo.

The Homeopathic Medicine Research Group, convened by the European Commission, examined 184 published and unpublished reports of controlled trials of homeopathic treatments. Their report (1996) concluded that only seventeen of these trials were conducted well enough to be considered, and whilst some cases may have demonstrated an effect greater than a placebo or no treatment, overall the number of participants in the seventeen trials was too small to permit any conclusions about the effectiveness of any given homeopathic treatment for a specific condition.

This is not surprising. The basic principles of homeopathy, laid down by Samuel Hahnemann in the late 1700s (that diseases are a manifestation of a 'psora' or suppressed itch; that the smaller the dose, the greater the effect), have no demonstrable relationship with each other or with what we now know about human biology. The only people for whom it could be said to 'work' are hard-pressed GPs, who can pass their more persistent and intractable patients on to an 'alternative' practitioner, safe in the knowledge that no great harm is likely to be done.

The best detailed critique of homeopathy is probably still Homeopathy and its Kindred Delusions, first delivered as two lectures by Oliver Wendell Holmes in 1842.

Michael Hutton, Camberwell, London SE5

In the early 1990s, BBC2's QED made a programme in which opponents of homeopathy claimed that its results were due to the placebo effect, and that in carefully conducted double-blind tests homeopathic treatment had failed. The programme makers then conducted an experiment to answer these criticisms.

Most dairy cows suffer from mastitis (an infection of the milk ducts) from time to time, treatment for which involves a vet and antibiotics, and during which the milk has to be discarded. You cannot fool a cow with the placebo effect so, at the suggestion of a homeopathic vet, a large herd was divided into two groups, each with its own water trough. From two similar but suitably marked containers, a liquid was poured into each trough (that is, only one dose was given) and two sealed envelopes, in which were the names of the substances added, were given to the programme makers for safe keeping.

Some weeks later, the farmer was asked about the incidence of mastitis. He explained that the incidence in one group had remained as before, whereas in the other group only one cow had required antibiotic treatment. The envelopes were opened and it was shown that the second group's trough had been treated with a homeopathic remedy and the other with just distilled water or a placebo.

Soroush Ebrahimi (licensed homeopath), South Woodham Ferrers, Essex

Medicines used by homeopaths are mostly diluted to the point where they could contain no molecules of the original substance. Since many scientists have had a materialistic training, their scepticism is understandable. However, the German scientist Fritz-Albert Popp, in a research programme at Kaiserslautern in the 1980s, found that all living organisms possess an electromagnetic energy field that correlates with the main vital functions. The energy readings (photon emission) of the organisms responded to the administration of potentized medicines, but not to placebo.

The French scientist, Jacques Benveniste, was ridiculed when he proposed that water retains a memory of a substance that has been dissolved in it and diluted beyond molecular level. However, scientists at the American Technologies Group in California recently discovered that, when a substance is dissolved in distilled water, shaken, then repeatedly diluted and shaken, clusters of minute ice-crystals form in the water. These ice-crystals remain stable at high temperatures and are maintained by electromagnetic energy, their structure being unique to the substance that was dissolved. This offers a credible explanation for the 'memory of water' concept. It appears therefore that the key to understanding the action of homeopathic remedies lies in the area of energy, as the founder of homeopathy assumed.

Alan Crook, Director of Studies, The College of Homeopathy, London W1

Alan Crook's answer is misleading in the extreme, giving the impression that there is a well-understood and widely accepted physical basis for homeopathic medicine. This is simply not true.

Since 1980 Fritz-Albert Popp has published some seventy-six papers on extremely weak light emissions from living systems. A few other authors have published similar work. It has no discernible relevance to homeopathy, and the physical mechanisms are routine: 142 papers cite Popp's work, and just three of them mention homeopathy in their titles or abstracts.

Jacques Benveniste's result has never been reliably replicated, and there is no explanation of it consistent with modern physics. The 'American Technologies Group' does not appear to publish its results in standard scientific journals, and the supposed explanations regarding 'electromagnetic energy' and the like use scientific parlance in an essentially meaningless way. The explanation regarding 'ice crystals' is anything but credible in conventional scientific terms.

But if an analysis of the literature or scientific data does not convince you of the implausibility of homeopathy, let's try a little common sense. The glass of water I drank with my supper has had innumerable substances dissolved in it during its history, many toxic, coloured or strong tasting. Curiously it was colourless, tasteless and did me no harm.

Professor Harvey Rutt, Highfield, Southampton

Isn't it strange how reading less about homeopathy makes one feel better? It struck me that this might indeed be a homeopathic effect, so I performed an experiment and cut out the two replies from the homeopathists, screwed them up and chucked them into the wastepaper basket. When I examined the hole where they had been in G2 I found, to my astonishment, that their meaning remained imprinted upon the very molecules of the atmosphere! And the meaning was that homeopathy is a load of wind.

Dick Bentley, Southampton

I was saddened to learn that homeopathy doesn't work. Our dog has suffered from car sickness since the day we brought her home from the RSPCA. Tablets from the vet made her groggy but didn't stop her emptying the contents of her stomach. A friend recommended a homeopathic remedy, which we now give her before each journey, and no more sickness. Now how do I tell her that it doesn't work and it's obviously been all in her mind?

Caroline Dearden, York

Proponents, despite the discredited efforts of Benveniste, are facing a century of solid thermodynamics – experimental, calculational and theoretical – which defies their explanations. This is not to say that homeopathy doesn't work, but no solution chemist will take the idea seriously until a homeopathist shows, by accepted method, how a solute-stabilized water envelope (one of Alan Crook's 'crystals') can re-form after the escape of its stabilizing molecule. The tools are available and in daily use; the event has not occurred while anyone was looking.

In addition, drinking water nowadays contains trace amounts of literally thousands of pollutants – carcinogens, teratogens and outright poisons – all of which should be exerting homeopathic effects. Wet chemistry being no respecter of human values, if homeopathy worked as it is described, one might expect us all to be long dead.

Ferren MacIntyre, Galway, Eire

Many years ago my two-year-old son suffered from allergic asthma. The conventional answer then was aggressive steroid treatment, which carried some risks, so my wife suggested the alternative of homeopathy. She was far from convinced about it and I was frankly sceptical but we found a local NHS doctor who also practised as a homeopath and he prescribed a dose of something very dilute.

The result was astounding. The blue, wheezing toddler turned pink within minutes, became able to breathe and would usually drop into a peaceful sleep. The effect was, in scientific terms, decisive, observable and entirely repeatable. Placebo effects, in this case, are as unconvincing an explanation as anything else I have read in twenty-five years. Like Professor Harvey Rutt, I find the ideas of water memory and enormous dilution apparently risible – but the corollary of this is to find a better explanation, not to damn homeopathy as impossible.

As Lavoisier, Pasteur and so many others understood, good science always fits the hypothesis to the evidence. History is littered with tales of the arrogant and the foolish who have preferred the easier route of reversing that logic or who have denied that something happens simply because they can't explain why it does.

Chris Woolf, Liskeard, Cornwall

I once saw a TV science programme in which the presenter encouraged a quietly steaming Icelandic geyser to dramatically 'blow' a few seconds later by tipping into it a large quantity of soap bars. Can anyone explain this phenomenon?

I have seen this done. The geyser pool is at the top of a hole in the ground, perhaps fifty metres or more deep, full of water that is continuously heated from the bottom by the adjacent mass of hot rock. Just prior to a natural 'blow', the water towards the bottom will have reached a temperature well above normal boiling point, but it is prevented from boiling by pressure from the column above. Left to itself, the water will eventually become too hot for this unstable situation to persist; steam-bubbles will form, and then the geyser spontaneously 'blows'.

To please an impatient audience, a travel guide can induce premature discharge by dropping soap into the pool. Arriving near the bottom, the soap starts to dissolve; as with any other solute, its presence depresses the boiling point of water, and steam-bubbles start to form and rise. Their arrival at the top usually causes a violent spillage of some water out of the pool. This reduces the weight of the column and its pressure, causing boiling of the whole column, as in a natural eruption.

Tom Hering, Kegworth, Derby.

Tom Hering is right to point out that the pressure exerted by the column of water above the geyser's reservoir suppresses boiling; water in a reservoir under a column fifty metres deep would boil at nearly 160°C. However, he explains the triggering action of soap in terms of boiling-point depression whereas, in fact, adding solutes to the water in the reservoir will produce a boiling-point rise – so the water would have to reach an even higher temperature to boil.

The same trick of triggering the geyser is carried out daily in New Zealand at the Lady Knox geyser near Rotorua. There, less than a kilogramme of soap flakes (much less than the forty kilogrammes used in Iceland) is dropped into the geyser spout. Very quickly, the liquid begins to foam and then the geyser 'blows' dramatically. A small concentration of soap will cause foaming in the water column; the density of the foam is considerably lower than the density of water, so the pressure in the reservoir falls and boiling can then occur.

Leo Pyle, Henley-on-Thames

What, generally, would have been the cause of death following a crucifixion?

Suffocation. The crucified person had to lift himself up in order to make each breath; as his strength gave out this became impossible. The gospel accounts suggest that Jesus deliberately gave himself over to suffocation when he felt his work was done. The legs of the two men crucified with him were broken to expedite their deaths; unable to lift themselves up, they would have died almost immediately.

Revd Dr Michael Hinton, Dover, Kent

Long before the supposed death of Christ, the Phoenicians carried out the first crucifixions using a single stake in the ground. The criminal would be tied to it and left to die of thirst or starvation. By the time the Romans, Greeks, Egyptians, etc. got the hang of it, it was considered the most humiliating form of death. Only slaves and the worst criminals were classed as crucifixion fodder.

After the single stake, crosses were brought into play, with sometimes three or four arms. Not forgetting, of course, St Andrew's cross. The Scottish flag was modelled on this design, after the patron saint was put to death on one such cross.

Death upon a cross was quick for the weak, but could linger if one was strong. Torment would be increased by the constant sun on the naked skin, the flies nibbling away and the choking desert sand. In years to come, crucifixions would take place with the cross (and victim) inverted. This was an improvement, as unconciousness would be mercifully quick.

Crucifixion was abolished by Constantine in the fourth century. The French ignored this, though, and crucified the killer of Charles the Righteous as recently as AD 1127.

Darren Hart, Great Barr, Birmingham

The rabbit has no apparent defence mechanisms. Given its vulnerability, what is the benefit of the white patch on its tail? Is it a target?

When a rabbit senses danger, he picks up his tail and runs. The white patch on his tail is a warning sign to those rabbits behind him that danger is at hand.

May Robertson, St Leonards, East Kilbride

Lack of defence mechanisms? What about its big eyes, big ears, high speed, burrow-dwelling habit, gregarious behaviour and potential to breed like rabbits?

Chris du Feu, Beckingham, Notts

Not only could our ex-laboratory rabbit throw an impressively thumping kick, his *coup de grâce* was the accurately aimed 'arc of urine to the eye'. Our cat Edward was unfortunately a frequent recipient of such tactics but Humphrey could also hit high enough to get humans too.

Judith Anderson, Whitchurch, Cardiff

My 1975 Shorter OED gives a definition for a word 'columbin', which is apparently 'an insulating substance . . . used for the sockets of Jablochkoff's candle'. However, it doesn't give a definition for the candle. I'm in the dark – could anybody illuminate me?

Paul Jablochkoff was a Russian telegraph engineer who set off to emigrate to America but only got as far as Paris in 1875. There he became interested in electric arc lighting. In this form of lighting an intense spark or arc is drawn between two pieces of carbon, which are gradually burned away. Most of the resulting light comes from the white-hot tips of the carbon. The gap between carbons has to be kept constant for the arc to be maintained, and various clockwork and other ingenious mechanisms were developed to do this.

Jablochkoff's solution was much simpler. His 'candle' consisted of two parallel carbon rods separated at a fixed distance by an insulating material (plaster of Paris initially). The tips of the rods were joined electrically by a thinner piece of carbon that burned out when the candle was 'switched on' and the arc established. As the carbon rods burned away, so the plaster of Paris crumbled away in the heat. Like a wax candle, the Jablochkoff candle was gradually consumed, each one lasting perhaps ninety minutes.

A later improvement to the efficiency of the candle involved replacing the plaster of Paris with certain insulating salts (including 'columbin') that glowed when heated. The candles were used for street lighting in Paris after being demonstrated at the 1878 Exposition Universelle. The Victoria Embankment in London was the first scene of their use in Britain, and then only when subsidized by French industrial interests. (Source: Brian Bower, *Lengthening the Day: A History of Lighting Technology*, OUP).

Richard Lawrence, Oxford

Are human brain transplants ever likely to become a reality?

In fifteen years or so brain repair will be established medical procedure, involving the transplantation of tissue into the brain. However, transplantations from one head to another are extremely unlikely ever to occur. Given what we know about things like memory and personality (not to mention the immune system), it is almost definite that one person will never be able to have a transplant of the 'mind' of another.

Tom Stafford, Department of Psychology, University of Sheffield

Can you repeat the question? My mind's elsewhere.

Ken Proud, Medan, Indonesia

Brain transplants cannot exist; what is meant is body transplants. The misunderstanding dates from long ago. The Greeks believed that the soul – the 'I' or the essence of the person – resided in the diaphragm. Most people these days would agree that the person is based in the brain.

The term decapitation is also nonsense; the person is deprived of the body so it should be decorporation. Perhaps a brain will get another body in the future but even if a body with an existing brain were connected to an extra brain, it should be called a body-sharing operation, not a brain transplant.

Douwe Verkuyl, Bulawayo, Zimbabwe

HIV is sometimes described as 'sophisticated', as it appears able to adapt its defences to resist attack by drugs. Are viruses generally highly evolved or are they primitive organisms, given that they appear to wish to kill their host? Are there viruses that develop a symbiotic relationship with their host?

When HIV infects human cells it starts making billions of copies of itself. As it does this it is unsophisticated, since it has no mechanism to check those copies. It makes lots of mistakes and these genetic mistakes may lead to a virus that has different properties, such as resistance to an HIV drug. A virus gains no advantage in killing its host. Some viruses live happily with one species but rapidly kill another if they accidentally infect it.

We are infected with many different viruses. You could not call this a symbiotic relationship as we probably do not benefit from it.

Our immune systems control these viruses and a few of them could cause problems if we had damage to our immunity.

Dr Simon Portsmouth, London N15

It is now generally agreed that mitochondria and chloroplasts were viruses which had invaded early primitive cells and helped distinguish the animal and plant kingdoms. They have their own DNA and are not inherited via nuclear mitosis, but via the oocite cytoplasm. As chemical factories, they are vital to cell function and provide the classic example of a symbiotic relationship.

David Spilsbury, Cannon Hill, Birmingham

Mr Spilsbury seems to have confused viruses and bacteria. Mitochondria and chloroplasts are in fact believed to be derived from cyanobacteria.

I am not aware of any truly symbiotic viruses, but there are many examples of highly sophisticated viruses that cause little disease. One example is Epstein-Barr virus (the cause of glandular fever). This is a highly complex virus that in the developed world is present as a persistent infection in the overwhelming majority of over-eighteens, of whom only a very small proportion develop illness. This is down to the many mechanisms that the virus has developed to mask its presence from its host's immune response, and to avoid damaging its host.

Rob Jordan, Department of Pathology and Microbiology, University of Bristol

It should firstly be pointed out that the 'wish' of viruses is not to 'kill their host', but to replicate their genetic material as much as possible. This can sometimes involve the killing of their host, but not always.

For example, there is a class of viruses known as 'temperate bacteriophages', which infect bacterial cells. When infecting a cell, one of these viruses makes a decision: if the cell that it has infected is in a harsh environment, then it uses the cell's replication machinery to make more viruses. It then bursts the cell, allowing the liberation of these newly formed virus particles. Alternatively, if the bacterial cell appears to be thriving, the virus lies dormant in the cell. In this way, it is still replicating its genetic material, because every time the bacterial cell duplicates its DNA, the viral DNA is duplicated also.

This latter process is called lysogeny. Whilst some dormant viruses appear to be merely 'taking their host cell for a ride', other viruses actually provide their host with useful genetic material, which can aid the chances of survival for the bacterium in certain environments. Indeed, some temperate bacteriophages provide their hosts with genes that cause disease (epidemic cholera is thought to have arisen in this way). As such, these bacteriophages are helping their bacterial hosts, at the cost of the human race. Though dormant viruses usually retain the capacity to kill their host, the dormant virus–host interaction can probably be described as a symbiotic relationship, and a rather sinister one at that.

Derek Thorne, Department of Jungle Biology, Cambridge University

From the 1920s to the 1960s, visions of the 'city of the future' often included some sort of monorail. What were the supposed advantages of this means of transport, and why was it rarely adopted in practice?

The great – indeed, almost insuperable – problem about the monorail is switching trains from one track to another, or adding and subtracting carriages to or from a train. On a conventional railway this is done by moving point-blades a couple of inches, but a monorail has to shift the entire load-bearing track. This requires a construction like a swing-bridge, and is prohibitively expensive. Therefore, with the exception of slow-moving amusement-park or garden festival lines, and short airport or university-campus links, where the cars are really horizontal lifts, the monorail has remained on the architects' drawing-board.

The exceptions are an electric line above the River Wupper in North-Rhine Westphalia and a funicular in Dresden. The Irish, though, managed to run the steam-powered Listowel–Ballybunnion line from 1887 to 1924, and the British authorities in Patiala, India, built a system – also quite long-lived – in which steam locomotives ran on a single rail with 'outrigger' road wheels.

Christopher Harvie, London N1

I saw an airliner leave a double vapour trail at high altitude. Soon this broke up into pairs of streaks, like 'equals' signs across the sky. Then each pair bowed outwards into two semicircles, so as to look like a row of 'colons'. Can anyone explain?

I have part of the explanation, but I left the Royal Aircraft Establishment before we had cracked all the mathematics.

The flows around an aircraft wing, which generate the lift force, result in a circulation of air that leaves the wing in the form of vortices, rotating clockwise from the starboard wing and counter-clockwise from the port wing. These tightly formed, rapidly rotating cylinders of air attract the vapour trailed from the jet engines, making the pair of vortices clearly visible. The subsequent patterns, described by the questioner, are formed by the phases of the breakdown of the vortices some distance behind the aircraft.

The research into vortex wakes of aircraft was particularly important in the 1970s, as the new generation of heavy jumbo jets developed and Concorde was being introduced. There was a concern that both the heavy conventional jets and Concorde could leave vortices in their wake during the approaches to landing that would upset following aircraft, particularly light aircraft. Landing separation distances were increased to ensure that safety margins were maintained.

William Sargeant, Diss, Norfolk

How did Amundsen know that he had reached the South Pole? Did Scott check that Amundsen's cairn was in the right place (or would that have been ungentlemanly)? Is the cairn still there?

Roald Amundsen closely followed the 170th longitude on the last part of his journey. He used all the navigational techniques available to him: several sextants, chronometers, an odometer on a wheel on one of the sledges and the current almanac. At the Pole on the summer solstice, the sun should circle the earth at a constant height. On 17 December 1911, just three days prior to this, the chronometer indicated that he was near the pole. So he began measuring the height of the sun over a twenty-six-hour period.

Like any observations, Amundsen's sextant measurements for the sun's height are subject to some error. His handwritten measurements, in Norwegian, are reproduced in his book *Sydpolen*. He did not give a numerical figure indicating how near he came to the pole, but only presented his raw data in his observation book.

We analysed his sun–height measurements, and by calculating the most probable error we believe he was within 0.45 kilometres of the pole. This degree of uncertainty along the whole length of the meridian is insignificant, but might become a point of debate as to who came nearest the pole rather than who was there first. To determine this we need Scott's data, but these are not available to us.

Drs Marjorie Barrett-Gultepe and Ercin Gultepe, Vail, Arizona, USA

I have heard it said that the Basque people have a higher proportion of people with O negative blood than other populations and that this is because they are the oldest, ethnically pure group in Europe. Is there any truth in this? Is blood group an inherited characteristic?

The origins of the Basques have long been debated. Mark Kurlansky in his book, *The Basque History of the World*, outlines many of these theories. The main reason that they are considered separate from other nationalities in Europe is that their language is not Indo-European and is unlike any other language in the world. Basques identify themselves by their language; to be a Basque – *Euskera* – means to be a speaker of the Basque language, not a member of a 'nation'.

One of the more scientific attempts to discover their origins was an investigation of their blood group. It was found that Basques have the highest concentration of type O blood in the world – more than 50 per cent of the population, with an even higher percentage in remote areas where Basque is more widely spoken. Basques also have a higher incidence of Rhesus-negative blood than anyone else in the world. Some scientists have argued that this demonstrates that Basques are direct descendants of Cro-Magnon man because other areas where Cro-Magnon man existed, such as the Atlas Mountains in Morocco or the Canaries, also have a high incidence of Rhesus-negative.

Rhesus-negative blood in a pregnant woman can fatally poison a foetus with Rhesus-positive blood, and the Basques still have a relatively high incidence of miscarriage and stillbirths. It has been argued that this is why the Basques remained a small population in a confined, mostly mountainous area while other populations in Spain, France and Portugal expanded.

Tim Chadwick, London NW5

Yes. In the smaller context, you inherit your blood group from your parents. In the larger one, your parents inherited their blood groups and other genetic markers from their ancestors.

Population frequencies of ABO, Rhesus and other gene markers are linked to racial ancestry and can be used to trace geographic origins. For example, North American 'native' groups have identifiable gene and blood group frequencies. Rarity in those populations of blood groups

A2, B, D and Rhesus suggests a narrow common original gene pool of Mongolian-Asian origin. Although analysis of more than blood groups is required and timing remains uncertain, such factors suggest that there were three, or possibly four, specific migrations into North America across the long-submerged Beingia land bridge.

Philip Hall, Faculty of Medicine, University of Manitoba, Winnipeg, Canada

The idea that the Basques might be a relic population that had suffered no significant admixture was put forward in the 1930s and 1940s. It was based on the observation that the Basques showed high frequencies of blood group O, the lowest frequency in Europe of group B, and the highest in the world of Rhesus-negative. The same idea can be dated back to at least 1539, although this time on linguistic grounds.

Blood groups are indeed inherited and therefore are genetic traits, but observations based on only one or just a few genetic systems cannot reliably reproduce the whole history of populations. A more recent and comprehensive work, including many genes, showed that although the main affiliation of the Basques was with the other European populations, they nevertheless showed some distinctive features. One interpretation was that Basques were a locally evolved population from prehistoric times (30,000 years ago) who resisted much of the genetic homogenization brought about by the expansion of early agriculturists across Europe about 10,000 years ago.

If the Basques were once very distinctive genetically, perhaps for socio-ecological reasons, that difference has largely been eroded by more recent interbreeding with surrounding populations. From the historical record it is clear that Basques, although aware of their cultural identity, have contributed significantly to the history of the wider world. They were skilful navigators and shipbuilders (some say they were taught by the Vikings), as well as successful entrepreneurs, who contributed to Spanish industrialization (which brought in a substantial number of workers from the poorest regions of Spain).

Santos Alonso and John Armour, Institute of Genetics, University of Nottingham

There is no such thing as ethnic purity. The blood factor in question is not O negative but Rhesus-negative, which has an incidence gradient: it is absent among Asians and the Amerind; rare among Africans;

present in 10–15 per cent of peoples of European origin and in around 25 per cent of Basques. One interpretation is that the pre-agricultural inhabitants of Europe were 100 per cent Rhesus-negative and gradually mixed with westward-expanding Rhesus-positive peoples from the East. The Basques would have mixed slightly less than other Europeans.

The concept of ethnic purity is scientifically unsound and politically tends to make people believe in 'ancestral rights'. That's why the title of the latest Basque Nationalist Party manifesto ('To be, in order to decide') curdles my Basque blood.

Anton Digon, Vitória, Basque Country

For many years the Japanese have been allowed to kill whales 'for scientific research'. What can there possibly be left to find out by now? Has anyone ever seen any of these reports?

There is still a great deal to be learned about whales. The issue is whether the knowledge gained through the Japanese Whale Research Programme is worth the cost to an arguably endangered species and to the integrity of the international ban on commercial whaling.

The Japanese take more than 400 minke whales each year in the Southern Ocean, ostensibly for the scientific research that is permitted under the terms of the worldwide ban. In 1997, the Japanese Institute for Cetacean Research published a bibliography listing more than 150 scientific papers written between 1989 and 1996, based on research conducted under special whaling permits. The topics included demographic parameters; reproductive segregation; the worldwide population structure of minke whales; and the fatty-acid composition of blubber oils. Some of the papers were published in standard scientific journals such as *Marine Mammal Science*; nearly all were published either in an annual report of the International Whaling Commission or by the Japanese government. Unpublished papers were presented to the IWC Scientific Committee or various veterinary, chemistry or fisheries symposia. The reports are available through the IWC headquarters in Impington, Cambridge.

However, because much of the whale meat finds its way into the Japanese market, where it sells for as much as US$100 per kilogram, there is widespread suspicion that the motivation behind the research permits is commercial.

William Dunlap, Quinnipiac College School of Law, Connecticut, USA

When Japan first launched its 'scientific' whaling programme in the Antarctic in 1987, its press reported that the intended purpose of the programme was to keep the commercial whaling industry alive until the moratorium on commercial whaling (which had come into effect the previous year) could be overturned. So far, Japan has killed 4,655 whales under the guise of scientific whaling – of which 2,037 have been taken from within the Southern Ocean Sanctuary. The meat from these 'researched' whales is sold on the domestic market.

When a special group of International Whaling Commission scientists convened a workshop to review the Antarctic programme after it had run for eight years, the group (which included Japanese scientists) unanimously concluded that the data produced by the programme 'were not required for management'. Every year the IWC passes a resolution calling on Japan to stop whaling and each year it is ignored, despite the fact that Japan is required under Articles 65 and 120 on the Law of the Sea to cooperate with the IWC.

The Greenpeace ship, *Arctic Sunrise*, is currently in the Southern Ocean Sanctuary, taking non-violent direct action against the Japanese whaling fleet, and while we will continue to do all we can at sea it is ultimately up to governments to make Japan stop.

Richard Page (whale campaigner), Greenpeace UK, London N1

Is there any actual cell or bone or fibre that remains in your body from birth until death, or does everything die or renew during a lifetime?

Female babies are born with a surplus (a lifetime supply) of fully formed eggs (oocytes) within their ovaries – and that's all they'll ever have. Those eggs that have not been ovulated over a woman's reproductive lifespan will remain with her until her death.

Rebecca Pritchard, St Andrews, Fife

Rebecca Pritchard is mistaken in her statement that the eggs (oocytes) of a woman that do not ovulate during her reproductive life remain with her until death. At birth a female child's ovaries contain about 2 million oocytes, a number that is reduced by degeneration and resorption (atresia) to about 300,000 at puberty. Atresia is the fate of all but about 400 of these eggs – those which undergo ovulation – and by the onset of the menopause very few remain. None is present after the establishment of the menopause.

Bob Heys (retired consultant gynaecologist), Ripponden, Halifax

One such site is the lens of the eye. Since these cells are not replaced, they must be protected from damage, especially by ultraviolet light.

David Kessel, Wayne State University School of Medicine, Detroit, Michigan, USA

You are born with your full complement of neurons, which are the cells of the brain. Loss of a neuron is irrevocable, hence the devastating effects of a stroke. Recovery of function after stroke results not from growth of replacement neurons, but from a rewiring of the connections of the brain, demonstrating the superb plasticity of the most complicated object in the universe.

On the other hand, the constituents of every cell, bone and fibre in your body, including every neuron, are constantly being replenished. Thus you die with different atoms, molecules, amino acids, proteins, fats, etc., throughout your body than those you started with. What keeps the entire body form from dissolving into mush as its pieces are being replaced is one of the great unanswered questions of biology.

Ralph Siegel, Center for Molecular and Behavioral
Neuroscience, Rutgers University, New Jersey, USA

Would mankind have evolved differently if the dinosaurs had not disappeared 65 million years ago?

If the dinosaurs had not disappeared, humankind simply wouldn't exist. At their apogee, the dinosaurs had a firm clawhold on just about every animal niche, from three-foot-tall egg-stealers up to forty-five-ton herbivores.

When the dinosaurs became extinct, the mammal line consisted essentially of scruffy little beasts that danced around their toes and tried not to get trodden on. It was only terrible luck that consigned the lizards to the evolutionary dustbin and let the versatile, but frankly pathetic, mammals enter the arena and flourish. Whatever it was that caused the demise of the dinosaurs, it must also have been enough to ensure that the peanut-brained placentals would eventually become intelligent primates. The potential for intellectual development had never solely been ours.

Duncan McMillan, Highgate, London N6

Yes, we would be able to run much faster!

Jeff Williams, Hengoed, Mid Glamorgan

There would be car-stickers with the message: 'A stegosaurus is for life, not just for Christmas.'

Graham Guest, London SE19

Probably. Some scientists think that evolution follows the path of contingency, which means that anything could alter the direction of evolution in such a way that its products would be very different if something important happened differently in a previous time. Mammals existed 65 million years ago, but they were small and shy; with the extinction of the dinosaurs, mammals had the chance to evolve into a more important and diverse group, from which humankind evolved. So, according to these scientists, without a larger 'ecological space' for the further evolution of mammals, it is probable that human beings would never have appeared.

Other scientists think that, given certain environmental pressures and provided that there are organisms on which natural selection can work, it is likely that some types of animals will evolve sooner or later. This means that perhaps human beings would not have appeared, but some kind of equivalent (maybe a bipedal and social animal with a big brain) would have.

Fernando Larrea, Department of Zoology, University of Western Ontario, Canada

The intervening years would have given ample time for adaptive

strategies to compensate for our giant reptile companions. Many of us would probably have evolved to be inedible (perhaps covered with poisonous sacs), or to stick in hungry dino throats (resembling large walking chestnut burrs with access to language).
Reuben Saunders, Ithaca, New York, USA

Is it theoretically possible to run on the surface of the sea (a) if you run fast enough or (b) if the salinity was increased? If (a), how fast would you have to run?

I have several times seen an animal run on the surface of a creek in the rainforest in Guyana, South America. This creature is locally known as the 'bush motorbike' and runs across creeks from one bank to the other when it has been sufficiently startled.

I hesitate to say 'seen' because it leaves only a blurred trace across the retina of the eye and some tell-tale ripples. I suppose that in making the crossing it owes all of its propulsion to the abandoned riverbank, rather than the surface of the water, and thus is not strictly running on water, but skiing.
Jeremy Doyle, Maputo, Mozambique

Further to Jeremy Doyle's reply: James Glasheen and Thomas McMahon of Harvard University deciphered the physics underlying the feat of the basilisk lizards of Central America. Apparently there are two components to the upward force that keeps the running lizard above the water surface.

1. The slap component: the force you feel when you rapidly strike a water surface with the open hand. In the case of the basilisk's foot the slap provides about 23 per cent of the upward force.
2. The stroke component. The fringed five-toed foot flares out, trapping an air pocket below it as it moves down through the water surface. This force component provides the rest of the support force. Most importantly, by slanting its foot backwards and slipping it out of the water surface while it is surrounded by the escaping trapped air, the creature avoids any drag. Incidentally a medium-sized lizard takes about twenty steps a second.

As for humans, there is little chance of emulating the basilisk's feat. To get close, a twelve-stone man would have to run at a speed approaching 65 mph and generate fifteen times as much power in his leg muscles as humans are capable of.

Dick Jones, Leigh-on-Sea, Essex

Is it ever 'too cold to snow'?

Freezing weather is always associated with anticyclonic conditions: that is, high pressure, clear skies and light winds. The cold air under these conditions is very dry; as evidenced by chapped lips, dry hands and static shocks when you get out of your car. The low moisture content of the air and the calm conditions make it impossible for clouds to form and for moisture to precipitate out as snow. It is, in effect, too cold to snow.

Snow only falls when an advancing mass of relatively warm air meets cold anticyclonic air. At this junction, the mass of cold air – being denser – pushes under the warm air, causing it to rise. As the warm air rises the water vapour in the air becomes saturated due to the falling pressure and some of it eventually condenses out to form cloud. If the conditions are right, the water droplets in the cloud form ice crystals, which coalesce and fall to the ground as snow. The air temperature at ground level has to be below 4°C for the snow not to melt and turn to rain on its way down, but this need not be the case and it is unlikely to be extremely cold. Indeed, the temperature will be slowly rising as the snow begins to fall.

Terence Hollingworth, Blagnac, France

Terence Hollingworth's answer is correct as far as the UK and maritime northern Europe is concerned. In more polar latitudes, or continental climates that are less affected by the tempering effects of the oceans, warm front conditions often occur at far lower temperatures. The 'warm' air merely needs to be warmer than the cold air that it meets and rises above.

My sister in Minneapolis reports that it snows plenty there with ambient temperatures of around -20°C for much of the winter.

Theoretically, there is no lower temperature limit for the mass of cold air although, as in the UK, it would generally feel slightly warmer once it begins to snow.
Peter Mackay, London SE24

Do you sweat when you are swimming? If so, how do you know?

After a thirty-minute swim in my local pool, I drink a half-litre bottle of water while drying and dressing. I drink because I'm thirsty. I'm thirsty because I'm dehydrated. I'm dehydrated because I have been sweating.
May Robertson, St Leonards, East Kilbride

May Robertson is surely mistaken as to the cause of her dehydration – unless she swims in a hot pool. The reason the body sweats is to lose heat and maintain normal body temperature, and, where I swim, vigorous exercise is needed to create heat to do that.

However, when the body is chilled, for example in your average swimming pool (by heat loss to the cooler water from parts immersed, and by evaporation of that water from the skin, from parts not immersed), the blood 'thickens'. This happens because peripheral blood vessels contract, to reduce heat loss, and the blood therefore has to lose volume to prevent an increase in blood pressure. Water is removed from the blood and leaves the body via the bladder.

Hence the dehydration experienced by Ms Robertson.
Amanda Fergusson, Galston, Ayrshire

If today's life expectancy is about double what it was in ancient times, why does the Bible assert that man's allotted span is 'threescore years and ten'?

'Life expectancy' is the length of life that the average baby could expect at birth. As such, it is purely a mathematical construct and has little to do with real lengths of life over historical periods. In times – and environments – where perinatal mortality is high and childhood illnesses are often fatal, the average lifetime will be consequently low. Also, fatal accidents are similarly related to ages and places where life is hazardous, for example, through unsafe working conditions and war.

However, the fact that large numbers of children die young does not mean that those surviving to adulthood do not live to a ripe old age. Visit any ancient cemetery and you will find plenty of septuagenarians, the odd octagenarians and even nonagenarians who lived and died 200–300 years ago.

David Spilsbury, Cannon Hill, Birmingham

'Lifespan', the maximum age to which any human being can live under ideal circumstances, is now thought to be 110–120 years.

J. D. Montague (*Journal of the Royal Society of Medicine*, 1994) compared the length of life of men who survived into adulthood in ancient Greece and Rome with similar samples from three other periods. He concluded that individuals born before 100 BC lived as long (median seventy-two years) as those who died in the periods 1850–1899 and 1900–1949 (median seventy-one and seventy-one and a half years). Only those who died between 1950 and 1990 had significantly longer lives (median seventy-eight years). So the Biblical statistician seems to have been both accurate about his/her own time and prescient about the future.

Michael Hutton, Camberwell, London

Michael Hutton is in error in attributing to some Biblical statistician the estimate of human lifespan of threescore years and ten. It comes from a psalmist together with a proviso that this may be extended to fourscore years (Psalm 90). Far more explicit is Genesis 6: 3 that 'his days shall be an hundred and twenty years'. This forecast has rarely been exceeded despite the passage of years.

John Wynne, Otley, Yorks

With the patriarchs living such long lives (Adam 930 years, Seth 912, Enos 905, Cainan 910, Mahalaleel 895, Jared 962, Enoch 365 not out, Methuselah 969, Lamech 777, Noah 950 — Genesis 5 and 9), the ancients could stand a lot of infant mortality and still have an average lifespan of seventy.

John Gill, Heswall, Wirral

What is the most successful genome DNA sequence in nature? Human? Virus?

Success biologically is the ability to reproduce, to pass on your DNA. In this, a virus is much more efficient than anything else, as it uses the host organism's materials and resources to replicate itself. A human must find a partner, become pregnant for nine months, give birth and then raise the baby until it can fend for itself. A virus does not have to do any of these, and so it can be said to be more successful.

Steve Cargill (biological sciences student), University of Edinburgh

In terms of numbers, bacteria, from which all other organisms have evolved, have always been the most numerous in terms of weight. A very rough estimate is given in Stephen Jay Gould's latest book, *Life's Grandeur*: the potential mass of underground bacteria is comparable to all the living mass (animal, plant) at the surface. Bacteria 'may represent life's only common mode throughout the universe'.

M. A. Reynolds, London E5

High on the list must be the genes coding for the respiratory enzymes in every cell, which are ultimately responsible for getting usable energy from foods like carbohydrates. They are found in every organism, from bacteria to humans.

Dave Headey, Faringdon, Oxon

Baron Frankenstein is popularly reputed to have harnessed electrical energy from thunderstorms. Could this ever be done? Could it be fed into the National Grid?

I do not know whether electrical energy from thunderstorms could be harnessed, but Frankenstein did not attempt it. Mary Shelley was, wisely, vague as to the means he used to bring his creation to life, although he seems to have had some sort of apparatus for generating electricity. Before writing the story, Mary had taken part in discussions with her husband, her friends and Byron, on 'galvanism' (electricity) and the experiments conducted by Erasmus Darwin.

Nor was Frankenstein a baron; he was a middle-class science student from Geneva. The questioner is drawing on Hollywood versions, not on Mary Shelley's creation.

Jim Fyrth, Totnes, Devon

Further to Jim Fyrth's answer, an account of Erasmus Darwin's medical use of electricity in treating Josiah Wedgwood's daughter Mary-Anne is to be found in Wedgwood's correspondence of 1779:

'Our little girl, Mary-Ann [sic], breeds her teeth very hardly, and unfortunately several of them are pushing forward at the same time. This brought on convulsions which lasted thirteen hours without intermission the first attack ... and when this left her we found she had lost the use of her arm and leg on one side ... Dr Darwin was here on Friday ... and ordered our little girl to be electrified two or three times a day on the side affected and to be continued for some weeks.'

A further description of an experiment to harness electricity to promote growth is to be found in Volume III of Arthur Young's A Six Month's Tour through the North of England (1771). Writing of Mr Clarke of Belford, he reports: 'An experiment he tried of the effect of electricity on vegetation, deserves attention; he planted two turneps in two boxes, each containing 24lb of earth: He kept them in the same exposure, and all circumstances the same to each, save that one was electrified twice a day, for two months, at the end of which time it was in full growth, the skin bursting, and weighed 9lb. The other, at the end of four months, did not quite reach that weight: a strong proof that the electric fire had a remarkable power in promoting and quickening the vegetation.'

Whether anything resulted from this experiment I have no idea, but I believe a Mr Raby related something similar to the Royal Society in 1788.

Lionel Burman, West Kirby, Wirral

Do magnets work in space? If so, where do they point to?

Yes, magnets do work in space. Ferromagnetic material (which the magnets used in compasses are made of) responds to the presence of a magnetic field, however and wherever that field is produced.

A magnetic field has a sense of direction, and magnets tend to line up with that direction. Whichever way a magnet points therefore depends on which direction the magnetic field points in the given place. In the case of a terrestrial compass this will generally be the direction of the earth's magnetic field, but this can change if you place another magnet near by.

Large astronomical bodies (such as the earth, the sun and even entire galaxies) tend to produce magnetic fields that pervade the space around them. The earth's magnetic field is thought to be generated by a kind of dynamo acting in its molten core. (The moon, on the other hand, generates virtually no magnetic field; it is too small to produce a dynamo.)

A magnet in space would feel the earth's magnetic field if it were near the earth and would tend to point towards the magnetic North Pole, just as it would on the earth's surface. The strength of the field drops off as you move farther away from the earth, so, at sufficiently large distances, the fields produced by other bodies can affect the magnet. Near the sun, for example, the earth has a negligible effect but the sun's own magnetic field is stronger, so the magnet would point towards the sun's 'North Pole'.

Farther afield, away from any stars, the Milky Way itself contains a magnetic field caused by the dynamo effect of galactic rotation. The magnet would therefore tend to line up in whatever direction this, rather complicated, galactic field was pointing.

Dr Peter Coles, Astronomy Unit, Queen Mary and Westfield College, London E1

What determines whether a tree becomes oil, coal or a fossil?

Oil, coal and natural gas were all created by the process of fossilization. What determines whether trees (or more commonly other, less robust vegetation) become coal is the conditions under which the dead vegetation finds itself after it dies. Most will rot away naturally on the surface, through the action of bacteria, insects, fungi and other parasites. However, this natural decay can be prevented when vegetation is quickly covered by layers of detritus and soil, or is silted under water.

The transformation into coal took place under these conditions, starting during the Carboniferous Period about 340–270 million years ago, and at high pressures, as layer upon layer built up. Basically, coal is fossilized vegetation.

Although peat is thought to represent the first stage in this process, the conditions that caused coal to be formed do not exist today. The Carboniferous flora were very different from what we know – much more abundant and more subject to be trapped in conditions that prevent decay.

Oil was formed in a similar manner, but in this case oil represents the remains of long-dead sea-creatures, not vegetation.

Iain Fenton, Tillicoultry, Clack.

I worked as a miner for several years, and when we removed the coal seam we would find fossil trees in the roof. The bark had changed to coal and showed as a thin ring perhaps two or three feet in diameter in the newly exposed roof. The wood that had been enclosed in the bark had apparently rotted away, leaving a cavity that had filled with sediment and turned to blue shale. We called these fossils 'caterenases' or 'cats'. They were regarded with some fear by miners because, as the roof squeezed down on to the supports, they were prone to slip out without warning like a huge piledriver.

George Storey, Morpeth, Northumb.

The Concise Oxford Thesaurus lists types of curve: for example, arc, spiral, etc. The list ends with a curve called the Witch of Agnesi. No other information is given. What kind of curve is this, and how did it get its name?

The Italian mathematician Maria Agnesi, born in Milan in 1718, was appointed Professor of Higher Mathematics at the University of Bologna in 1749 by Pope Benedict XIV. In her book *Instituzioni Analitiche ad Uso della Giovent Italiana* (1738), she thoroughly studied the curve known as Witch of Agnesi, whose analytic equation can be written as $y = a^3/(x^2+a^2)$ where a is the amplitude of the curve at $x = 0$.

The reason for the curve's name is a translation error. In Italian *versiera* means curve, but over time it was misprinted as *avversiera*, which means she-devil or witch.

Agnesi gave up mathematics after her father's death in 1752. She dedicated the rest of her life to helping the poor of Milan, becoming director of the Pio Albergo Trivulzio in 1771. She died in her native city in 1799.

Dr M. J. F. Cortina Borja, Department of Statistics, University of Oxford

Why do sharks swim with their dorsal fin above the surface? What benefit does this give them?

This is a fallacy brought about by cartoonists and their ilk. The dorsal fin is in fact a highly effective balancing mechanism – a keel in reverse, if you like. The fact that most sharks are encountered by human swimmers at the surface doubtless has more to do with the habits of humans than of sharks.

Daleep Heyer (marine biologist), Oxford

Sharks are frequently seen on the surface because that is where they feed. Hence the only useful advice to any swimmer who finds a potentially dangerous shark near by: dive, get below it and there is a real chance that it will ignore you and swim away – or even swim around benignly and let you take its photo, as Jacques Cousteau's boys discovered many years ago.

Chris Jones, St Albans, Herts

Has anyone ever seriously researched time travel?

J. W. Dunne's *An Experiment with Time* (1927) caused a sensation when first published. It proposed a concept of time in which time travel seemed possible. Max Planck could not fault Dunne's maths but said that his premises were incapable of proof and so were unscientific. *Reverse Time Travel* (1995), by the scientist B. Chapman, explores the subject in depth and, while not ruling out time travel, makes it sound pretty unattractive.

Of course, cosmologists have a deep interest in the arrow of time and the following works have information of interest to the potential time tourist: *The Mind of God* by Paul Davis (1992); *The Anthropic Cosmological Principle* by Barrow and Tipler (1996), and *A Brief History of Time* by Stephen Hawking (1988).

I hesitate to promote my own book, *Time Travel for Beginners* (2005), published by Farland Press.

Peter Sharp, Warkworth, New Zealand

I believe Margaret Thatcher had the British returning to the Victorian era. And let us not forget that Curtis LeMay was bombing the Vietnamese back to the Stone Age.

Ken Frank, Claremont, California, USA

There is a fascinating (and readable) explanation of 'The Quantum Physics of Time Travel' by David Deutsch and Michael Lockwood in *Scientific American*, March 1994. It explains how although common sense may rule out such excursions, the laws of physics do not. It also rebuts some oft-heard criticisms, such as that time travel can't exist, otherwise we would have swarms of visitors from the future!

Tom Farrow, Sheffield

Diego Torres at the University of Sussex was quoted in various newspapers in March as having discovered 'wormholes' in the space–time continuum, which may allow instantaneous travel to the farthest parts of the galaxy, as well as travel in time.

John Radford, Brighton, Sussex

J. W. Dunne's *Experiment with Time* was not concerned with time travel, as Peter Sharp seems to suggest. It was an attempt to explain the sensation of déjà vu and apparent precognition.

Dunne kept notes of dreams and reinterpreted them to fit later events. His explanatory theory depended on the idea of time flowing like a river, on the banks of which the dreamer stood in Time 2, observing the flotsam of Time 1 events approaching and departing. This leads to an infinite regression of serial times, T3, T4, etc., and conflicts with the idea of a space–time continuum within which events

occur rather than being swept along by a current.
Martin Simons, Stepney, South Australia

What does a flame look like in zero gravity?

In 1992, I and colleagues from the Fire Research Station flew a fire experiment on a series of parabolic flights with engineers and astronauts from the European Space Agency. Parabolic flights involve periods of 'free fall', giving rise to short periods of zero- or (more accurately) micro-gravity conditions within the aircraft. Since each parabola lasts only twenty seconds, we mostly burned small gas flames and small pieces of paper.

The gas flames, which started as 'normal' yellow flames (such as are seen from a Bunsen burner), became spherical like a bubble and turned from yellow to blue, finally becoming invisible. They turned yellow again once the period of zero gravity ended. The flames on the paper died back and went out.

These effects are due to the lack of gravity-driven convection, which on earth enables oxygen (in the air) to reach the fire. In space this can be simulated by a fan. Where oxygen is available within the material on fire, such as happened on Mir, a more normal fire results.
Martin Shipp, Fire Research Station, Garston, Herts

If the dinosaurs had been intelligent enough to develop complex civilizations, could any evidence of this possibly have survived the 65 million years that they've been extinct?

It would depend on whether the dinosaurs could have achieved our level of technology. The natural processes of the earth's crust would have destroyed much evidence. Fossils survive for millions of years, so perhaps artefacts made out of composite materials such as carbon fibre could survive, although buildings would have been buried.

The only sure way of leaving a trace of civilization is to go into space. The artefacts left on the moon by the Apollo astronauts will still be there in millions of years' time – if they have not been removed by future

tourists. The Pioneer spacecraft, bearing messages to beings it may encounter, will still be voyaging through the stars for billions of years.
Peter Stockill, Berwick Hills, Middlesbrough

Dinosaur scientists may have predicted the catastrophe that destroyed their population long enough in advance to have built a huge spaceship containing a sample of the dinosaur ecosystem – thereby enabling a small community of dinosaurs to make a timely escape into the cosmos. Perhaps they will soon be back to reclaim their home planet.
Stephen Shenfield, Providence, Rhode Island, USA

Any complex civilization could not exist without the use of metals and many other minerals, and that means widespread mining. If geologically ancient shafts and tunnels had existed, we should have found some. For instance, in the stable, mineral-rich 'shield' rocks of Canada, Australia and southern Africa, 'fossil' geological faults well over 100 million years old are not uncommon; and tunnels – which would in time have infilled through detritus and metasomatism, etc. – would proclaim their presence by unusual shapes and mineral assemblages. Even areas outside the stable shields would occasionally offer evidence bared by erosion and so on.

Add the fact that we humans have found that eucalypts were still confined to Australia and New Guinea, ginkgo trees to China, and maize to the Americas, and it seems that the denizens of any 'complex civilization' didn't even travel.
Len Clarke, Uxbridge, Middx

Civilization is not defined by the use of metals and minerals, nor by the mining associated with them. That's like defining civilization as the obliteration of rainforests for the provision of toilet seats.

Had dinosaurs been ecologically enlightened, the constructions of their civilizations would have biodegraded long ago and no evidence would remain. If civilization is a product of the making and upkeep of societal laws, the dinosaurs' extinction might have been the result. Carnivores might have agreed to give up meat and herbivores might have ceased grazing out of sympathy with defenceless plants. Egg-thieving mammals might have been encouraged to go into rehab. The

tyrannosaur might have lain down with the diplodocus and never got up again. We may have missed the first truly civilized end of an era.
Trevor Lawson, Amersham, Bucks

It's not impossible that several so-called 'anomalous' fossils bear witness to incredibly ancient civilizations, although it is impossible to ascertain anything about such societies.

At least two artefacts have been discovered in coal: an 'iron instrument' resembling a drill bit was found completely sealed in a coal seam in 1852; and a piece of gold thread was found in a rock eight feet below ground level in Rutherford, Scotland, in 1844.

Two apparent prehistoric nails have also been found: a two-inch nail in gold-bearing quartz (reported in *The Times*, 1851); and a seven-inch nail in a block of granite in 1845.

In 1968, in Antelope Spring, Utah, a two-inch-thick slab of rock was split to reveal a 'human' footprint, wearing a shoe, in rock 300 million years old. This find pre-dates the evolution of the dinosaurs. Moreover, the foot, whatever it belonged to, had trodden on a trilobite (a marine invertebrate extinct for 280 million years).
Garrick Alder, Kempston, Beds

What's the difference between a herb and a spice?

Not a lot. Plants have been used for medicinal (mainly) and culinary purposes since ancient times. Any part of the plant used for either purpose is referred to as 'a herb'. All grand houses would have had their own herb(aceous) gardens growing plants suitable for temperate climates.

The term 'spice', on the other hand, refers mainly to the pungent, aromatic parts of those plants that are native to tropical Asia and the Moluccas, which became known as the Spice Islands. 'Spices' are used mainly for culinary purposes. Many of these plants also produce essential oils, where 'essential' means 'essence or distilled spirit'.

Even though we speak of herbs and spices, there is no clear distinction and a spice can be thought of as a rather pungent herb of non-temperate origin.
Leslie Kennedy, Lenham, Kent

Herbs have blue tops, spices have brown tops. (Source: J. Sainsbury plc.)
Joseph Clinton, Norwich

Leslie Kennedy is insufficiently explicit. 'Herb' is a common, general botanical term meaning a green plant that contains no woody structures. A banana plant is a herb – not, as is commonly stated, a tree. Pungent spices come mainly from the warmer parts of America and Asia. The milder herbs are largely temperate in origin: that is, those most common in cooking.

The inference, common in much writing, that spices come mainly (or wholly) from the Spice Islands (the Moluccas) is incorrect. H. N. Ridley's classic book *Spices* (1912) describes some fifteen spices. Only three originate in the Moluccas: cloves (*Syzygium aromaticum*), mace and nutmeg (*Myristica fragrans*).

Paul Holliday, Uppingham, Rutland

Are there any areas on the surface of the planet where the process of fossilization of organic material is beginning?

Yes, most notably in the remaining peat bogs of the United Kingdom. These form as centuries of organic material such as sphagnum moss gradually grows on top of itself with the resulting death and degradation of the ancestor plants.

Through the analysis of pollen from core samples of peat bogs, scientists have been able to ascertain what crops were growing in the past. Also, at the very bottom of the oceans where there are enormous pressures and little disturbance, marine life will gradually sink to the bottom and, over many millions of years, become fossilized.

There are other examples – such as coral reefs, mangrove swamps and coniferous forests – but in each case a lack of disturbance is probably the most important ingredient.

Liz Maidment, Chester

The House of Lords.
Roger Darby, West Moors, Dorset

Which is more intelligent, my seven-month-old baby or my seven-year-old cat?

Your cat. If you abandoned both right now, only the cat could survive without your help.

Christine Brandon-Jones, London SW8

It depends on your understanding of intelligence. Your cat will outdo your baby on 'what a cat needs to know' specialities, whereas your baby will excel in 'appropriate responses to silly human faces and sounds' subjects. Your cat probably thinks it's more intelligent than you!

Megan Cupid, Birmingham

Having observed the behaviour of our eight-month-old baby and our cats, aged eight and ten years, I would say that if the questioner's cat has learned to keep out of the way of his baby, the cat is more intelligent.

Chris Pentney, Blaydon on Tyne

There is an unbridgeable gulf – recognizable from birth – between human intelligence and animal behaviour. By six months a baby will laugh, chuckle, squeal with delight, scream with frustration and have vocalized 'conversations' with you. Most importantly, despite being usually unable to speak recognizable words, a seven-month-old already has a considerably more sophisticated understanding of language than any animal can ever have.

Cats, dogs, rabbits, hamsters, snakes, stick insects – all make interesting pets. It does not do, though, to be seduced by their surface characteristics into attributing to them human qualities that are simply not there. Animal behaviour is sufficiently diverse and fascinating without anthropomorphism of this kind.

Gerald Haigh, Bedworth, Nuneaton

Cat IQs are measured by opening doors. Most of mine will rise up on their hind legs and charge any door that hasn't gone click. Roughly half the doors don't open and they can't work out why, but a particularly bright girl pondered the problem and tried pushing the wall instead.

The cleverest puss pats the door handle, looks appealingly at the nearest human and goes 'waaah'. It works every time. I'm afraid a seven-month-old baby wouldn't do very well in this test.

David Brinicombe, London W5

I have just seen a spider build a web across my twelve-foot garden without intervening support. How does it get the first thread started?

There are at least three methods used by spiders to span such gaps, but they all depend on a fine gossamer thread being wafted by air currents until it becomes fixed at some point.

In the first case the spider simply points its spinnerets into the wind, emitting a a fine gossamer silk, which is carried away. The spider tests this every so often and, if it appears to be anchored, will use it as the bridge thread for a new web.

Alternatively, while issuing the gossamer, the spider lowers itself to the ground on a somewhat thicker support line. Once there, it tests the gossamer to see if it has achieved a connection.

Or, the spider attaches both the gossamer and the support line to the original site and lowers itself (keeping the threads separated by a hind leg) to the ground. There, it releases that end of the gossamer and climbs back up the support line to retrieve the fixed end of the gossamer and test it to see if a bridge has been formed. (Source: Theodore H. Savory, *The Spider's Web*, Frederick Warne, 1952.)

Gus McNaughton, Otley, West Yorks

In the book and film *2001*, the hero survives a brief exposure to a vacuum. In other stories, vacuum is instantly fatal and very, very gruesome. What would really happen?

Although there would be a huge temperature gradient between the 37°C of the human body and the (almost) absolute zero of space, heat cannot be lost in a vacuum by conduction or convection but only by radiation; so you would freeze eventually but not instantaneously. However, all moisture on the skin and inside the mouth, throat and lungs would vaporize instantly. The loss of the residual air inside the lungs would cause oxygen to diffuse back out of the bloodstream, leading to unconsciousness and then death within a few minutes.

Fictional accounts often describe bodies as 'exploding' but this seems unlikely. The body is probably constructed strongly enough to withstand a pressure difference between the interior and exterior of just one atmosphere.

Mike Hutton, St Bart's and Royal London Medical School, London SE5

Mike Hutton doesn't answer the question. In *2001*, even if the shuttle-craft pressurization wasn't already lower than one atmosphere, the astronaut would have been able to gradually reduce the pressure in the airlock to about half an atmosphere before letting himself be hurled out by the rush of escaping air.

All then depends upon his being able to reach the appropriate button before losing consciousness due to the sudden depressurization. If he were able to do this quickly enough, the airlock would repressurize without his help. It is unlikely, upon again regaining consciousness, that he would suffer no ill effects at all, but he would live to tell the tale.

Terence Hollingworth, Blagnac, France

In 1956, whilst employed as a welder for the then Atomic Energy Authority, I helped make a pressure vessel. It was tested by a vacuum process.

Meter tests showed that a foreign body was inside the tank shell. We cut open the vessel and found that someone had left a hammer inside it. The steel hammer head was removed, as was the very fine dust that had once been the wooden hammer shaft.

Mike Mitchell, Failsworth, Manchester

How can I estimate, in megabytes, the amount of memory in my brain?

The conversion of information into binary digits is a gross simplification of processes in the brain. A single, static, well-resolved picture on a video display screen might need 1.5 megabytes of a machine's memory.

If anything moves, this will increase – and that is just one scene. How many scenes do we remember throughout a lifetime? What about language, literature, maths, science, music, to say nothing of neuro-muscular coordination?

Machines are mere extensions of brains, devised to perform set programmes quickly. Garry Kasparov is no more inferior to a chess machine than is a bicyclist to a fast car.

Michael Dearden, Carnforth, Lancs

How does a 'controlled explosion' avoid blowing up the bomb that is being made safe?

Although the detonation of a bomb sounds like an instantaneous event, it invariably consists of a sequence of events, albeit too fast and too quiet for the ear to perceive.

For example, an anti-handling switch, which may be so placed as to close an electric firing circuit if the bomb is lifted, might take a couple of milliseconds to move. And a mechanical striking mechanism has to complete its action to cause a non-electric detonator to explode. This explosion usually has to be transferred to a further intermediate explosive charge before the main charge begins to explode.

The trick of a 'controlled explosion' is to knock the bomb apart before the train of initiation events can run its course, but to avoid knocking it so hard that the impact of the intervention detonates it anyway. In the case of most improvised devices, the most common disrupter consists of a short gun, which fires a blank cartridge and propels a gun-barrel full of water at the target. A mass of water, if travelling fast enough, can smash its way through the case of many bombs and, once inside, bursts violently enough to propel the bomb components in all directions before they have time to perform their various functions.

The only sense in which a 'controlled explosion' is fully under control is that the operator knows that a bang will occur when he presses the button, but the size of the bang involves an element of luck. Actuation of the disrupter alone typically causes a modest bang. If the controlled explosion results in the detonation of the target bomb with the violence that the maker intended, the event becomes an 'uncontrolled explosion' – or cock-up.

Sidney Alford (explosives engineer), Corsham, Warks

Why do males of the human and related species have nipples?

Because males are genetically defective females. The basic blueprint for humanity is female. A foetus with XX or XO chromosomes will develop as female. If, however, one chromosome is deformed into a Y shape, then at a crucial stage of development a hormone surge will change the normal development pattern, and among other physical changes the male human will fail to develop breasts in adolescence.

Jane Carnall, Edinburgh

In case a sex-change operation needs to be carried out later in life.

Vic Fisher, Kingston on Thames, Surrey

Jane Carnall's statement that 'males are genetically defective females' requires some examination.

She appears to believe that every foetus begins its development with two X chromosomes, and that males are produced when one of these is 'deformed' into a Y chromosome. In fact, males begin their development with one X and one Y chromosome. When genes are mixed in sexual reproduction, the female contributes one or the other of her X chromosomes, and the male may contribute either his X chromosome or his Y chromosome. If he contributes a Y, the child will be male; and if an X, female.

This gives rise to the curious paradox that, whether you're male or female, your sex is inherited from your father. For this reason it is necessary for the male genotype to incorporate some instructions on how to build a female body, nipples and all. It is interesting to notice that women have a similar bit of surplus flesh: the clitoris, which has no biological function.

T. Hardcastle, Groby, Leics

All embryos, irrespective of sex, develop rudimentary gill structures in the early stages of pregnancy. Of course, these features are lost in later development. Nevertheless, I would ask Ms Carnall: does this makes us all genetically deficient fish?

Robert Greenland, Dorchester, Dorset

If it were possible for a spaceship to reach the point in the universe where the Big Bang occurred, what would it find there now?

The basis of the Big Bang theory is the so-called Cosmological Principle: that the universe is, roughly speaking, the same at every point in space if observed at the same time. Wherever you went in your spaceship you would therefore see pretty much the same thing as we see around us from earth.

The mistake implicit in the question is to think of the Big Bang as occurring at a point in space; the Big Bang creation event represents the origin of space. This event was infinitely small and can therefore be regarded as a point, but the point in question contained all of our present universe (in an infinitely compressed form). There is therefore no need to travel to visit the point where the Big Bang happened. It happened everywhere (including here) but, in the beginning, everywhere was in the same place.

Dr Peter Coles, Astronomy Unit, Queen Mary and Westfield College, London E1

The expansion of the universe is more like the three-dimensional equivalent of the surface of a balloon as it is inflated. The single point of the Big Bang has been 'stretched' to form the universe we see today.

Steven Hall, Leigh, Lancs

Deaf aliens.

John Ward, Fareham, Hants

The answers so far seem to miss the point. Surely, since the Big Bang occurred a finite time ago and matter cannot travel infinitely fast, the entire universe must be a sphere of finite diameter. Does not a sphere have a centre? The location of the centre relative to the earth could be found if the distance from the earth to the 'edges' of space could be measured. As light travels faster than matter, a sufficiently sensitive telescope should be able to observe some, if not all, of the universe boundary.

Angelo Valentino, London SW3

Angelo Valentino's reply would appear to make perfect sense, but although the universe is finite, it has no boundary, hence no identifiable centre.

In accordance with the theory of General Relativity, space curves round on itself like the skin of a balloon. If one were to go on a rocket in a straight line, one would not reach 'the edge' but would, eventually, come back to where one started. As a result of this, the universe must not be thought of as a three-dimensional sphere, but as the three-dimensional surface of a four-dimensional 'hypersphere'.

As to an answer to the question: 'What happens to the part of the hypersphere underneath the surface?' – the answer is, I think, unknown to science.

Donald Baillie, Penicuik, Midlothian

Why is water wet?

Water isn't wet. Wetness is a description of our experience of water; or what happens to us when we come into contact with water in such a way that it impinges on our state of being. We, or our possessions, 'get wet'. A less impinging sense experience of water is that it is cold or warm, while visual experience tells us that it is green or blue or muddy or fast-flowing. We learn by experience that a sensation of wetness is associated with water: 'There must be a leak' or 'I must have sat in something'.

Jacqueline Castles, London W2

Any fluid could be said to be wet if wetness is a result of the sensation caused by the movement of a fluid over the skin. Have you ever noticed that you can't feel wetness if you hold your hand perfectly still while it is submerged, or that a drop of water on the skin doesn't feel wet?

Chris and Shewy Ould, Chesterfield, Derby.

The wetness of water is thought to be due to its high moisture content.

(Dr) Jason A. Rush, Department of Mathematics, Edinburgh University

Water is wet to make it a more marketable commodity.

Sam McBride-Dick, Colchester

The questioner will be little enlightened by the previous replies and you must surely give him or her another chance. Two answers were humorous; two were just wet.

As an amateur photographer, I am familiar with what is, I think, properly called wetting agent, which is added to water – to the final washing after developing and fixing – to make it wet with respect to the surfaces of photographic film. Without this agent the water resides on film in blobs, resulting in drying marks; with it, most of the water drains off and the rest dries evenly.

So in response to the query I would say: (a) water isn't always wet; wetness is always relative to a given substance and/or type of surface; and (b) as to why it is wet when it is, presumably the answer is in terms of surface tension.

Laurie Hollings, Brighton

Water is wet, in the sense of being a liquid that flows easily, because its viscosity is low, which is because its molecules are rather loosely joined together. The sensation of wetness is largely due to the cooling caused by evaporation, and water has a rather high latent heat of vaporization, which is the amount of heat it removes from its surroundings in order to convert liquid water into water vapour.

John Geake, Handforth, Cheshire

None of the answers given to this question so far quite gets to the chemical explanation for water's 'wetness'.

Wetness is here synonymous with 'clingingness' – water wets because it clings. Water, of course, is molecularly H_2O and this compound of hydrogen and oxygen is electrically neutral. However, there are also in water many free charged hydroxyls (-OH-, negatively charged) and hydrogen ions (H+, positively charged). These charged particles retain the ability to attract other charged particles (with the opposite charge) just as magnets do. In this way they stick or cling, involving other neutral H²O molecules at the same time.

If water was made up entirely of neutral particles it would not cling, or wet, because the component elements would 'prefer' to stick to each other rather than to make bonds with other substances.
Ian Flintoff, London SW6

Ian Flintoff has surely misrepresented the chemistry behind water's properties.

Hydroxyl ions and hydrogen ions in water, far from being 'many', are very few (pure water contains some 556 million water molecules for every hydrogen ion). Water molecules are indeed 'electrically neutral' but are highly polar molecules: that is, they have a positive 'end' and a negative 'end', although neither 'end' carries a full unit of charge. It is this polarity that causes water molecules to 'stick to' one another and, given the chance, to other molecules of a polar nature.

Other liquids can be wet, even those that contain molecules that are entirely non-polar (for example, octane, benzine and even liquid nitrogen – don't try 'em!), but only in relation to another substance, because wetness is to do with surface tension and that implies an interface between two substances.

For this reason water is rather poor at wetting things: try washing your hands without soap! The molecules of water do prefer to stick to one another rather than to molecules of other substances, but this effect is easily overcome by introducing another substance that interferes with the interactions between the water molecules. This allows the water molecules to interact with the molecules in the other surface instead.
C. A. Mitchell, Reading, Berks

Are scientists any closer to answering the question: which came first, the chicken or the egg?

Assuming that the chicken evolved from two other birds that were not quite chickens, then these two latter birds must have produced, at some time in the past, an egg out of which came the first chicken.

Geoffrey Samuel, Lancaster

We must remember that the chicken is an actual chicken, whereas the egg is only a potential chicken. Philosophically speaking, actuality always precedes potentiality, so the chicken came first. Probably.

Kishor Alam, London N14

Kishor Alam argues, on the basis of actuality preceding potentiality, that the chicken must come before the egg. But from the egg's point of view, a chicken is only a potential egg (just as human beings are simply the way in which genes manage to perpetuate themselves).

David Lewis, St Albans, Herts

The chicken is, of course, *Archaeopteryx*, the oldest fossil bird. It comes from the Solnhofen lithographic limestone, from the Late Jurassic rocks of Bavaria (that is, about 150 million years ago). Its skeleton is so like that of contemporary dinosaurs that it is generally agreed that its ancestors were in fact small, lightly built dinosaurs. The dinosaurs were reptiles, and in some cases are known to have laid eggs; therefore it is likely that the egg came first.

However, most fossil reptile eggs date from the later Cretaceous Period (144 million to 65 million years ago) and are those of large dinosaurs. Being big and relatively strong, they have a better chance of preservation than smaller ones. The oldest find reported (from the Early Permian Period of Texas – about 270 million years ago) is so poorly preserved that palaeontologists are uncertain about its true identity. It may be the remains of an inorganic nodule – a chemical growth within the sediment.

The earliest reptile fossils come from even older rocks: the Early Carboniferous of Scotland (350 million years ago). So it is probable that the earliest eggs date from this time – 200 million years before *Archaeopteryx*. The egg is no chicken!

(Dr) Denis Bates, Institute of Earth Studies, University College of Wales, Aberystwyth

Readers may be interested in the rather tongue-in-cheek article by Walter N. Thurman and Mark E. Fisher: 'Chicken, Eggs, and Causality, or Which Came First?' (*American Journal of Agricultural Economics*, May 1988).

The authors conducted so-called 'Granger causality tests', using annual data from the US Department of Agriculture on egg production and chicken population, covering the period 1930–1983. Such tests can be used to see if there is an asymmetry between the value of the information provided by past observations of the variables in predicting each other's current values. Using regression analysis one attempts to discover whether variations in Series Y (say, chicken population) can be adequately explained by its own past values, or whether lagged values of a second variable X (say, egg production) contribute significantly to the equation.

A similar regression would be carried out reversing the role of the variables. If it can be shown that X is needed to help explain Y (after accounting for the influence of past values of Y) but that Y is not needed to explain movements in X, then one may conclude that X 'Granger-causes' Y (named after Clive Granger who first proposed the procedure).

Using this approach in what Thurman and Fisher called 'the most natural application of tests for Granger causality', they concluded that the egg came first. However, readers may feel that this result should be taken with a pinch of salt, especially when they hear that other applications of the test have given rise to such perverse findings as 'GNP "causes" sunspot activity'!

Guy Judge, Emsworth, Hants

How can I weigh my head?

Fill a water butt until water flows out of the overflow. Let the water settle and then immerse the head completely, keeping it submerged until the water level has settled, having first arranged some method of collecting the displaced water that will flow out of the overflow. The volume of water displaced should then be measured and the experiment repeated, this time immersing the whole body. Again the volume of displaced water should be recorded. The ratio of the first volume to the second, multiplied by total body weight gives the proportion of body weight that is due to the head. This method assumes the human body has a uniform density and does not take into account the contribution of any pegs on the nose needed to prevent drowning.

(Dr) N. J. Mason, University of Oxford

Dr Mason's method does not allow for the dense nature of the head, which contains much bone. A more accurate method is to float in the barrel, adjusting your lung volume to leave the head completely out of the water. While holding your breath, top up the barrel to the overflow and then submerge yourself completely, collecting the displaced water and measuring its volume. Climb out of the barrel, without further spillage, and then refill the barrel, measuring the volume needed. The floating volume of the body (the volume to keep the head up) can be calculated from the difference of the two volumes measured above. The weight of the head is the floating volume (in litres) less the body weight (in kilos).

J. B. Diamond, Hertford

J. B. Diamond's formula yields a head weight of zero, which cannot be right, even in J. B. Diamond's case.

M. J. Lloyd, London EC1

Find a long board with pivotal centre mounting (for example, a see-saw). Weigh yourself unclothed, then lie on the board with the pivotal point coinciding with the base of the skull. Have someone place weights on the head end of the board up to a distance not exceeding the length from the pivot to the heels in the opposite direction. When the see-saw is balanced, deduct the sum of the added weights from your total body weight to obtain the weight of your head.

Jane Pepper, Canterbury

Entertaining, but wrong. If it worked, so would perpetual motion.

An approximate answer would be got with the aid of a muscle relaxant, a gravity meter and a blow from Michael Watson. But for a less dramatic method, take a see-saw, a ruler and a large inanimate object. Balance flat on your back on the see-saw, then bend your head

forward on to your chest. The see-saw will tilt; shuffle along to restore the balance. Measure the distance you have to shuffle and divide this by the amount by which you moved (the centre of) your head. This gives the weight of your head as a fraction of your whole body weight.
Peter Green, Department of Mathematics, University of Bristol

Peter Green gives a neat answer but I am left wondering what to do with the 'large inanimate object'.

Here is an alternative solution that, again, assumes you can estimate the position of the centre of gravity of the head. Take a plank longer than your body and place it across two weighing scales that act as pivotal points. Lie along the plank with head to the left of the left pivot, and move the right pivot until it reads the same as the left one. (Each reading will equal half the combined weight of body and plank.) Saw off and weigh a length of plank to the right so that the shortened plank overhangs each pivot equally. The weight of the head is equal to the weight of this off-cut, multiplied by the distance of the centre of gravity of the head from the left pivot and divided by the distance from the centre of the off-cut to the right pivot.
Rob Johnsey, Redditch, Worcs

Is a fourth – or higher – spatial dimension a reality that exists but eludes human senses and imagination, or is it an abstract concept for which there is no room in the real universe?

The fact that we cannot comfortably fit our right-hand foot into our left-hand shoe is evidence that space has only three dimensions.

Consider a two-dimensional experiment: two paper shapes are laid out on a table, one in the shape of an R, the other a mirror-reversed R. By simply moving the shapes around on the two-dimensional surface of the table, you cannot make them exactly coincide. (The reason is that they have no axis of symmetry. In contrast, an E, which does have an axis of symmetry, can be made to coincide with its mirror image.)

However, if you let one shape move in the third spatial dimension, by lifting it up and turning it over, you can make it coincide with its mirror-image counterpart. The apparent differences between these two-dimensional objects disappear once they are allowed to move in three spatial dimensions. The three-dimensional right foot and left foot are just like these shapes: they cannot be made to coincide as can things (having no plane of symmetry). But were they able to rotate in a fourth spatial dimension, their differences would disappear.

Nature is full of objects that have no plane of symmetry. A molecule of adrenaline, for example, has no plane of symmetry and can occur in either a 'right-handed' form or a 'left-handed' form. The fact that these different forms have different physiological properties should convince us that there is no fourth dimension of space.

Dr Robin Le Poidevin, Department of Philosophy, University of Leeds

The fourth spatial dimension is simultaneously at right angles to any direction in which we care to point. However, being 'trapped' in the three dimensions, we can't actually point in this direction. Also, even if we could detect the extra dimension, we would not be able to 'see' it because our retinas are two-dimensional surfaces, and to see a four-dimensional object in its entirety we would need three-dimensional retinas. The best we could hope for would be to see three-dimensional slices of the objects in series as we scanned it, just as hospital scanners are used to view slices of the human body.

There exist some computer programs that show the projection of, say, a hypercube (the four-dimensional analogue of an ordinary cube) rotating. The images are perplexing, although some people claim to be able to get an idea of the appearance of the actual hypercube through watching these real-time images.

According to some of the latest theories in physics, space consists of many more dimensions than we can actually detect. The fourth and higher dimensions are postulated to be a physical reality.

Dr Khurram Wadee, Ealing, London W13

The contradiction between the two respondents can be resolved by analysing what we mean by 'space'.

Dr Le Poidevin's symmetry examples certainly show us that there are only three dimensions to our everyday, commonsense kind of 'space', the 'space' that we can perceive and move our feet in. Yet physicists dealing with superstring theory have developed persuasive theories using an extra six spatial dimensions. These higher dimensions, however, are curled up into tiny circles, or similar closed surfaces, and are so small that they are invisible on casual inspection (something in the range of $1/10!33m$ across). This curling up of dimensions is analogous to our observing, say, a piece of string from a distance and seeing it as a line, then moving closer and observing that it actually has an extra, circular dimension.

If we could observe any point (say, a subatomic particle) at a large enough magnification, we would similarly see that it is not a point, but has further dimensions in unexplored directions.

Mark Howard, London NW6

Why is a mirror image not upside down as well as being the wrong way round?

The short answer is that a mirror image is not the wrong way round (in the sense of a left/right reversal).

Try this experiment: instead of designating your hands 'left' and 'right', place a glove on (say) the right hand and call them 'gloved' and 'ungloved'. Now stand in front of a mirror so that you are facing north. Your (right) gloved hand points east. So does the mirror image's gloved hand. Your (left) ungloved hand points west. So does that in the mirror. Your feet point down and your head up – so do those in your reflection. What has changed? You face north – your mirror image faces south. This is the only reversal.

R. Thomson, Brighton

Consider looking at a book in a mirror. The key is that one has to turn it round to face the mirror. If you turn it around its vertical axis, right and left are reversed, so you get 'mirror' writing. If you turn it around its horizontal axis, you do not get mirror writing: it is upside down, and not right–left reversed in the mirror. In every case, you see what you have done to make the book face the mirror.

The same holds true for yourself. Usually you turn around vertically to face a mirror – but you could stand on your head, in which case you would be upside down and not right–left reversed.

The history of this ancient puzzle dating back to Plato, and its solution, are discussed in R. L. Gregory, *Odd Perceptions* (Routledge, 1986) and in *The Oxford Companion to the Mind* (OUP).
Professor Richard Gregory, CBE, FRS, Department of Psychology, University of Bristol

I tried various contortions with books in front of mirrors, trying to fathom Professor Gregory's reply. All I got when I turned the book on its horizontal axis was mirror writing, which was also upside down.

Maybe I don't know my Plato from my Aristotle but I think the professor is pulling our legs. It all depends on how you define 'wrong way round'. A mirror simply reflects every point straight back. There is no left–right inversion and also quite consistently no top–bottom inversion either. Our feet remain on the floor, our heads remain in the clouds, our left hands remain on the left and our right hands remain on the right. Inversion only occurs if we imagine ourselves to be our mirror images . . . Perhaps that's where Professor Gregory's speciality – psychology – comes in.
Brian Homer, Gwynedd

Professor Gregory is certainly not 'pulling our legs', as Mr Homer suggests. Quite the reverse(!). Mr Homer claims that he saw mirror writing that was also upside down, which would be a refutation of the original question.

Writing seen in a single mirror can be either upside down or the wrong way round but it cannot be both. Write the word 'bow' on a piece of paper. Turn it around a vertical axis to face a mirror. In the mirror it looks like 'wod', which is right–left reversed. If the paper is instead turned around a horizontal axis to face the mirror, the word looks like 'pom', which is upside down but not right–left reversed. The word Mr Homer would claim to see is 'moq'. It would not be possible to observe this with only one mirror.

The rest of Mr Homer's answer is sensible and is not inconsistent with Professor Gregory's perfectly reasonable answer.

Nevertheless, the really intriguing question is psychological: why do we think of people or objects seen in mirrors as being the 'wrong way round' and why do we find it disturbing to see them? It is contrary to our perception of the 'real' world, where people greet each other by shaking their right hands, and the hands of a clock go round in a clockwise direction.

(Dr) Roger Owens, Wedmore, Somerset

What would be the smallest possible nuclear explosion? I seem to remember that in Isaac Asimov's 'Foundation' trilogy a nuclear booby-trap destroyed someone's bedroom.

If all the uranium in an amount the size of a sweet fissioned, it could destroy a building. However, such small nuclear-fission explosions are impractical because a chain reaction cannot be sustained in such a tiny amount. The minimum amount of fissile material required is called the critical mass and this depends on the design of the device. It is thought by some that the critical mass for a conventionally designed booby-trap made from uranium is about ten kilograms, which is a lump about the size of an orange. But if the design were improved, the quantity could be much less.

Tayakan Kapinakhish, Balsall Heath, Birmingham

The smallest nuclear delivery system was the US army's Davy Crockett rocket-powered projectile, which was deployed in Germany in 1962. It had a warhead of about 0.5 kilotons yield and a blast radius of between 200 and 600 yards. The complete system (launcher, sights, rocket motor and warhead) weighed sixty-eight kilograms.

Nuclear reactions can take place between hydrogen atoms, neutrons, etc., so I imagine there is no theoretical minimum size of an explosion but there may be practical limits due to the complexity of trigger mechanisms.

The incident referred to in Dr Asimov's works occurred in *The Stars Like Dust*, where Biron Farrill's bedroom is occupied by a radiation bomb that later turns out to be a fake.

John Waters, Port Talbot, West Glamorgan

The Davy Crockett project was eventually vetoed by President Kennedy on the grounds that it might lead to soldiers of NCO rank taking the decision to 'go nuclear'.

Roger Sabdell, Richmond, Surrey

Is it true that the average height of Britons has increased by a foot or more over the last few centuries? Is this phenomenon caused by improved diet? When will we stop growing?

In 1873, the medical officer and the natural science master at Marlborough College measured the height of 500 or so of the pupils, aged sixteen and a half. The average height of the boys was 65.5 inches. When a comparable sample was measured eighty years later, the average was 69.6 inches – equivalent to a gain of half an inch a decade.

James Tanner (in *Foetus into Man*, 1978) makes the point that such trends in children's height are at least partially accountable in terms of earlier maturity. The so-called secular trend at completion of stature in adulthood is in the region of four inches in a hundred years. He did not detect a slowing down in the trend.

Although improved standards of nutrition are cited as one possible cause, Tanner also invokes a genetic explanation, which in turn hangs on the increased incidence of marriages and procreation outside the village community. He notes that a key factor in the growth of this 'outbreeding' was the introduction of the bicycle.

Peter Barnes, Milton Keynes

The study of skeletons from archaeological excavations has shown that the average height of the population within the British Isles (and elsewhere) has varied over time, and there is no doubt that the single most important influence is that of diet.

In this present era of food surpluses and balanced diets in Europe, most people will grow to their full genetic potential (unless other factors such as smoking or ill health intervene). But earlier generations were acutely prone to the fluctuations of harvests, poverty and starvation – unless they were members of privileged groups.

Skeletons of wealthy lay-people found in excavations that I directed at Norton Priory in Cheshire showed their height to be little different in range to that of the present-day population. The peasant population of the same era tended not to grow as tall and would usually die much younger.

Dr Patrick Greene, Director, Museum of Science and Industry in Manchester

The height of the average young male around 1750 was about 160 centimetres (63 inches) and in 1980 it was 176 centimetres (69.3 inches); there is no evidence in earlier centuries of a growth leap as great as another six inches.

The answer is complex because there has always been significant variation in height between social classes, although the inequality has narrowed over time; it therefore matters whom you measure. The average height of public schoolboys has risen less than that of working-class children. This fact helps to answer the second question: the primary cause of growth is increased income, which means that people can eat more, although levels of disease and pollution can have an effect. But it also means that the increased income inequality since 1979 may be affecting average heights and variation between classes.

We do not know when we will stop growing; in Britain we still have a long way to go to catch up with richer nations such as the Netherlands, where young males average over 180 centimetres (71 inches).

Roderick Floud (co-author Height, Health and History, CUP),
London Guildhall University

Let's assume that there have been humans or human-like beings for some 2 million years or, say, 100,000 generations. If their average height increased per generation by a mere one-thousandth of an inch, we should now be eight feet four inches taller than our remote ancestors. It seems likely, therefore, that there are powerful influences restricting humans to a fairly narrow variation in height, even over long periods of time.

Louis Judson, Penrith, Cumbria

When a fly is making its approach to land on a ceiling, does it fly upside down or does it flip over in the last microsecond before landing?

This question was asked on the *Brains Trust* programme on the radio a few years ago when Commander Campbell, Dr C. E. M. Joad and Sir Malcolm Sargent treated it as a joke, but Professor Julian Huxley was quite angry that he didn't know what he thought he ought to have known. The following week, I believe, he returned to say that he had conducted experiments that showed that the fly flew close to the ceiling until its first two legs could be put over its head to touch, and adhere to, the ceiling, bringing the rest of its body up to leave the creature on the ceiling and facing in the opposite direction.

V. Beilby, Fareham, Hants

This question was the subject of intensive study by an American convict. After many years of observation he said that, in the process of landing on the ceiling, flies always perform a half-upwards loop. To start flying again, they have to complete this loop.

To prove it, the convict invented this way of catching flies: nearly fill a glass with soapy water, beat up a bit of a foamy head on the surface and raise the glass slowly from directly beneath the fly. Once the surface of the foam is about an inch and a half from the fly, it is doomed. In completing the interrupted loop, the fly cannot but dive into the foam.

Dulcie Kirby, Franschhoek, South Africa

Professor Joad, in the *Brains Trust*, 1941, said: 'It all depends on what the fly had for lunch. Normally it lands on the ceiling by a loop-the-loop, but if it had too much to drink it does a roll.'

Peter Helsdon, Chelmsford, Essex

6

Odds and Ends

What is the plural of 'computer mouse'?

This conundrum prompted Microsoft to prefer to use the term 'hand-held pointing device'. Sony suffered the same problem with Walkmans/Walkmen. It reminds me of the apocryphal keeper in charge of mammals at London Zoo who wrote to his supplier: 'Please send me a mongoose. Please send me another one with it.'
Tom Cutler, Hove, East Sussex

After scanning dictionaries (online and off) I can only conclude that the world is as yet undecided – many dictionaries list both 'mice' and 'mouses'. But it is worth noting that the pronunciation of mouses doesn't seem to follow houses ('hauziz') and appears to be more like 'maussis'. And since most computers usually only have one mouse, there is little need for a plural in everyday use. Mice, however, often come in large numbers (like lice) and perhaps deserve a special plural. Mouses, like houses, are often considered in ones.
Sam Shepherd, Eastbourne, East Sussex

I have seen several computer catalogues that list varieties of computer mouse under 'rodents'.
Natalie Lyons, Hornchurch, Essex

In his reply, Tom Cutler mentions the plural of 'mongoose'. Most people say it is either 'mongeese' or 'mongooses'. Every mathematician, however, knows it is 'polygoose'.

Peter McBurney, Department of Computer Science, University of Liverpool

Further to previous replies: the plural is 'mouses', for the same reason that you may take a Mickey Mouse exam and two of them are Mickey Mouses: an exam is not a mouse and therefore the plural follows the regular pattern, adding '-s'. Mailmen are men, but Walkmans are not. A mongoose is not a goose and so the plural is mongooses. The Toronto hockey team consists of men, not leaves, and so they are the Maple Leafs, not the Maple Leaves. I know whereof I speak: my family are people, not feet, and so in groups we are Lightfoots not 'Lightfeet'.

David Lightfoot, Bethesda, Maryland, USA

David Lightfoot is logical, but incorrect. It is not a brand name or compound word, which would follow normal plural practice. It is not even called a 'computer mouse'. Its inventor in the 1960s simply called it the mouse (adding the word 'computer' just puts it in context).

Usage in the computer industry is overwhelmingly in favour of 'mice'. Just look at any catalogue of computer peripherals. As a product, the mouse first appeared as part of what was originally known as the WIMP interface (Windows, Icons, MICE, Pull-down menus). But people do use mouses (the word seems to appeal to some academics – possibly because they use real mice in their research and it would be so easy to confuse the two). So, by dint of usage, both are correct.

However, linguistically, you could make a case for using 'mousen', or cartoon fans could say 'meeces', or you could adopt the Microsoft cop-out: 'mouse devices'.

David Fox, London

What is the religious significance of the ladybird? 'Lady' comes from the Virgin Mary; its German name translates as 'Maria beetle'; in Dutch, it translates as 'Our dear Lord's little creature'.

I grew up in Norfolk where the ladybird is called a 'bishy barney bee'.

I had always assumed this was an obscure dialect expression, but perhaps the name derives from a Bishop Barnaby?

T. W. Tilford, Marlow, Bucks

In Irish the ladybird is *bóín Dé*, meaning 'God's little cow'.

Ciarán Ó Maoláin, Armagh

Ladybirds belong to the family of coccinellidae beetles, from *coccinatus*, Latin for 'clad in scarlet'. The common English ladybird is red with seven black spots and the name is derived from 'Our Lady', based on artistic representations of the Virgin Mary wearing a red cloak, the seven spots symbolizing the 'seven joys and seven sorrows' of the Virgin. There is no scriptural basis for this, however, and ladybirds are not mentioned in the Bible.

W. A. Exell's *History of the Ladybird* cites 329 names for ladybirds in fifty-five different languages. A quarter of these are dedicated to the Virgin Mary, but many are dedicated to God, Jesus and the various saints of Christendom. In India the name is a dedication to Indra. In Hebrew the ladybird is referred to as 'Cow of Moses our Teacher'.

Rosemary Capriolo, North Balwyn, Victoria, Australia

I don't know the religious significance of the ladybird. However, its Kernewek (Cornish language) equivalent, *bughik-Dyw*, also translates as 'God's little cow'. More highly thought of, though, is the butterfly, *tykki-Dyw*, meaning 'God's toy' or even 'God's darling'.

Milo Perrin, St Just, Cornwall

In France, ladybirds are known as *bêtes à bon Dieu*, which means 'God's creature'. If you see one, it is regarded as a sign of good luck and if you can catch one and have it walk on your hand, you make a wish.

Ramona Wilkins-Carlier, Enfield, Middx

And here in Japan they are called *tentou-mushi*, which translates as 'Heavenly path insect'!

John Ryder, Kyoto, Japan

'Heavenly path' is a literal translation of the kanji characters used for *tentou* in the Japanese word *tentou-mushi*. But the word is also a commonly used, rather old-fashioned word for 'sun'. In olden days it was also a name used for gods or divine beings (presumably derived from Shintoism, whose supreme deity is the sun goddess). So it's either 'sun insect' or 'divine insect'.

Satsuki Oba, London NW3

I have heard professional comedians claim that there are only eleven jokes in the world. What are they?

Tottenham Hotspur's first team.

Sean Cronin, London N1

It is not eleven jokes, but eleven butts of jokes that can be listed. My own version reflects the proportion of male to female comedians fairly accurately.

The wife; the missus; 'er; 'er indoors; 'er cookin'; 'er in bed; 'er trying to compete wiv the blonde; the muvver-in-lor; the wife's mum; 'er mum; his penis size.

Murray Weston, Stevenage, Herts

If the questioner were to attend my comedy classes at City University, he would discover there are ten forms of joke category: mis-understanding/farce; slapstick and visual humour; innuendo, wordplay and puns; exaggeration; reverse analogy and comic metaphor; inappropriate response; repetition; irony, sarcasm and black humour; mimicry, parody and satire; oh, and repetition.

Needless to say, if you're Jim Davidson, ignore the above.

Marc Blake, London SW14

Maybe there's only one, as the poet Robert Frost intimated when he wrote: 'Forgive, O Lord, my little jokes on Thee,/And I'll forgive Thy great big one on me.'

Malcolm Johnson, London SW16

In a number of mainland southern European towns, some households place one or two plastic bottles filled with water on their doorsteps or porches. I have been told that it discourages dogs from fouling the area. If true, why does it work?

This phenomenon also exists in Japan. At first I thought it was related to earthquakes and that when Tokyo finally succumbs to 'the big one', survivors could crawl from the rubble and find supplies of water with ease.

However, I was reliably informed that these bottles are to deter cats from going to the toilet against people's houses. Apparently the water acts as a kind of mirror, which the cats see themselves in and which makes them scared and unable to do the deed. I wonder if it works to deter burglars?

Anthony Gardner, Tokyo, Japan

After noticing such bottles of water scattered along nature-strips beside footpaths and in some gardens of suburban Adelaide, I was told that cats and dogs instinctively avoid fouling near what might appear to them a potential drinking source. I've seen it so often and for long enough to imagine that if it didn't work it would have been easily disproved by now.

Keith Bushnell, Penneshaw, South Australia

Ten years ago this practice was very popular in New Zealand and many front lawns were covered with bottles of water. Finally a researcher did a survey and found that lawns with bottles were fouled by dogs four times as often as lawns without. However, it was still a 'rare event' for a lawn to be fouled and most lawns were 'spared', so it was easy for a homeowner to believe that his lawn was being protected by the bottles.

Professor Neil Pearce, Centre for Public Health Research,
Wellington, New Zealand

We optimistically did this for years until a fellow New Zealander made a slightly shamefaced public confession. Having heard a relative complain about the dog poo on her front lawn, he had extemporized, inventing what to his amazement soon became a national myth. New Zealand loved the way it had been fooled. The myth, however, spread abroad and appears to be indestructible.

Kathryn Smits, Auckland, New Zealand

Argentina witnessed a rash of this a few years ago. The result was just another hurdle in walking along Buenos Aires pavements. Not only did we have broken pavements, poop and puddles but bottles as well. However, after a year or so, it just fizzled out naturally, having made no impression on the dogs' habits.

Alice Adamson, Buenos Aires, Argentina

Here in Ceará, Brazil, people hang clear plastic bags full of water in the kitchen to frighten flies with their own magnified reflection. If it does work I would hate to think how many flies there would be if there were no plastic bags of water!

Incidentally, many kitchens here are ornamented with strips of orange rind hanging down like fly-paper – but I have yet to find out what it is for.

Mark Greenwood, Fortaleza, Brazil

In Mel Brooks's film *The History of the World: Part 1*, Moses is depicted descending from Mount Sinai and dropping a third tablet of stone, so destroying commandments eleven to fifteen. What might these missing commandments have been?

11. Thou shalt not lie through thy teeth when in government.
12. Musicians, actors and celebrities all count as false gods.
13. Shop on the Sabbath day – but remember thine credit limit and keep it holy.
14. Confession and absolution are not a licence to repeat the sin.
15. Don't believe everything you read.

Marc Blake, London SW14

One would be: 'Thou shall not use a mobile phone in a restaurant.'

Michael Carey, London N11

Avoid the A64 on Bank Holidays.
John Morrison, Hebden Bridge, West Yorks

11. You shall take proper care of your children.
12. You shall be just, kind and forgiving to all who depend on you.
13. You shall not go to war other than in self-defence.
14. You shall not perform any act that involves cruelty.
15. You shall not pursue financial gain with detriment to others.
Rafael Scharf, London NW11

Killjoys will doubtless inform you that if you read Exodus and Numbers you'll find not only another five commandments, but a further 598 or so to follow.

But of course everyone knows the eleventh commandment:
11. Thou shalt not get caught.

Fewer are aware of the next four:
12. If caught, blame someone else.
13. If that doesn't work, don't apologize.
14. If forced to apologize, don't resign.
15. If forced to resign, get a good book deal.
Charles Harris, London NW3

11. Thou shalt not drive thine ass at more than 30 mph in a built-up area.
12. Thou shalt not suffer thy cat to use thy neighbour's garden as a toilet.
13. Thou shalt not curse thy supermarket trolley. It knoweth not what it doeth, and neither do youeth.
14. If a cyclist should smite thee upon the pavement, thou shalt not shove him into the oncoming traffic.
15. Curse not thy neighbour's barbecue, for a burnt sacrifice is pleasing unto the Lord.
Robert D. Hill, Reigate, Surrey

11. Thou shalt not believe in IMF prescriptions.
12. Thou shalt not worship Millennium Domes.
13. Thou shalt not kill the downtrodden for throwing stones.

14. Thou shalt not sit idly by while oil companies rip thee off.

15. Thou shalt not believe Hollywood's version of anything.

A. Kassam, The Hague, Netherlands

Can anyone tell
Me if this
Is a poem or
not?

The problem with definitions of poetry is that they are either too limiting or too general. At the end of the day, it is poets, publishers and audiences who decide. As the questioner implies, this means that there are areas of great disagreement. Chaucer's *Canterbury Tales* is written in what we call 'verse' and yet we don't usually call the whole cycle, or even one of the individual tales, a 'poem'. Proverbs, aphorisms, slogans and formulaic jokes such as riddles often display the characteristics that we associate with poetry: pattern, rhythm, compression, musicality and the like, but they are rarely called poems.

Ever since people started writing free verse, there have been some readers who thought that what these poets had written was indeed poetry, while there were other readers who were sure that it wasn't. Interesting problems arise with the 1611 Authorized Version translations of the Psalms and the Song of Solomon. Nowadays, many readers would regard these as poetry. These can be contrasted with John Donne's sermons, including the famous 'For whom the bell tolls' piece or Martin Luther King's 'I have a dream', both of which have the rhythms one might associate with free verse poetry, and yet few would call these poems.

This said, it is quite possible to take up a non-categorizing position on all this: 'I don't care what it's called; do I like what I'm reading or hearing?' After all, when we're in conversation with people not many of us ask ourselves if we have just heard an example of irony or sarcasm, litotes or hyperbole, ellipsis or deixis and the like. If we can avoid getting stuck in the 'What is it?' position, it's perhaps easier to enjoy the way that all kinds of language-users create patterns with words that intrigue us.

The questioner has written what is a classic self-referential sentence and laid it out on the page according to the tradition of free verse. Nice

one, but not worth sweating over whether it's a poem or not.
Michael Rosen, London E8

A poem, like all literary forms, is a set of highly mutable conventions, agreed between producer (poet) and receiver (reader). These conventions are open to continuous revision and transformation – but it is usually (not universally) accepted that a poem is a poem if it is produced with the intention of it being poetry, and if it is possible for a reader to recognize it as poetry. The questioner's lines were produced with the concept of poetry in mind, and I was able to recognize them as such (primarily because of the punctuation and line structuring) – so they are poetry. Or perhaps, to do justice to the ambiguity of this issue, I should say:

Your poem
Is Poetry
If this
Is.

A famous example of a poem being forged out of the purposeful arrangement of everyday speech is 'This is Just to Say' (1934) by William Carlos Williams, which reads:

I have eaten
the plums
that were in
the icebox
and which
you were probably
saving
for breakfast
Forgive me
they were delicious
so sweet
and so cold.
Andrew Teverson, London SW9

Prose,
I suppose.
Nick Cutler, Inglewhite, Lancs

I shan't
as I can't.
But I would
if I could.

Simon Maddison, Hitchin, Herts

Yes
it is
not.

Dan Usiskin, London N12

It's a poem if the line format imparts a different meaning, emphasis, or sonority. Otherwise it's just a fancy layout. You might try passing it off as 'Art', though.

Norman Henderson, Southampton

It is not a poem as it has none of the essential elements of poetry: subject, meaning, theme, mood, imagery, language that draws attention to itself, rhyme, rhythm and form. But this is:

Well, is it memorable
Or easily forgot?

Professor Edward Black, Sydney, Australia

According to Jeremy Bentham it would be a poem. He is reported to have said: 'Prose is when all the lines except the last go on to the end. Poetry is when some of them fall short of it' (quoted in M. St J. Packe, *The Life of John Stuart Mill*).

Carrie Osborne, Alstonefield, Derby.

Why do wine bottles have a large indent in the base?

Wine bottles used for still wine don't have an indent in the base. However, bottles used for champagne and other sparkling wines do – for two reasons.

First, the indent is designed to prevent the bottle exploding. The curved wall of the bottle makes for a very strong structure, and the indent makes the base as strong as the wall.

Second, during the fermentation process the bottles are stacked upside down. Because of this, the solid matter that results from the fermentation comes to rest on the underside of the cork (it is later expelled and the bottle is topped up during the degorgement process). The indent allows the bottles to be safely stacked with the neck of one resting in the indent of the bottle below.

Nigel Shaw, London SW19

I was startled to read the explanation for the indent in the bottom of wine bottles given by Nigel Shaw.

Wine bottles for still wine most certainly do have an indent, especially those in the 'burgundy' shape, and particularly those containing the more expensive wines. My son developed a theory that if in doubt at the off-licence, feel a few bottoms.

Second, champagne (plus fizzy wine with aspirations) isn't stacked upside down 'with the neck of one resting in the indent of the bottle below' but is placed neck first in a set of holes made in a wooden board about six feet by four feet. Starting at the horizontal, each bottle is given daily a fifteen-degree twist and a slight upward tilt, until it is as close to the vertical as possible. The sediment spirals down the bottle to the neck for degorgement.

I agree with Mr Shaw that strong bottles are necessary for fizzy wine, but that still leaves us wondering why the bottles for still wines have the indents.

Stephen Hill, Hobbs Pavilion Restaurant, Cambridge

Wine bottles used to be individually blown and hence were spherical, somewhat like Chianti bottles. The more stable straight-sided bottles were produced with the aid of an iron rod pressed into the bottom of the bottle while the glass was still workable, leaving this indentation. The iron rod was called a 'punto' and so the indentation it made while rolling the bottle became known as the 'punt'.

As for Stephen Hill's theory that you should always go for the bottle with the deepest punt: I used to subscribe to that myself but experience has taught me that some clever vintners have learned to exploit it!

Bill Watson, Chorlton-cum-Hardy, Manchester

Many wines continue to develop in the bottle and this process produces sediments. These fall to the bottom of the bottle over time and form a layer. When wine is poured from a flat-bottomed bottle, this layer is easily disturbed and the poured wine ends up cloudy, spoiling its appearance and sometimes its taste. Having an indent in the bottom means that the sediment is deeper, with a smaller surface area, so it is thus easier to avoid disturbing it.

This also provides an explanation of why Stephen Hill's son noticed the connection with more expensive wines. Most cheaper wines are filtered or whirled in a centrifuge before bottling, avoiding their being clouded by sediment and thus the need for the more expensive punt-bottomed bottles. Many wine buffs consider that wine only achieves its full complexity if allowed to develop without filtering, which explains the link between punts and quality (or expensive) wines.

Nigel Duncan, London SW20

I drink two bottles of supermarket red wine a week, none of it sparkling, and I rarely pay more than £3.49 for a bottle. The wines come from various parts of the world; some have punts and some do not.

Nowadays wine bottles are machine moulded. Small differences in the shape of the bottle may mean that the mould has to be more complicated and thus more costly, but the effect on the cost of each bottle would be negligible.

As to clever vintners exploiting the punt, I don't see how they can do that, now that the volume is stated on the label. I suspect that the punt is another of those wine snobberies like the ridiculous practice of stuffing the neck with a piece of bark, which tends to taint the wine and is no cheaper than the much more efficient screw cap. And if someone writes to say that corks 'breathe', I would like to see them prove it.

Ray Cobbett, Billericay, Essex

Ray Cobbett believes that vintners cannot exploit the punt because 'the volume of wine is stated on the label'.

The EU permits a variance of 20ml per bottle, following a plea from producers who stated that this was necessary to allow for inaccuracies in the bottling machines. So your 750ml bottle should in theory contain between 730ml and 770ml but, uncannily, it will generally contain 730ml. This is perfectly legal and gives the producer a bonus bottle for every three dozen.

T. George, School of Leisure, Hospitality and
Food Management, University of Salford

Ray Cobbett is right and T. George is wrong: vintners 'cannot exploit the punt because the volume of wine is stated on the label'.

Sure, the law permits a tolerance on individual bottles to allow for variability in the performance of bottling machines but there is an overriding requirement that the average of all bottles in a batch must not be less than the quantity declared on the label. So for every bottle found to be underfilled, there will be another that is overfilled – no profit to the vintner. If Mr George has evidence to the contrary he should pass it forthwith to his Trading Standards authority for legal action.

Michael Ranken, Hythe, Kent

Ray Cobbett, who considers wine corks to be a 'ridiculous snobbery', might like to consider the following.

The traditional management of cork oak forest in Portugal, which supplies 80 per cent of the world's wine corks, is vital both to the economy of one of the poorest regions in Europe and to the sustainability of one of the world's richest ecosystems. The cork oak forest – habitat of the Iberian lynx, the black stork, Bonelli's eagle and the Spanish imperial eagle, among other highly endangered species – is under severe threat from the increasing use of plastic 'corq' (manufactured by Supremecorq, in which Bill Gates is a major investor).

Right-on wine drinkers should express concern to their supermarkets and off-licences.

Clare Butler, Milton Keynes, Bucks

Is there any evidence that Wilbur and Orville Wright actually made their unwitnessed 1903 flight? Even the Smithsonian Institution originally doubted the claim, which was made only after Santos-Dumont's witnessed flight had been publicized.

The Wright brothers' flight on 17 December 1903 was witnessed by five of the crew of the Kill Devil Life Saving Station, one of whom took the famous photograph. It was also reported in the following day's issue of the aptly named *Norfolk Virginian-Pilot* newspaper.

The Smithsonian Institution did not doubt the date, but disputed the Wright brothers' claim to have produced the first successful flying machine. The secretary of the Smithsonian Institution, Professor Samuel Pierpont Langley, had been granted $50,000 by the US War Department to develop an aircraft, and had flown several quarter-scale models of his *Langley Aerodrome* between 1900 and 1903. However, attempts in October and December 1903 to launch the full-scale version from a platform on a houseboat in the Potomac River ended in failure. The Smithsonian claimed that this craft could have flown before the Wrights'.

Other aircraft designers later tried to deny the Wrights' claim in order to overturn their patents on many of the design features. The Wright brothers made a flight of twenty-four miles in thirty-eight minutes in October 1905; by contrast, Santos-Dumont made the first officially recognized flight in Europe, lasting twenty-one seconds, in November 1906.

The whole subject of first-flight claims was dealt with at length by the British aviation historian, C. H. Gibbs-Smith, leading to his conclusion that the Wrights made the first powered, sustained and controlled flights, supported by witnesses and photographic evidence.

Vic Smith, Ickenham, Middx

If Lent lasts forty days, why is Ash Wednesday six and a half weeks before Easter? Surely it ought to be the following week?

The simple answer is that Sundays are not counted as part of Lent. This is because every Sunday is the Feast of the Resurrection of Our Lord and as such cannot be taken as part of the Lenten fast.

The Forty Days of Lent were chosen by the Early Church as a period of preparation for baptism at Easter (the only time that baptisms were then usually held) and for the reconciliation of penitents. Later on, all Christians were encouraged to fast during Lent. The tone is set on Ash Wednesday when believers are marked on their foreheads with the ashes of last year's palm crosses as a sign of their mortality.

The Forty Days of Lent are associated with the fasting of Jesus prior to beginning his public ministry (Matthew 4: 2; Mark 1: 13; Luke 4: 2). Acts 1: 3 sets another forty days between the Resurrection and the Ascension.

Forty days is a ritual period of preparation recurring throughout the Bible: Noah's flood, (Genesis 7); the embalming of Joseph (Genesis 50); Moses on the holy mountain (Exodus 24); the spying out of Canaan (Numbers 13); the boasting of Goliath before his death at the hands of David (1 Samuel 17); Elijah fasting in the desert (1 Kings 19); Jonah's warning to Nineveh (Jonah 3).

The Church's Year also keeps the forty days of Christmas, from Christmas Day to Candlemas (2 February).

Revd James Little, Newark, Notts

In the Bible and Church calendar – as everywhere else until recent times – exact counting is not a strong point (see David Ewing Duncan, *The Calendar*).

The four Sundays leading to the first Sunday in Lent were traditionally called Septuagesima, Sexagesima, Quinquagesima and Quadragesima; that is, respectively, the seventieth, sixtieth, etc., day before Easter! There is also an element of doubt about other claims: that the Israelites were exactly forty years on their wilderness wanderings; that both Saul and David reigned for forty years; and that the Exile in Babylon lasted seventy years.

There is no telling whether Jesus was exactly forty days in his wilderness experience. Even the Resurrection supposedly occurring after three days boils down to a period of about thirty-six hours between the death of Jesus on the cross and the rolling back of the stone.

Therefore the alternative answer is: don't expect precision!

Revd Peter Robbins, Tamworth, Staffs

At various times and places in the Early Church, Lent has lasted seven weeks (omitting Saturdays and Sundays) or six weeks (omitting the

Sundays – a total of thirty-six days). Also three (or even two) weeks have been referred to as *tessarakosté* (forty days).

During the first three centuries of the Church, a pre-Easter fast of only a few days was customary – although the fasting was probably much more strict than it is today. It was not until the seventh century that the Western Church added the four days from Ash Wednesday to the following Saturday, and the thirty-six days of fasting became a forty-day Lent.

Revd Julian Dunn, Great Haseley, Oxford

I know only the first two lines of a poem:

> **An Austrian army awfully arrayed**
>
> **Boldly by battery besieged Belgrade ...**

The next two lines end in 'come' and 'doom' and I believe it continues right through the alphabet. Can anyone complete it?

The following poem, by Alaric A. Watts (1797–1864), is found in several anthologies, my source being the *New Oxford Book of Light Verse* (1978):

> An Austrian army awfully array'd,
> Boldly by battery besieged Belgrade.
> Cossack commanders cannonading come
> Dealing destruction's devastating doom:
> Every endeavour engineers essay,
> For fame, for fortune fighting-furious fray!
> Generals 'gainst generals grapple, gracious God!
> How Heaven honours heroic hardihood!
> Infuriate – indiscriminate in ill –
> Kinsmen kill kindred – kindred kinsmen kill:
> Labour low levels loftiest, longest line,
> Men march 'mid mounds, 'mid moles, 'mid murd'rous mines:
> Now noisy noxious numbers notice nought
> Of outward obstacles, opposing ought –
> Poor patriots – partly purchased – partly press'd
> Quite quaking, quickly 'Quarter! quarter!' quest:
> Reason returns, religious right redounds,

Suwarrow stops such sanguinary sounds.
Truce to thee, Turkey, triumph to thy train,
Unwise, unjust, unmerciful Ukraine!
Vanish, vain victory! Vanish, victory vain!
Why wish we warfare? Wherefore welcome were
Xerxes, Ximenes, Xanthus, Xavier?
Yield, yield, ye youths, ye yeomen, yield your yell:
Zeno's, Zimmermann's, Zoroaster's zeal,
Again attract; arts against arms appeal!
Maureen Jewess, Wimbotsham, Norfolk

The whole poem, which follows all the letters of the alphabet except 'J', appeared in the *Faber Book of Comic Verse* (1942), which was edited by my father, Michael Roberts.

In the preface my father stated: 'I have followed tradition in ascribing the lines ... to Alaric A. Watts who, according to his son and biographer, contributed them to the *Literary Gazette* in 1820. There is, however, some evidence that they first appeared a few years earlier in the *Trifler*, a periodical written by the boys of Westminster School.'

After the bombing of Serbia in 1999 I began working to put these lines into modern dress:

An Allied air arm, Albrightly arrayed,
By Bill, Blair bidden, boldly bombed Belgrade ...

The effort is shaping up slowly.
Adam Roberts, Professor of International Relations, Balliol College, Oxford

I was delighted to read the full poem, but was a little surprised that there was no line of Js. I offer the following:

Jostling, jowled, janissaries, joust, jab, jeer.

Although it has the right number of feet, and even has a Turkish reference, I could hardly be expected to find a rhyme for 'ill' and 'kill' — except 'Jill', perhaps, and that didn't seem quite relevant.
Philip Bour, Huntingdon, Cambs

Following Adam Roberts's attempted update, here is my contribution:

An Allied air arm, Albrightly arrayed,
By Bill, Blair bidden, boldly bombed Belgrade.

Clinton censors counter-cleansing campaign
Destroyed, devastated Dictator's domain
Engineers exacting enormous exploding
Futilely fulfilling fundamental foreboding.
Greatly gathered gunnery giving general gusto,
Hysterical humiliations, hounded high-low
Indiscriminate internecine immolations inapt
Kosovans' kindred killed, kith kindlessly kidnapped.
Lifelong liberals loathing limited liabilities
Milosevic's marauders, murderous mentalities
Noisily noxious needing notoriety
Oblivious outsiders opposing opprobriously.
Patriotic purpose prepaid, pursuing penury,
Quixotic quest, quickly quandary.
Reason redundant Religion rightly replies.
Supersonic surveillance, somnambulant secret spies.
Tyrant turned tail, timorously truculent,
Underbelly undercut, ultimate unwisdom unimplement.
Vainglorious victory, vanish vain vanquished.
Warlords weeping, warplanes weak willed.
Xanthippe-like xenophobes, xantho-livered xantho-eyes,
Yielded yet yearning Yugoslavia's yesterdays.
Zanily zealous zeitgeist zeroed.
Allied aggrandisement, aggressors arraigned.

R. F. Jones, Liverpool

Are the words 'their' and 'they' as substitutes for 'his or her' and 'he or she' now acceptable through constant (mis)usage? Surely a new word for 'he or she' would be preferable?

This use of 'they', 'them' and 'their' has a long history of use, even in written English. William Caxton, the first printer in England, writes in 1470, 'Each of them should make themself ready'; William Shakespeare prays that 'God send everyone their heart's desire.' It was only in the eighteenth century that grammarians labelled 'they' as ungrammatical, on the grounds that the pronoun should be singular if it corresponded to a singular noun. (These grammarians were less worried about gender: their solution was to use 'he' and pretend it included females.)

But a living language is stronger than grammarians: the singular 'they' has resisted two centuries of attempts to regulate it out of English. In the 1970s feminists drew attention to the fact that grammar rules in books were at odds with common usage, and that the rules also discriminated against women. There were some attempts at compromise: newly invented sex-inclusive forms, among them 'tey', 'co', 'per' and 'E', were put forward, but none of them caught on. Why should they? A solution already existed. Major British grammar and usage books now consider this use of 'they' as acceptable. They are doing their job: recording what many educated speakers of the language say and write.

Catherine Walter, Chilton, Oxon

Is there any English word that rhymes with 'orange'?

Perhaps it will make you cringe
Or even cause you to binge
To find that the word infringe
Actually rhymes with orange,
Plus several more that hinge
On sounds of a similar tinge.

Rollo Bruce, Horsforth, Leeds

The 1985 *Penguin Rhyming Dictionary* considers the final syllable only and thus claims to rhyme 'orange' with the likes of 'syringe', 'scavenge' and 'lozenge'. These, though, are plainly weak rhymes. *Walker's Rhyming Dictionary* offered 'sporange', meaning a spore-case, which is indeed in the OED. I'd like to see you use it in a casual couplet, though . . .

Ian Shuttleworth, London W10

There is a hill in Monmouthshire called Blorenge (near Abergavenny).

Mrs J. Tanner, West Wickham, Kent

It's rumoured that William of Orange
Was one bracket short of a door hinge
So unkempt and hairy
Was the old fruit, that Mary,
(His consort), renamed him Will More Fringe.
Deborah Jackson, Combe Down, Bath

The store's been shut for years now, but did Gorringe's sell oranges?
Roger Crosskey, London W10

The questioner should take a leaf out of Shakespeare's book – he coined one-tenth of the 17,667 words in his vocabulary, many of which are still in use today: 'lonely', 'majestic', 'critical' and 'excellent', to name but a few. Who knows, future linguists may applaud the questioner's genius for discovering a word that rhymes perfectly.
Emily Morris, Beaumaris, Anglesey

Other words for which it is well nigh impossible to find a rhyme are: 'month', 'silver', 'purple' and 'chimney'.
Peter Sharp, Snells Beach, New Zealand

I cooked some oats in boiling milk,
And ate it from a porringer.
Next time I'll add some citrus juice
To make my breakfast oranger.
Connell Wagner, Spring Hill, Queensland, Australia

What is the term for getting the lyrics to songs wrong?

Malapopism.
John Docherty, Paisley, Glasgow

The correct term for this is dislyrhythmia. This condition is mainly a dysfunction of memory, particularly in the speech centre of the brain, but strangely it does not affect the brain's ability to remember rhythmic patterns. The net result is that the person tries to fit words that they think are right to the tune, with disastrous consequences to the rhythm. I have been a sufferer of this for many years.

There is also an associated condition called amlyralinesia, where the sufferer has the ability to remember only the first line or two of a song and sings 'la-la-la' for the rest of the lyrics. Research by a colleague and myself some years ago discovered this to affect some 60 per cent of the population. This could be why so many Eurovision song contest winners in the past had few lyrics and lots of la-la's and boom-bang-a-bang's.

Tom Bush (subject adviser, Learning Disabilities),
Institute of Health Studies, University of Plymouth

The term for mishearing a lyric – if, for example, you think Bob Dylan is singing 'The ants are my friends, they're blowin' in the wind' – is 'mondegreen'.

This term was coined by Sylvia Wright in a 1954 *Atlantic* article. She revealed how, as a child, she had wept over a folk song that included the lyrics: 'They had slain the Earl of Moray/And Lady Mondegreen.' Much later, she realized that the song was not about the tragic fate of Lady Mondegreen, but rather the continuing plight of the good earl: 'They had slain the Earl of Moray/And laid him on the green.'

From sifting through thousands of mondegreens to compile four book-length collections, I can report that the most frequent error is probably the title of my first volume, ''Scuse Me While I Kiss This Guy' – a common mondegreen for Jimi Hendrix's lyric: ''Scuse me while I kiss the sky.' But my favourite is from my brother, who was always convinced that Paul Young was singing: 'Every time you go away, you take a piece of meat with you.'

Gavin Edwards, Camden Town, London NW1

A child returning from Sunday school reported that he had sung about an animal called Gladly who had trouble seeing straight. The hymn was: 'Gladly the Cross I'd bear.'

A. C. da Roza, Northwood, Middx

Gavin Edwards misquotes the Scottish ballad 'The Bonny Earl of Moray'. It should be: 'They hae slain the Earl of Moray/And hae laid him on the green.' This is made quite clear from the final stanza:

O lang will his Lady
Look owre the Castle Downe
Ere she see the Earl of Moray
Come sounding through the town.

James Baxter, Sunbury-on-Thames, Surrey

I disagree with Tom Bush as to the cause of this phenomenon. When we listen to words or music, or look/read, the brain is actively constructing sense out of what we are taking in very quickly. It begins to construct sense from relatively little information and is, in consequence, running 'parallel' with the sensory aspects of the brain, frequently checking between the two. More often than not what the brain is predicting from its previous knowledge will be the word or phrase or image that it was expecting. But, of course, things do not always turn out that way.

Consequently, we mishear, mis-see, misunderstand – that is, we construe incorrectly. Pop music is often unclearly sung, hence the frequency of this phenomenon in this field. It happened to Sylvia Wright when a young girl because her model of the world was much less sophisticated and, hence, was more likely to construct an error. It is a perfectly normal working of the brain, and a symptom of disorders for a very few.

David Freedman, London NW2

A Round John?

In the mid-1950s our neighbour worked at a school in Pomona, New York State. One day around Christmas time one of the young students painted the manger scene. There were the cows and the donkey, the farmyard animals, Mary and Joseph, the angel in attendance, and on one side was a little fat boy.

'Who's that?' the teachers asked.

'That's Round John,' the boy replied. 'Y'know, like in the song, "Round John, Virgin, Mother and Child."'

Mark Antrobus, Kodaikanal, India

What are the determining factors that distinguish a hamlet from a village, a town and then a city? How does a settlement move up or down in status – for example, through population size?

Our family has simple rules on this. Hamlet or village? The latter has a pub. Village or town? The latter has a Woolworth's.

R. Sanderson, Leamington Spa, Warks

The smallest settlement, a hamlet, is just a few houses, quite often around a farm. When in earlier times the hamlet increased in size and was deemed big enough to warrant its own priest, a church was built and it became a village. As the village grew, and had sufficient farmers and traders to establish its own market, it became a town. When the town was of sufficient importance to warrant a cathedral or abbey, it became a city.

Peter Ward, Lansdown, Bath

In Britain there are no criteria that set out how a place is classified. For example, a town has to apply to the Queen to become a city and then on certain royal occasions the Queen decides to allow a couple of applications. Those that succeed and those that fail are never informed why.

Almost every other country has a clear process for identifying a city. In China, centuries of bureaucracy and civil service practice have arrived at highly detailed and inflexible criteria, including, for example, that the non-agricultural population of the town must exceed 120,000, of whom no fewer then 80,000 must be engaged in non-agricultural industries. By contrast, in the United States some states may label an area a city regardless of population size (Spring City, Tennessee, has an approximate population of 2,000).

In Peru, criteria include population growth and the existence of educational institutions and hospitals. In Japan, rather differently, a city must have a population of 50,000 or more, and its inhabitants must be engaged in commercial or industrial pursuits. Thus, Tokyo contains several cities.

Jane Griffiths MP, London SW1

In 1873 John Shortridge, an emigrant to North Carolina, remarked that the small cluster of houses surrounding his woollen mill at Mark's Creek would, in his native England, have been called a hamlet. 'This is not a hamlet yet,' he said, 'but I believe it will be one soon and perhaps in years to come a city; so we will name this tiny village Hamlet and christen the baby town by planting a little tree.'

The tree grew and so did the settlement, and with the rapid expansion of the railroads and attendant industries, the strategically placed Hamlet soon became a flourishing terminal for rail passengers and freight. By 1903 it had official city status and to the present day has enjoyed the distinction of being the City of Hamlet.

Gill Barker, Cambridge

In England, Lamb and Bacon are common surnames, but few people are called Beef. In France, Le Boeuf seems to be a fairly common surname but not L'Agneau or Le Bacon. Why?

The etymological origins of the words 'lamb' and 'bacon' lie in Old German, which arrived in England during the Saxon invasions of the fifth and sixth centuries. They were used in the Anglo-Saxon language until the Norman invasion in 1066, along with the bovine descriptors, 'cow' and 'bull'.

From 1066 until around the end of the fourteenth century, Norman French and Latin were the languages spoken by the Norman ruling elite. These were the people who ate the most meat (the peasantry was not able to afford it). Hence the words we use in modern English for cooked meats — beef, mutton and ham — come from the French *boeuf, mouton* and *jambon*. The peasants were the ones who looked after, killed and prepared these animals for their Norman lords and so we describe live animals with the Anglo-Saxon words cow, sheep and pig.

It is not surprising that the modern English surname 'Beef' is rare as it is not an Old English word. Surnames that include the words 'cow' and 'bull' are very common, however (for example, Cowan, Cowburn, Cowland, Cowley, Cowking, plus Bull, Bulman and Bullock).

I cannot say why L'Agneau (the modern French for 'sheep') is not a common surname in France, but the English surname Agnew is quite common.

As for Le Bacon, this is an English word. I don't think any person would be happy with its modern French translation of 'Le Lard'.
Simon Wilkinson, London NW7

Is there a collective term for words such as 'figment' that can only be used in conjunction with one other word (that is, 'imagination')? Alternatively, can someone come up with a sentence that contains 'figment' but not 'imagination'?

It is used alone in 'making figments feel' (Hardy); 'a monstrous figment' (Thackeray); 'figments of the mind' (Berkeley); 'a figment of abstraction' (Caird on Kant). 'This was no figment' appeared in a newspaper quite recently.
Mike Lyle, Llangynog, Carms

I can't think of a single sentence that just contains the word 'figment'.
William Martin, Exeter, Devon

If the next sperm in the queue had fertilized my mother's egg, would I have been in various ways different or would someone else have been conceived in my place?

The idea – that I would still exist even if my mother had married a different father, or if conception had taken place a month later than it actually did, or if the second spermatozoon had won the race to the ovum – originates with Thomas Aquinas, who held that the soul is infused into the body at the moment of conception. Presumably my soul was positioned somewhere, to join with the newly formed embryo as soon as the egg was fertilized. If fertilization was delayed, so was I.

If we disregard the notion of 'soul' and look at what happens when a fertilized egg splits to form identical twins, we realize that we get two discrete human identities where before there was only one. The same is true when the connection is cut between the two upper hemispheres of the brain: two separate spheres of consciousness are created – that is, two different identities in one body. Clearly a particular human identity originates with a particular functioning human brain, and we must therefore deduce that if the next sperm in the queue had fertilized my mother's egg, I would not exist. That means that my existence depended on 'my' spermatozoon arriving at 'my' ovum before the 3 billion or so other spermatozoa who were having a go.

(Dr) André Blom, Waterloo, Ontario, Canada

I would like to go on *Mastermind* but I don't have a specialist subject. Which topic of research would give people the impression that I've spent years in a library, whilst consuming the smallest time to master?

Try:

1. Yourself.
2. Accurate unemployment statistics 1979–97.
3. The successful war on poverty/drugs/crime/pollution, etc.

Tony Beswick, Tapton, Chesterfield

Try the Peloponnesian War. There have been many books on the subject, but the sole contemporary source for all subsequent works is *The History of the Peloponnesian War* by Thucydides.

Thucydides did not include anecdotal information, he personally interviewed the protagonists and he excluded anything that could not be checked from another source. It was hundreds of years before other historians took a similarly rigorous approach, and by that time no other contemporary sources from the war were available.

Quentin Langley, Woking, Surrey

This reminds me of a glut of jokes over thirty years ago about the smallest books in the world: for example, *The Very Best of German Humour*; *Famous Italian War Heroes*; *A Hundred Years of Jewish Cricket*, etc.

I suggest the questioner hunts out one of the following: *Men of Probity in the Conservative Party 1979–96*; *English Sporting Success since 1967*; *Altruism in the Privatized Utilities*; *The Secret Life of Princess Diana* ...

Richard Handford, Chichester, West Sussex

In the story of Goldilocks and the Three Bears, why is it that Daddy Bear's porridge was too hot, Mummy Bear's porridge was too cold and yet Baby Bear's was 'just right'? These observations appear to place the temperature of the smallest portion between that of the largest and middle-sized portions. Is there some simple explanation of the anomalous cooling rates of the three bowls?

Ignoring for a moment the insulating properties of the Bear family's breakfast porcelain, let's apply Newton's law of cooling.

Heat loss varies as temperature difference (which at the start is the same for all three) multiplied by surface area. Rate of cooling varies as rate of heat loss divided by volume. Suppose that Baby Bear had half as much porridge as his mother and one-third as much as his father. In most families, adults use the same set of dishes while babies have their own smaller dishes, usually prettily decorated (Baby Bear's may have had pictures of cuddly little men on it). Mummy's shallow pool of porridge cools more quickly than Daddy's deeper portion; as long as the radius of the adult dish is between 1.45 and 1.8 times that of Baby's dish, Baby's porridge will cool at a rate partway between that of his father and that of his mother.

This is of course a simplified calculation. As different rates of cooling take effect, it becomes necessary to take temperature difference into account, involving the use of calculus. The insulating power of the dishes would also have to be allowed for, together with any difference in insulation between the two types of dish.

(Miss) C. A. Bryson, West Kirby, Merseyside

When considering the problem, one must surely examine the character of the porridge thief herself. Given that Goldilocks has trespassed on the property of the three bears and stolen their porridge, would we be correct to take her testimony concerning temperatures of the porridge at face value? I contest that it is simply wilful whim that causes her to eat the porridge of Baby Bear and the temperature argument is a smokescreen to divert attention from her theft. Why are our sympathies aroused by Goldilocks when it is the three bears who suffer the trauma of coming back to find that their home has been invaded, that they have been robbed, and that the interloper is asleep in one of their beds?

Bruce Beattie, London EC1

Bear society is male dominated ... The intended time of consumption was when Daddy Bear's porridge was just right, at which time Baby Bear's would have been too cold and Mummy Bear's would have congealed. It's just that Goldilocks got there early.

John Higgs, Stoneygate, Leics

The questioner assumes that Mummy Bear had the middle-sized portion. The fact that her porridge was cooler than her child's suggests that this was not so.

There are two probable reasons for Mummy Bear's small serving; both reflect badly on the state of equality in ursine society. Times were hard in the woods of fairytale land and porridge was often a rare commodity. If stocks were running low, it is all too likely that noble Mummy Bear would go without in order to fill the stomachs of her husband and child. Or, after pressure from the media and her partner, Mummy Bear may have become depressed about her ample figure (height: seven feet, weight: twenty-two and a half stone) and felt obliged to go on a diet.

M. Hewett, Connahs Quay, Clwyd

Nursery tales, like nursery rhymes, are hotbeds of cultural propaganda. Daddy Bear is a macho male – red-hot porridge, rock-hard bed. (You even see him on television, drinking beer with the lads.) Mummy Bear is a wimp. Baby Bear, with whom readers are intended to identify, is superior to Mummy, doing his level best to emulate Daddy, and the little brat is always right.

(Professor) Ian Stewart, Mathematics Institute,
University of Warwick, Coventry

Question: I once read a nonsense poem that removed the apparently negative prefixes of words like 'inept', 'inert' and 'uncouth' to make new words: 'ept', 'ert' and 'couth'. I've searched for the poem since, but no luck. Can anyone help?

The poem to which I think the question refers is 'Gloss' by the American poet, David McCord, which runs:

> I know a little man both ept and ert.
>
> An intro? extro? No, he's just a vert.
>
> Shevelled and couth and kempt, pecunious, ane.
>
> His image trudes upon the ceptive brain.
>
> When life turns sipid and the mind is traught,
>
> The spirit soars as I would sist it ought.
>
> Chalantly then, like any gainly goof,
>
> My digent self is sertive, choate, loof.

I hope this is of sistance.

J. D. Trehearne, Ealing, London W5

The poem is probably:

> I dreamt of a corrigible nocuous youth,
>
> Gainly, gruntled and kempt;
>
> A mayed and sidious fellow forsooth –
>
> Ordinate, effable, shevelled, ept, couth;
>
> A delible fellow I dreamt.

Quoted by Willard R. Espy in his book, *The Game of Words*, (Bramhall House, New York).

C. Sherris, Billingham, Cleveland

It is a much-quoted maxim that there are only seven stories in fiction and that all others are based on them. Is it true, and what might these seven stories be?

I'm not sure about plots for stories, but plots for plays are a subject that my father, the Irish playwright Denis Johnston, had a lot to say about. Originally he thought there were seven, but then he realized that there are in fact eight:

1. Cinderella – or Unrecognized Virtue at last recognized. It's the same story as 'The Tortoise and the Hare'. The central figure doesn't have to be a girl, nor does it even have to be a love story. What is essential is that the Good is despised, but is recognized in the end: something that we all want to believe.

2. Achilles – the Fatal Flaw, which is the groundwork for practically all classical tragedy, although it can be made into comedy too, as in the old standard Aldwych farce. Lennox Robinson's *The Whiteheaded Boy* is the Fatal Flaw in reverse.

3. Faust – the Debt that Must be Paid, the fate that catches up with all of us sooner or later. This is found in all its purity as the chase in O'Neill's *The Emperor Jones*. And, in a completely different mood, what else is *The Cherry Orchard*?

4. Tristan – that standard triangular plot of two women and one man, or two men and one woman. *The Constant Nymph* or almost any French farce.

5. Circe – the Spider and the Fly. *Othello*. *The Barretts of Wimpole Street* if you want to change the sex. And if you don't believe me about *Othello* (the real plot of which is not the triangle and is only incidentally jealousy) try casting it with a good Desdemona but a poor Iago.

6. Romeo and Juliet – Boy meets Girl, Boy loses Girl, Boy either finds or does not find Girl – it doesn't matter which.

7. Orpheus – the Gift taken Away. This may take two forms: either the tragedy of the loss itself, as in *Juno and the Paycock*, or it may be about the search that follows the loss, as in *Jason and the Golden Fleece*.

8. The Hero Who Cannot Be Kept Down. The best example of this is that splendid play *Harvey*, made into a film with James Stewart.

These plots can be presented in so many different forms – tragedy, comedy, farce, whodunnit – and they can also be inverted, but they still form the basis of all good writing. The fault with many contemporary plays is simply that they do not have a plot.

Rory Johnston, London NW3

Rory Johnston's listing of eight basic plots for plays seems very inadequate.

Georges Polti, in his famous book, *The Thirty-Six Dramatic Situations*, classified these not by legendary/mythological tales of archetypes or personalities (Faust, Circe, etc.) but by the situation itself; for example, no. 10, 'Abduction'; no. 25, 'Adultery'; no. 3, 'Crime Pursued by Vengeance', etc., etc. Nobody to my knowledge has improved on Polti's thirty-six possible plots, although some of his subdivisions taken from classical models are, to say the least, tenuous (Situation 26e: 'A woman enamoured of a bull').

John Pilkington (playwright), Exeter, Devon

To Mr Johnston's eight plots for plays you can add David and Goliath – the individual against the repressive/corrupt powers of the state or community, or their rival claims. As in *Enemy of the People*, *The Visit* and, of course, *Antigone*.

Leslie Caplan, London NW3

Consider the following application of Mr Johnston's eight prototypical plots:

1. Cinderella. Rick, an ex-pat Yank bar-owner in wartime Morocco, begins as a drunken cynic but his 'essential goodness' is at last celebrated.
2. Achilles. Like the Greek warrior, the proud, 'fatally flawed' Rick – once a doer of great deeds – spends most of the story sulking in his tent. He is forced into selfless action only for the sake of the refugee Ilsa, the woman he loves.
3. Faust. Rick's good looks, fame and wealth may be parochial but they are Faustian and gratuitous. Inevitably, Rick's debt is called in and he gives up his business, his girl and everything he has lived for.
4. Tristan. Manly Rick (Tristan) loves and is loved by sultry Ilsa (Isolde) but she is already married to wimpish Victor Laszlo (King Mark).
5. Circe. Ilsa's wiles entice Rick into her service only to destroy him.
6. Romeo and Juliet. Once, in Paris, Rick and Ilsa loved and lost each other. Here, in Morocco, they get back together but are finally parted again.
7. In a concrete sense the gift taken away is a Letter of Transit, which would enable Rick to go back to America but which he is forced to give up to Laszlo. More symbolically, the gift is of personal happiness and is sacrificed to political necessity, since to save Laszlo is to save the world for democracy.
8. The Irrepressible Hero is Rick personified.

There is also a ninth archetypical storyline, 'The Wandering Jew', which is bafflingly excluded from Mr Johnston's list. Rick is, of course, the persecuted traveller who will never return home. Thus, instead of eight (or nine) stories, there is only one, and it is called *Casablanca*.

Robin Blake, London WC1

There are only about seven themes in fiction, and they include Love, Money, Power, Revenge, Survival, Glory and Self-awareness. It is the quest for these that makes a story. Most stories have more than one theme and it is the superimposition of themes, with the arising conflicts, that makes a story interesting.

Robin Blake's suggestion that all stories can be imposed on the *Casablanca* plot is really saying that *Casablanca* contains several basic themes, which it does, although most of them are not resolved and in general are badly written. Nevertheless, the film is good because of its dramatic tension, partly created by the fact that actors were given their scripts on a daily basis and so never knew the ending themselves.

It might also have been quite a different film if the original actor chosen for the lead had played the part: Ronald Reagan.

Stan Hayward (author of Scriptwriting for Animation), London NW2

Is it really feasible that a chimpanzee with a typewriter and an infinite amount of time would be able to produce the complete works of Shakespeare?

According to the Darwinian theory of evolution, a chimp did just that.

George Armstrong, Silloth, Cumbria

Let's give the chimp a chance and provide a special keyboard with just twenty-six capital letters, a few punctuation marks and an oversized space-bar, the size of ten regular keys. Assuming, say, sixty words per minute and no breaks, we can expect to wait about eight hours before the word 'To' (with a space leading and following) comes into view. Extending to the phrase 'To be' would require another twelve hours of labour. 'To be or' would warrant a lot of patience, some 140,000 years' worth, not to mention around 4,500 million pages of paper used in the process.

A fraction of a sonnet, let alone an entire play, would require 'more books than could fit into the whole world' (John 21: 25), as the gospel writer enigmatically puts it.

Thus, for practical reasons, the answer has to be no.

Christopher R. Palmer, Department of Community Medicine, Cambridge University

Assume that the chimpanzee has the unusual benefit of a keyboard with only twenty-seven keys: one for each letter of the alphabet and one for space. Assume the beast hits these keys completely at random at a strike rate of one per second. And assume the chimpanzee's immediate task is to type the word 'Macbeth'.

The chimpanzee has a 1 in 27 chance of striking the letter 'M' with its first tap; this is relatively quick and easy. There are 729 (27 × 27) possible two-letter sequences: to type at random 'M' followed by 'A' with one second between each strike would take (according to the laws of probability) twelve minutes and nine seconds.

'Mac' is one of 19,683 possible three-letter sequences; and 19,683 seconds is five hours, twenty-eight minutes and three seconds. If one continues to multiply by twenty-seven as the sequence grows, it will be found that the six letters of 'Macbet' will, in probability, not be reached for twelve years. It will be 331 years before the word 'Macbeth' is stumbled over by accident.

Of course, a chimpanzee with an awful lot of luck could do the job in just seven seconds.

R. D. Phillips, Chorlton-cum-Hardy, Manchester

It all depends on what you mean by 'really feasible'.

Given an infinite amount of time, anything that could happen will happen. The complete works of Shakespeare produced by a typewriter-toting chimpanzee is such a possibility; that is, it is not logically self-contradictory.

Whether an infinite amount of time is 'really feasible' is the crunch question. The problem thus is not to do with the chimpanzee but with the lifespan of the universe. If the universe lasts for ever, the chimpanzee will make it. My bet is that it won't, because it isn't.

(Dr) William Johnson, Arnside, Cumbria

I have had this problem with apes before. As soon as they learn to type a twelve-line essay, such as 'How I Spent My Summer Holiday', they think they are God's gift to literature. Before you can say 'Twelfth Night', they are off looking for something better. Those who show any real promise may make it to Hollywood as scriptwriters, where they will find there is no shortage of people prepared to slap them on the back and hand them a banana daiquiri. After a while the novelty wears off and the decline is normally rapid – from hack writer to bit parts in *Tarzan* films, then Skid Row.

Murray Allison, London N8

All the answers so far assume that the only restriction is the amount of time available. But ribbons and typewriters wear out, trees have to be cut down to make paper, chimps have to be fed. So unlimited resources would be needed. One thing that cosmologists seem to be agreed on is that the amount of matter in the universe is finite (the great astrophysicist Arthur Eddington reckoned that it contained only ten raised to the power of seventy-nine protons), so even with infinite time the odds against stochastic Shakespeare are even longer than those calculated by your correspondents.

S. K. Epton, Whitby, South Wirral

The chimpanzee must be understood as an example of randomness, and the complete works of Shakespeare as an example of an enormous number of symbols of twenty-seven different types (the letters of the alphabet plus the space bar for separating words), arranged in a specific order.

Knowing how long it would take to type just one word even if working at a good speed, and knowing that the chimp will succeed in typing the complete works of Shakespeare (because given that amount of time it is necessarily so), we realize that infinity is a concept quite difficult to understand.

So the answer is: of course it is feasible, but only as long as you think of the chimpanzee as not being a real one, and the same with the typewriter and the paper it uses. It's only a way of picturing an abstract idea.

Alex Guardiet, Fulwood, Sheffield

The complete works of Shakespeare would never occur by chance.

The chimpanzee is faced with twenty-seven keys and may press any of them. Therefore, all letters (and the space bar) would have an equal chance of being selected and in any large sample each would occur approximately the same number of times. Absolute equality would be approached more and more closely as the amount of typing increased.

The letters comprising the complete works of Shakespeare are far from a random selection. In English the letters 'A', 'D', 'E', 'I', 'N', 'O', 'R', 'S' and 'T' occur far more frequently than 'J', 'K', 'Q', 'V', 'X' and 'Z'. It would be impossible for a chimpanzee to produce a lengthy, random sequence of letters that reflected this inequality. One might expect the letters towards the centre of the keyboard to be hit more frequently than those towards the ends.

However, this possibility does not improve the chances of the works of Shakespeare being typed by chance. On a standard QWERTY keyboard, 'A' occurs to the extreme left, whereas 'J' and 'V' are near the middle.

Gregory Beecroft, Welwyn Garden City, Herts

Gregory Beecroft appears to have been hitting a few random keys himself when he claims that the complete works 'would never occur by chance' because the letters of the alphabet are not equally frequent in English but are hit with equal probability by the chimpanzee.

Even if two events – say the typing of a 'Z' and the typing of an 'E' – are equally probable, this does not necessarily mean they will occur equally often in a given random sequence. Similarly, there is no guarantee that any sequence of tosses of an unbiased coin will produce equal (or even approximately equal) numbers of heads and tails. A thousand consecutive heads, although exceedingly unlikely, is not an impossibility with a fair coin; neither is Shakespeare with a chimpanzee.

The letter frequencies used by Shakespeare are irrelevant. Any pre-specified sequence of letters is just as likely to occur as any other, regardless of its composition. Thus a sequence consisting entirely of 'Z's is no more and no less likely to be produced than any other given sequence (including Shakespeare's works). Even if Shakespeare's works consisted entirely of 'zzzzzzzzzzzzz ...' (*A Midsummer Night's Dream*, perhaps?) the chimp's chances would not have changed.

Ben Craven, Stirling

Disregarding practical considerations such as typewriter wear and the expiry of the universe, and assuming the chimp continues to press the keys at random, Mr Guardiet claims it will 'necessarily' produce a copy of the works of Shakespeare, and Mr Beecroft that it will never achieve the feat.

Both are wrong. In an infinitely long random series of typewriter symbols, you can expect any finite string of such symbols – whether a short one such as 'to be' or a longer one such as Shakespeare's complete works – to occur an infinite number of times. In this case, Shakespeare's works should appear just as often in the ape's typescript as any given string of the same length that contains unusual letters of the alphabet in the same proportion as common ones.

However, there remains a tiny chance that the string sought will never occur. Infinite number theory gives fascinating results and it is hard to illustrate how small this chance is. If you imagine enough eternally typing chimps to completely fill a Newtonian universe of infinite size, then you would still need more before probability favoured one of them omitting the works of Shakespeare from its script.

Graham Haigh, Milnthorpe, Cumbria

Scandalously, the literary implications have hardly been considered by previous correspondents.

In order to produce one 'complete works' the chimp would first have to produce, in addition to millions of pages of complete garbage, thousands of incomplete works (it would also be certain to pass through several minor poets on the way). If it were possible to do it at all, then it should be possible to improve on the original. Some of the many variant versions would be free of all sexism, racism and militarism. That would indeed be a complete edition of Shakespeare.

Gabriel Chanan

Perhaps if the problem involved a monkey producing the complete

works of Jeffrey Archer, people would find it easier to believe that the feat would, unfortunately, be achieved.
M. J. Moody, Beeston, Notts

I am currently engaged in trials with some chimpanzees to find out whether, given an inexhaustible supply of materials, they can produce a nuclear missile.
A. P. Eines, Southbourne, Dorset

Why is it that the keys on push-button telephones are numbered from the top downwards, but vice versa on computers?

Research as far back as 1955 showed that the 1–2–3 arrangement conforms to people's expectations better than the 7–8–9 arrangement, but the same research also showed that people did not expect there to be any performance difference between the two layouts.

In 1963, the 7–8–9 arrangement was adopted as the British Standard (BS 1909) and the first research on performance with the two arrangements was conducted in Cambridge. Unfortunately the research demonstrated that the 1–2–3 layout led to significantly better performance than 7–8–9.

This research has been replicated on a number of occasions. Companies designing numeric keypads therefore had two conflicting pieces of information and I do not know how their decisions were made. However, whatever the issues were then, the problem now is that neither industry can easily change without upsetting many experienced users.

The same problem occurs for alphanumeric keypads, where we now know that QWERTY is not the best arrangement, but the major difficulties of changing to better keyboards (for example, the Dvorak keyboard) are deemed to outweigh the benefits.
David Gilmore, Psychology Department, University of Nottingham

A friend recently told me that the term for a group of ravens is 'an unkindness'. What's the origin, and are there any other similarly bizarre names for groups of animals?

The origin of the term is presumably related to an old (now obsolete) sense of the word 'unkindness', meaning 'unnatural conduct'; the raven was traditionally regarded as a bird of evil omen, and mysterious or unnatural conduct. The word as used for a flock of ravens dates from the mid-fifteenth century and is included in a list of 'proper terms' in the *Book of St Albans* (1486).

Other group terms include: 'a hastiness of cooks', 'an observance of hermits', 'a shrewdness of apes', 'a cloud of flies', 'a blush of boys', 'a piteousness of doves', 'a desert of lapwings' and 'a bevy of ladies'.

Judy Pearsall, associate editor, Oxford English Dictionaries,
Oxford University Press

Judy Pearsall defines an 'observance' as the group name for hermits. Surely a group of hermits constitutes a contradiction in terms?

Greg Mackay, Rome, Italy

The collective term for our financial advisers must be 'a wunch of bankers'.

David Lambert, Harlow, Essex

No one has yet mentioned James Lipton's book, *An Exaltation of Larks*, which includes not only this but a comprehensive catalogue of collectives.

Some of the other ornithological ones are delightful: 'a charm of finches'; 'an ostentation of peacocks'. Others are racy, humorous, sardonic or serendipitous, like: 'a wince of dentists'; 'a piddle of puppies'; 'a stampede of philatelists'.

(Mrs) Else Pickvance, Northfield, Birmingham

How about 'A morbidity of majors', which is included in the 'Groups of a Kind' listed in the 1990 Penguin edition of the *Quickway Crossword Dictionary*?

Tom Egan, Eglwyswrw, Dyfed

I was once told by college lecturers that the collective noun for a group of college principals was 'a lack'.

Ian Lucraft, Sheffield

My research has elicited the following: 'sac' – a group of gastroenterologists; 'colony' – a large group; 'bellyful' – a large group in a small room; 'appendix' – a splinter group; 'rumbling appendix' – a noisy splinter group; 'burst appendix' – a splintered splinter group; 'abdomination' – a group of splinter groups; 'eructation' – the hot air generated by an abdomination.

John Hazlehurst, Cumbria

What was the good news that they brought from Ghent to Aix?

Aix is besieged and about to surrender; the good news is that help is on the way. This is the implied meaning of line 46 of Robert Browning's poem, 'the news which alone could save Aix from her fate'. The explanation is Browning's, but he gave it with reluctance; he always insisted that the ride itself was what mattered. He said that he wrote the poem 'on board ship off Tangiers', when he 'had been at sea long enough to appreciate even the fancy of a gallop'.

There is no historical foundation for the episode: according to Browning it reflects a 'general impression of the characteristic warfare and besieging that abounds in the annals of Flanders'.

D. Karlin, co-editor, with John Woolford, of
The Poems of Browning, Longman Annotated English Poets (1991)

Did Adam and Eve have navels?

In Genesis 1: 26, God (displaying his own disconcerting tendency to plurality) says: 'Let us make man in our own image, and let them have dominion over the fish of the sea.' So 'man' was a collective being from the beginning.

As for Adam and Eve, the names occur much later on in the text, after the Fall, and mean something like 'red' or 'earthy' and 'living' or 'lively'. So they're symbolic qualities and were presumably consciously attached to symbolic persons. It took a later, less-aware culture to start treating these allusive stories as literal histories.

So the first humanity wasn't very different from present-day humanity, belly buttons and all, and the power of creation stories can

still be recaptured by those who gaze beyond their own navels.
David Newton, Chelmondiston, Suffolk

'Yes' is the short answer. It could be argued that the Adam created in God's own image was navel-less; sexual reproduction only came on to the scene after the expulsion from Eden, and the navel is a mark of our fallen state.

In the last century a creationist rearguard action against Darwinism centred on Adam's navel. Philip Gosse's book *Omphalos* (Greek for 'navel') argued that, although Adam was created, his body looked as if he had once been born; similarly, although the animals in the Garden of Eden were created as adults, they looked as if they had been born and grown in the normal way. Gosse's master stroke was to extend the argument to the earth itself, which 'appeared' as if it dated back millions of years.

However, neither creationists nor evolutionists were impressed with this, and the case for a scientifically respectable creationism duly perished.
Phil Edwards, Manchester

My theory is that when God had finished making man he realized that Adam just didn't look right with that expanse of smooth featureless abdomen, so he created the belly button. Later, when placentation became just the thing, it was the perfect place for the umbilical cord to attach to the foetus.
Dr Kitty Smith, London N8

Index

666: why number of the beast? 108–11
£2 coin, wording round edge 32–3

Acts of Parliament
    oldest with current powers 7–8
    unauthorised amendments 61
Adam and Eve, navels 315–16
age, definition of 'old' 189–90
Agnesi, Maria: and her curve 250–1
air temperatures, and snow 244–5
aircraft
    first powered flight 289–90
    vapour trails 235–6
airships
    mysterious, late 19th century 76–7
    propelled and steered
        by sails 89–90
Aix: good news and siege 315
Alaska, sale by Russia 99–100
Ali, Chaudhry Rehmat, and name of
    Pakistan 4
All Blacks, origins of name 8–9
amlyralinesia 297, 298
Amundsen, Roald, navigational techniques
    236
ancient civilizations, evidence
    left by 253–5
angels: dancing on the head
    of a pin 40–1
angling, effect of screaming fish 174–6

animals
    anthropomorphism 257
    collective nouns 313–14
    homeopathic remedies 226, 228
anniversary dates, effect of adoption
    of Gregorian calendar 105–7
archers, physical requirements 183
Arkansas, origins of
    name/pronunciation 6–7
arrests, law on 176–7
art, definition of 210–12
Ash Wednesday, date of 290–2
Ashoka, conversion to
    Buddhism 123–4
asthma, homeopathic cure 228
atheism
    consequences if declared by
        heir to throne 197–9
    proof not required 162
attractiveness, and glasses 179–80
augmented fourth: 'chord of evil' 86
'awl', meaning/use of 18

babies, intelligence, vs. cats 257–8
Bacon, as surname 300, 301
bacteria, prevalence of 247
bacteriophages 234
bar-codes, and number of
    the beast 111
basilisk lizards: running on

water 243–4
Basque people, origins and
    blood groups 237–9
battle
    between 3 opposing sides 122–3
    last Western head of state to
        die in 129
bear: Wojtek, Polish army 66–7
Beef, as surname 300
beer, watered down 184–5
Begin, Menachem, and Nobel
    peace prize 186
benefit concert, first 34
Benidorm, meaning of
    name 136, 137, 138
Bennett, Gordon, identity 39–40
Bentham, Jeremy, definition of
    poetry 286
Benveniste, Jacques, and
    homeopathic medicine 226, 227
Bible
    Adam and Eve's navels 315–16
    Amalekites, war against 124
    counting, accuracy of 291
    David, killing of messenger 24
    eagles 171–2
    Eve, eating of fruit 38
    forty, significance of 291
    ivory tower 35
    Lent 291
    life expectancy 245–6
    manna 115
    'missing' commandments 282–4
    Mothering Sunday 13
    Noah's Ark, size 84–5
    number of the beast 109–10
    peace of mind 169
    Peculiar People 89
    Samaritans 100–2
    wearing of clothes 153
    year of Christ's birth 120, 121
'Big Apple', as name for
    New York 41–3
Big Bang, place of occurrence 262–3
blackened windows, photographs
    through 191

blame culture, responsibility for 150–1
Bligh, Captain, survival strategy 220–1
blood groups, Basque
    people/ethnic origins 237–9
'blue blood', origins of phrase 13–14
blue sky, and trouser material 5
'Bob's your uncle', origins
    of phrase 44–5
body transplants 233
bones, uses of 173–4
books, early uses of
    dust jacket 10–11
books quoted/discussed
    see also Bible
    2001 258–9
    Abecedarium Anglico Latinum (Huloet)
        22–3
    An Exaltation of Larks (Lipton) 314
    An Experiment with Time (Dunne) 251,
        252–3
    The Anthropic Cosmological Principle
        (Barrow and Tipler) 252
    The Authentic History of the Great Box
        (Robertson) 64
    The Basque History of the World
        (Kurlansky) 237
    Beneath the City Streets (Laurie) 80
    The Birth of Christ (Seymour) 121
    A Blueprint for Survival 192
    The Book of Heroic Failures (Pile) 93
    Book of Lists (Wallace) 91
    Book of St Albans 314
    Brewer's Dictionary of Phrase
        and Fable 199
    A Brief History of Time
        (Hawking) 252
    The British Apollo 75
    Canterbury Tales (Chaucer) 284
    Collins Field Guide to the Mammals
        of Africa 130
    Concise Oxford Dictionary 153, 207
    Concise Oxford Dictionary of the Christian
        Church 13
    Concise Oxford Thesaurus 250
    Country Lasses (Johnson) 29
    De Anima (Aristotle) 130

The Discovery of Insulin (Bliss) 187
The Dream of Poliphilus (Colonna) 38
Eminent Edwardians (Brendon) 44
Encyclopaedia of Islam 142
The Encyclopedia of Word and Phrase Origins (Hendrickson) 19
The End of an Age (Inge) 209
The End of Time (Barbour) 162
Everyday Book (Hone) 106
Faber Book of Comic Verse 293
Fights, Feuds and Heartfelt Hatreds (Kerr) 93
Flashman's Lady (Fraser) 45
Foetus into Man (Tanner) 274
The French Revolution (Carlyle) 46
The Game of Words (Espy) 305
The Handbook of Russian Literature 186
Historical Slang (Partridge) 45
A History of English Drama (Nicoll) 15
History of the Ladybird (Exell) 279
The History of the Peloponnesian War (Thucydides) 302
History of the World (Roberts) 31
Hitch Hiker's Guide to the Galaxy (Adams) 206
Homeopathy and its Kindred Delusions (Holmes) 225
The Ideology of Fascism (Gregor) 135
Interpreter of Hard Words (Bailey) 29–30
The Iron Wall 136
Keepsake (Heath) 10, 11
Landscape and Memory (Schama) 38
Language, Truth and Logic (Ayer) 195
Lark Rise to Candleford (Thompson) 125
Le Débâcle (Zola) 129
Life's Grandeur (Gould) 247
London Labour and the London Poor (Mayhew) 83, 84
The Long Walk (Rawicz) 27
The Lore and Language of Schoolchildren (Opie and Opie) 12–13, 86–7
The Lost Continent (Bryson) 69
Made in America (Bryson) 19, 47
Maid Marian (Peacock) 37
Man Must Measure (Hogben) 147

The Man Who Saved London (Martelli) 98
The Meaning of Art (Read) 210
The Mind of God (Davis) 252
Miscellany-at-Law (Megarry) 61
The Newcomes (Thackeray) 37
Odd Perceptions (Gregory) 272
Omphalos (Gosse) 316
Oxford Companion to the Mind 272
Oxford Dictionary of English Place-Names 117
Oxford Dictionary of Saints (Farmer) 147
Oxford English Dictionary 2, 17, 29, 114, 204–5, 231, 295
A Pageant of History 58–9
Parable of the Cistern (Combe) 197
Paradise Lost (Milton) 41
Penguin Rhyming Dictionary 295
Peveril of the Peak (Scott) 58
Pirates (Mitchell) 44
Quickway Crossword Dictionary 314
The Quiet Don (Sholokhov) 186–7
A Return to Modesty (Shalit) 153
Reverse Time Travel (Chapman) 251
Rights of Man (Paine) 215
The Serpent and the Rainbow (Davis) 72
Shared Pleasures (Gomery) 25
The Shell Book of Firsts 26
A Six Month's Tour through the North of England (Young) 248
So Many Hungers (Bhattacharya) 128
Soldier Bear (Morgan & Lasocki) 67
Spices (Ridley) 256
The Stars Like Dust (Asimov) 273
The Strange Death of Liberal England (Dangerfield) 102
The Suffragette Movement (Pankhurst) 103
Sydpolen (Amundsen) 236
Symbols of Church Seasons and Days (Bradner) 171
The T-Shirt Book (Gordon and Hiller) 1

Tasty Trails of Northumbria
  (Harrison) 36
The Thirty-Six Dramatic Situations
  (Polti) 306–7
Torrington Diaries (Byng) 106
The Trail of the Serpent (Braddon) 5
Ulysses (Joyce) 39
Ur of the Chaldees (Woolley) 21
Vocabulary of East Anglia (Forby) 37
Waiting for Godot (Beckett) 209
Walker's Rhyming Dictionary 295
Wellington: Pillar of State
  (Longford) 93
Wellington: The Years of the Sword
  (Longford) 122
Westward Ho! (Kingsley) 117
What is Art? (Tolstoy) 210
boredom, as cause of death 208–9
bottled water, as animal fouling
  deterrent 281–2
brain
  cells, irreplaceability 241
  memory, estimation of size 259–60
  memory/sensory interaction 298
  transplants, likelihood 232–3
Brains Trust (radio programme) 40, 275–6
Bristol, and twin-towns 154–5
Browning, Robert, and fate of Aix 315
Buckingham Palace, secret tunnels 79–80
Buddhism, koans, and attainment of
  Nirvana 160
Buenos Aires
  origins of name 136–7
  pavements 282
bull, occurrence in surnames 300
'bulls' and 'bears', origins as financial
  terms 28–9
burials, and Necropolis railway 75–6

cafés and restaurants, optional payment
  for food 64–6
can-opener, invention of 33
Canada
  failure to buy Alaska 99–100
  origins of name 112, 115
'canard', meaning as false report 21

capitalism
  and destruction of civilization 191–4
  and economic cycles 197
  global: how to bring down without
    loss of job 157–8
car sales, by price sticker on
  windscreen 181–2
cats
  fouling, and bottled water 281
  intelligence, vs. babies 257–8
ceiling walkers 83–4
cells (human): any remaining from birth
  to death? 240–1
censuses, biblical times 120–1
change, as essence of life 163
chicken or egg: which came first? 265–7
chimpanzees, typewriters and
  Shakespeare 308–13
China, definition of city 299
'chord of evil' (augmented fourth) 86
Christ, uncertainty over birth year 120–2
church lecterns: why eagle-shaped? 171–2
church music, use of augmented
  fourth 86
churches, length of time to
  complete 125
cinema, and popcorn 25
circuses, names of buildings for 14, 15
citizen's arrests 176–7
city, definition of 299
civilizations, evidence left by 253–5
clothes
  and arrival of prudery 153
  classical musicians 3
  jeans, early 2–3
  sea water and sweating 220–1
  T-shirts 1–2
coal, formation of 249–50
'cobblers', slang use of 18–19
Cockney rhyming slang 18–19
coded messages, to staff 163–5
Cold War: did Americans and Russians
  ever kill each other? 119
collective nouns 313–15
colours, associations with seasons 203–4
commandments: what would 11 to 15

have been? 282–4
commercial organization, oldest currently
  functioning 16–17
computer keyboards, layout of
  numbers 313
computer mouse, plural of 277–8
constitution, UK
  declaration of atheism by heir to throne,
    consequences 197–9
  and electoral crises 165–6
construction project, longest to
  complete 124–5
controlled explosions 260–1
corks, wine bottles 288, 289
cotton wool, phobia of 151–2
cow, occurrence in surnames 300
crescent moon symbol, origins of 141–2
crucifixion, cause of death 230–1
cucumbers, glowing from electricity 85
cults see sects

Danson, Yvonne: marathon runner 184
Darwin, Erasmus, electrical experiments
  247–8
death
  and boredom 208–9
  by crucifixion, cause of 230–1
  from famines, accountability for 126–9
deed poll: any names prohibited? 201–2
deepest penetration below Earth's
  surface 59–61
Denham, and twin-town 153–4, 155
dinosaurs
  effects on evolution of human race
    241–3
  evidence left by 253–5
dislyrhythmia 296–7, 298
divorce, by unauthorised amendment of
  Act of Parliament 61
DNA sequence, most successful 247
dog faeces
  and bottled water 281–2
  and leather tanning 173–4
Dorgan, 'Tad': cartoonist 19, 20
dreams, causing heart attacks 88
drilling below Earth's surface,

deepest 59–61
drum kit, invention of 8
duels, last 'traditional' 92–3
dust jackets (books), first uses of 10–11
dusters: why yellow? 203–5

email, first 31
eagles, and church lecterns 171–2
Earth
  extinction of human race, effects
    on 212–14
  lengthening day 220
  magnetic field 249
  and moon, gravitational effects 219–20
  self-survival mechanisms 208
economic cycles, causes of 197
economic growth, and destruction of
  civilization 191–4
economists: unworthy of Nobel
  prize 185–6
Edward the Martyr, location of
  remains 78–9
effigies of Judas, burning of 86–7
eggs (human)
  fertilization, and identity 301–2
  time present in body 240–1
Einstein, Albert
  and Nobel prize 221–2
  theories of relativity 161, 163, 221–2
election crises, and UK constitution 165–6
electricity, unconventional uses 85, 247–8
elephants, African, trainability 140–1
environmental catastrophe (Cretaceous
  Period): how did soft-skinned creatures
    survive? 222–3
environmental degradation, and
  growth 191–4
Epstein-Barr virus 234
erotica and pornography, difference
  between 200
eternity, as essence of life 161
'ethnic cleansing', origins of phrase 21–2
evolution of mammals/human race, and
  dinosaurs 241–3
ex-smokers: when become
  non-smokers? 149–50

explosions
  controlled 260–1
  nuclear, smallest 273

famine deaths, accountability for 126–9
Father Christmas, visiting schedule 77–8
feminists, and rules of grammar 295
fiction: only 7 basic stories? 305–8
'figment', sentences containing 301
films
  2001 258–9
  Casablanca 307–8
  The History of the World: Part 1 282
  Ring of Spies 108
fire station: ever burned down? 70–2
fire-walkers: unburned feet 52–3
firemen's poles, first use 36
fishing, effect of screaming fish 174–6
flags
  France 46, 47
  Jolly Roger 43–4
flame, appearance in zero gravity 253
flies
  and bagged water 282
  landing techniques 275–6
flight, evidence of first powered 289–90
food
  'bulking-out' by manufacturers 102–4
  first preservation in tin cans 33–4
  influence on body height 274–5
  in UK, before imports 125–6
formal dress, classical musicians 3
fossilization
  current 256
  trees 249–50, 256
fountains
  first 38–9
  flowing with wine 82–3
fourth dimension
  nature of 162–3
  spatial: does it exist? 269–71
France
  ladybirds 279
  National Assembly 46–7
  and origins of 'OK' 48–9
  units of measurement 94, 95, 96

Franco, General Francisco, and World
  War Two 98–9
Frankenstein, use of electricity 247–8
freedoms
  relationship to legislation 170–1
  restrictions in society 215, 216
freezing times of water, hot vs.
  cold 218–19
Frenacapan, Fred and Fanny,
  identity 5–6
Frinton, Freddie, and *Dinner for
  One* 69–70
fruit seeds, wooden 102–3

Gandalf's Garden: optional payment
  café/spiritual centre 64, 65–6
gastroenterologists, collective nouns 315
gender, determination of 261
Genuine Progress Indicator (GPI) 193–4
gephyrophobia (bridges) 180–1
Germany, units of measurement 95
geysers: soap causing blowing 229–30
Gilgamesh 31–2
glasses, and enhancement of
  attractiveness 179–80
global capitalism: how to bring down
  without loss of job? 157–8
Goldilocks and the Three Bears, porridge
  heat loss 303–4
golf croquet 183
Goodge Street, tunnels/underground
  transit camp 80, 81, 82
gravity, effects on flame 253
Greece, culmination of war of
  independence (1827) 123
'green room', origins of name 15–16
Gregorian calendar, effect of adoption on
  anniversary dates 105–7
growth, and destruction of
  civilization 191–4

Haiti, zombies 73
Hamlet, City of 300
hamlet, definition of 299–300
Hannibal, importance of elephants 140
'hat-trick', origins of phrase 45

head, weighing of 267–9

head of state, Western, last to die
in battle 129

heart attacks, caused by dreams 87–8

heat loss, Three Bears' porridge 303–4

height increases (over time),
human body 274–5

heir to throne, consequences if an
atheist 197–9

herbs and spices, difference
between 255–6

Hippodrome, use of name in
circuses/theatres 14–15

Hitler, Adolf, meeting with Franco 99

HIV: sophisticated virus? 233

Hollard, Michel: 'the man who saved
London' 97–8

homeopathic medicine, proof of
effectiveness 224–9

'honeymoon', origins of word 22–3

'hot dog', origins of phrase 19–20

Hudson, Sir Jeffrey: 'dwarf' 57–9

human body
any cells remaining from birth to
death? 240–1
body transplants 233
height increases over time 274–5

human race
and continuation of dinosaurs 241–3
effects on Earth of extinction 212–14

'humble pie', origins of 36–7

Hunt, Leigh, and Shelley's heart 90–1, 92

Hutton, William: compulsive walker 54

Huxley, Professor Julian, and flies' landing
techniques 275–6

identity, and sperm fertilization
race 301–2

inch, standardization of 96

India
famines, causes of 126, 127–8
World War Two, loyalties of soldiers
134–5, 136

individual, first authenticated named in
history 31–2

infinity: chimpanzees, typewriters and

Shakespeare 308–13

innumeracy, as source of pride 194–5

insulin, discovery of, and Nobel prize 187

intelligence, babies vs. cats 257–8

Islam
'clergy'/religious leaders, job titles and
ranks 152–3
and crescent moon symbol 141, 142

'ivory tower', original 35

Jablochkoff, Paul: and his
'candle' 231–2

Japan
bottled water, and cats 281
definition of city 299
ladybirds 279–80
'scientific' whaling 239–40

jeans, early 2–3

jelly baby, invention of 28

Jerusalem, meaning of 136, 138

jokes: only 11 in the world? 280

Jolly Roger, origins of name 43–4

Judas, burning effigies of 86–7

Kandahar, as name of ski-bindings 7

Kansas, origins of name 6

Keighley, and twin-town 154

keyboards, layout of numbers 313

Kissinger, Henry, and Nobel peace
prize 185

Kneale, Nigel, works by 156–7

Koh-i-noor diamond, history of 118–19

Korean War, involvement of Soviet
Union 119

ladybirds, names for 278–80

Lamb, as surname 300

laws, legitimacy and consent 214–17

lecterns: why eagle-shaped? 171–2

left and right wings, politics 46–7

Lent, timing/significance of 290–2

life
essence of 161–3
meaning of 206–8

life expectancy, past and present 245–6

'life of Riley', origins of phrase 41

lifts, plummeting, injury
   minimization 205–6
lighting: Jablochkoff's candle 231–2
lions: ever found in Europe? 129–30
lizards, basilisk: running on water 243–4
London
   City of: why separate police force? 178
   secret tunnels 79–82

Macleod, John, and Nobel prize 187
magnets, use in space 248–9
males, reasons for having
   nipples 261–2
marriage, to two or more
   heads of state 117–18
mathematics, value of 194–5
Melksham, claims to fame 138, 139, 140
memory (brain), estimation of size
   259–60
messages to staff, coded 163–5
metric system, and alternatives 94–7
MI (Military Intelligence) numbers, less
   well-known 203
microdots, use of 107–8
mirror image: why not upside
   down? 271–3
mixer taps, slow adoption in UK 187–9
'mondegreens' 297
'monger', meaning/origins of word 9–10
mongoose, plural of 277, 278
monkeys, typewriters and
   Shakespeare 308–13
monorail 235
moons, rotation and orbit 219–20
Moran, Jim: disprover of popular
   fallacies 67
morning sickness, cures for 195–7
Mothering Sunday: why Sunday? 12–13
mouse (computer), plural of 277–8
museum, first 20–1

names
   changes by deed poll 201–2
   deriving from misunderstandings of
      words 112–16
   duplication in 113, 114, 116

inappropriate 50–1
including punctuation 117
ironic 136–8
restrictions of 202
surnames, meaty 300–1
Napoleon Bonaparte, and metric
   system 94
NASA, units of measurement
   used 95, 96
Native Americans, blood groups 237–8
navels: possessed by
   Adam and Eve? 315–16
Nazi-occupied Europe, fate of Black, Asian
   and Arabic people 134–6
Necropolis railway 75–6
needle in a haystack: has anyone
   looked? 67–8
Nero
   and number of the beast 108–9, 110
   as a real Caesar 110–11
Netherlands
   height of males 275
   units of measurement 95, 97
New York: why 'Big Apple'? 41–3
New Zealand
   black as sporting colours 8–9
   dog fouling, and bottled water 281–2
Newton, Isaac 32
nipples: why do males have
   them? 261–2
'nitty-gritty', origins of phrase 35–6
Noah's Ark, minimum size 84–5
Nobel prize
   Albert Einstein 221–2
   least deserving winner 185–7
notices, giving 'helpful' information 143–6
nuclear explosions, smallest possible 273
number keys, layout, computers and
   telephones 313
number of the beast: why 666? 108–11
numerical notation, and mathematical
   calculations 147

oil deposits, origins of 60–1
'OK', origins of 47–9
old age, definition of 189–90

'oldest trick in the book': what is? 37–8
one hand clapping, benefits of
contemplation of 160
'orange', rhyming words 295–6
orienteering, physical demands 183

pagan worship, continuation after
Christianity established 130–2
pain, whether felt by
non-mammals 174–6
'paint the town red', origins of
phrase 17–18
Pakistan, origins of name 3–4
Panacea Society 61–2, 63
Pankhurst, Sylvia, jam-making 102–3
paper industry, use of rags
and bones 174
parachutes, first testing/
development of 43
parliaments, adversarial seating
arrangements 169–70
passports, first issue of 26–7
peace of mind: where
to be found? 168–9
Peculiar People 88–9
Peloponnesian War, as *Mastermind*
specialist subject 302
phobias
bridges 180–1
cotton wool 151–2
photoelectric effect, first explanations
of 221–2
photographs, through blackened
windows 191
phrases see words and phrases
pickles, glowing from electricity 85
pilot's 'self-destruct' protest,
Suez Crisis 104–5
pirate flag: why 'Jolly Roger'? 43–4
planets, rotation and orbit 219–20
playing cards
'curse of Scotland' 74–5
invention and development of 34–5
plays: only 8 basic plots? 305–8
poems
An Austrian army awfully array'd...

(Watts) 292–3
Gloss (McCord) 305
This is Just to Say (Williams) 285
poetry
definition of 284–6
lines following letters of alphabet
292–4
prefix removal 304–5
police forces, 2 or more in same
city 178–9
politicians, time taken to 'go bonkers'
155–6
politics, left and right wings 46–7
popcorn 25
Popp, Fritz-Albert, and homeopathic
medicine 226, 227
pornography
as art 211
and erotica, difference between 200
Powell, Foster: compulsive walker 53
prison vans, photographs through
windows 191
Prohibition, effects on brewers/
distillers 111–12
Proust, Marcel, duel fought 93
prudery, arrival of 153
pubs, and watered-down beer 184–5

Q-Whitehall 80
'quack', origins of meaning as bogus
doctor 29–30
Quatermass, origins of name 20
rabbits, defence mechanisms 231
rag and bone men 173–4
railway, Necropolis 75–6
ravens, collective noun for 313–14
religion
see also Bible; sects
ever stopped a war? 123–4
ladybirds, significance of 278–80
relationship to cults 200–1
rhyming words, difficult 295–6
rights
consent, and state power 214–17
and legislation 170–1
Roman Empire, continuation of

pagan worship after Christianity
    established 130–1
Roman numerals
    calculations using 147
    and number of the beast 109, 110
'Round John' 298
Russia
    Gregorian/Julian calendars 106–7
    sale of Alaska 99–100
    spacecraft, meaning of names 11–12

sales of cars, by price sticker on
    windscreen 181–2
Samaritans (religious sect) 100–2
sand, grains on Earth 223–4
Sanders, George, reasons for
    suicide 208
Sands, Richard: ceiling walker 83–4
Santa Claus, visiting schedule 77–8
Scotland, 'curse of': which playing
    card? 74–5
sea water
    and prevention of sweating 220–1
    running on 243–4
seasons, associations with colours 203–4
sects
    belief that all matter evil 213
    Samaritans 100–2
    when become a religion? 200–1
security messages to staff, coded 163–5
sex, determination of 261
Shakespeare, William
    chimpanzees and typewriters 308–13
    Henry V 29
    Julius Caesar 18
    vocabulary 296
sharks, and swimming 251
Shelley's heart, rescue from funeral
    pyre 90–2
Sholokhov, Mikhail: author of
    The Quiet Don? 186–7
'shoot the messenger': did
    they ever? 24–5
Shriners 68–9
signs, giving 'helpful' information 143–6
singing, and breaking glass 73–4

ski-bindings, Kandahar 7
'Sloppy Joes' 2
smokers (ex): when become non-
    smokers? 149–50
snake-oil salesmen 27–8
snow
    ever too cold for? 244–5
    water content 223
soap, causing blowing geysers 229–30
soft drinks, additives 103–4
song lyrics, forgetting/mishearing 296–8
South Pole, and Amundsen's navigational
    techniques 236
Southcott, Joanna: and her box 61–4
space
    place of origin/shape 262–3
    use of magnets in 248–9
spacecraft, Russian, meaning of
    names 11–12
Spain, 'neutrality' in World War Two 98–9
sperm, and race to ovum 301–2
spices and herbs, difference
    between 255–6
spiders' threads 258
sport: which could start in late 20's and
    make national team? 182–4
St George, as popular national
    saint 147–8
'*stan*', meaning of as suffix 4
'standing on the shoulders of giants',
    origins of phrase 32–3
stars, number in universe 223–4
Suez Crisis, pilot's 'self-destruct'
    protest 104–5
sumo bouts, length 177–8
swastika, non-Nazi uses of 55–7
sweating
    and sea water 220–1
    and swimming 245
Sweden, units of measurement 95, 97
swimming
    and sharks 251
    and sweating 245

T-shirts 1–2
Tajikistan, meaning of name 4

taps, mixer and single 187–9
telephones
    number keys, layout 313
    Theatrephone 52
television programmes
    The Day Today 79
    Dinner for One 69–70
    Horizon 208
    Interview with a Zombie 73
    Mastermind 302
    QED 225–6
    Tomorrow's World Live 53
    Who Wants to Be a Millionaire? 158–9
    The Year of the Sex Olympics 156–7
television weather forecasters, hand
    movements 172–3
tennis, scoring 41
The Bonny Earl of Moray (ballad) 297–8
Theatrephone 52
theatres
    colour green, use of 15–16
    Hippodrome, use of name 14–15
'they', use of 294–5
Tiananmen Square massacre,
    causes/evidence of deaths 132–4
time, as essence of life 161–3
time travel, research on 251–3
tin cans, first use for food
    preservation 33–4
torpedo, land-based 54–5
towns
    definition of 299
    with no claim to fame 138–40
trees, fossilization of 249–50, 256
tunnels, secret (London) 79–82
Twelve Days of Christmas, origins
    of song 30–1
twin-towns: excuse for councillors'
    perks? 153–5
typewriters, chimpanzees and
    Shakespeare 308–13

UFOs, first reported 77
Ultimate (frisbee game) 182
units of measurement, metric and
    alternatives 94–7

universe, place of origin/shape 262–3
USA
    and Alaska 99–100
    city, definition of 299
    constitution, and electoral crises 165–6
    Prohibition, effects on brewers/distillers
        111–12
    T-shirts 1–2
Uzbekistan, meaning of name 4

vacuum, effects of exposure to 258–9
vapour trails, patterns 235–6
Vauxhall, use in Russian language 113,
    114–15
village, definition of 299
viruses
    reproduction of 247
    sophistication of 233–4
voice, and glass breaking 73–4

walking, compulsive 53–4
war: ever stopped by religion? 123–4
water
    amount in snow 223
    bottled, as animal fouling deterrent
        281–2
    freezing times, hot vs. cold 218–19
    'memory' of 226–7, 228
    running on 243–4
    soap, and boiling point/density 229–30
    supply, and tap styles 187–9
    'wetness' of 263–5
Waterloo, 'friendly fire' casualties 122
Watts, Alaric A. 'alphabetical' poem
    292–3
wealth: is it wrong? 166–8
weather, blue sky and trouser material 5
weather forecasters, hand
    movements 172–3
wedding ring: why left hand? 199–200
Wellington, Duke of
    duel fought 92–3
    uncertainty over birthday/place 122
Westminster (parliament), adversarial
    seating arrangements 169–70
'wetness' of water 263–5

whaling, 'scientific', by Japan 239–40
Wilson, George: compulsive walker 54
wine bottles, shape/volume issues 286–9
wineglass: breakable by human
   voice? 73–4
winnings, division of, *Who Wants
   to Be a Millionaire?* 158–9
Witch of Agnesi (curve) 250–1
Witchcraft Act (1735), repeal of 102
Wojtek: Polish army bear 66–7
Wollstonecraft, Mary, site of
   burial/memorial 91, 92
words and phrases
   'awl' 18
   'blue blood' 13–14
   'blue sky', and trouser material 5
   'Bob's your uncle' 44–5
   'bulls' and 'bears' 28–9
   '*canard*' 21
   'cobblers' 18–19
   'ethnic cleansing' 21–2
   'figment', sentences containing 301
   'hat-trick' 45
   'honeymoon' 22–3
   'hot dog' 19–20
   'humble pie' 36–7
   'ivory tower' 35
   'life of Riley' 41

'mondegreens' 297
'monger' 9–10
'mouse' (computer), plural of 277–8
'nitty-gritty' 35–6
'OK' 47–9
'oldest trick in the book' 37–8
'orange', rhyming words 295–6
'paint the town red' 17–18
'quack' 29–30
rhyming words, difficult 295–6
'shoot the messenger' 24–5
'*stan*', as suffix 4
'standing on the shoulders
   of giants' 32–3
'they', use of 294–5
World War Two
   British/Allied troops fighting for Axis
      23–4, 134–5, 136
   fate of Black, Asian and Arabic people,
      Nazi-occupied Europe 134–6
      Spanish 'neutrality' 98–9
      V1 'flying bomb', action against 97–8
Wright, Sylvia, and 'mondegreens'
   297, 298
Wright, Wilbur and Orville, evidence
   of 'first flight' 289–90

zombies: real? 72–3